New York Entertains

New York
Entertains

By the Junior League
of the City of New York

Illustrations by Patricia Whitman

DOUBLEDAY & COMPANY, INC.
GARDEN CITY, NEW YORK
1974

THE NEW YORK JUNIOR LEAGUE is a volunteer organization whose purpose is to train its members for service and leadership in the New York community.

The profit realized from the sale of *New York Entertains* will be spent on the League's community program. Since 1901, the New York Junior League has devoted its energies and its resources to this vital work and it is to these undertakings in the New York community that we dedicate our book.

Copyright © 1974 by The Junior League of the City of New York, Inc.
All Rights Reserved
Printed in the United States of America
Design by Paul Randall Mize
First Edition

Library of Congress Cataloging in Publication Data

Junior League of the City of New York.
   New York entertains.

   1. Entertaining. I. Title.
TX731.J79   1974   641.5'68
ISBN 0-385-09651-8
Library of Congress Catalog Card Number 74-2515

THE JUNIOR LEAGUE OF THE CITY OF NEW YORK, INC., would like to thank the many people who contributed to this book: its members and their friends who contributed recipes, the numerous testers, the editorial committee:

Lynn McDonald Hathaway
Penelope Johnson Wartels
Sally A. Ball
Betsy B. Bigelow
Barbara C. Conwell
Barbara W. Cook
Travers Moncure Evans
Duane F. Hampton
Molly O. Parkinson
Georgeanne M. Rousseau
Bobbie Brewster Scarff

The Junior League would also like to thank its Financial Vice President, Julia S. Hansen, and its President, Anne K. O'Neil, for their support.

Introduction

Where can blinis, blintzes, tacos, crêpes, or pancakes be found around almost any corner? Where else but in New York? For unlike the other great American cities, New York is a capital of the world. It encompasses a greater variety of nationalities, stronger ethnic influences, more exciting diversity than any other city in the country. It's a melting pot that never quite melted with a diversified populace. In fact—since this is a cookbook—we might compare New York to a stew; like a proper one, it is a city in which each ingredient contributes to the whole without losing its own integrity. And without Chinatown, Little Italy, Harlem, Spanish Harlem, or that little bit of Germany—Yorkville— what would New York be? Each of these neighborhoods, and many others, provide the adventurous shopper with authentic ingredients characteristic of its own cuisine. One goes to Mott Street in Chinatown for salted black beans, sesame paste, Szechuan peppercorns. East Harlem for sofrito, cilantro, and chorizos. The Lower East Side for bagels, lox, and kosher dills. The Upper West Side for a little bit of everything.

New York's diversity also helps to create its many-faceted personality—the mood, the magnetism, the magic. It's never dull. Glamour, glitter, and brashness—humanity, wit, and warmth—it's a feast for all the senses. This cookbook draws its inspiration from that infinite variety, the many cuisines, plus the seasonal aspects of celebrating and shopping and translates them into the art of entertaining—New York style.

Sample these pages and these recipes season by season, and you will find that flavor—the style—of New York. It's a style that can range from ultra chic to ultra casual, from veddy formal to very friendly, from totally traditional to utterly original. Sample these menus and party ideas that are spiced with seasonal produce—and you will soon discover that when New York entertains it is never dull.

Here spring is greeted with shad roe or a tribute to New York's Dutch heritage—an asparagus recipe that's authentically *old* Amsterdam. Summer's bounty is savored with tomatoes, squash, cold soups—a dinner aboard a boat, a Mediterranean feast, or back-terrace barbecue. For fall you will find something to fit everyone's taste: a tail-gate picnic, a Thanksgiving dinner, elegant pre-opera feasts, a salute to the game season. Welcome winter with Christmas: shopping, gala parties (with and without children), a New Year's Day celebration, sporting parties.

Most ingredients used in these recipes are available country-wide, either in supermarkets or specialty food shops. If you cannot find them locally, those shops can probably advise you where to write for them. The menus were devised of dishes that complement each other—but the recipes should not be considered rigid within the framework of a particular suggested menu. For instance, a first course in one menu might well provide a light luncheon or supper; a rather complicated vegetable accompaniment might prove a perfect first course. The alternatives are many—the choice is yours.

We offer a dessert with every menu, but keep in mind that fresh fruit with cheese is always an appropriate alternative. And coffee accompanied with a tray of cordials is an elegant finale to any dinner.

These recipes were contributed by many of New York's finest cooks, developed into menus by some of the city's most hospitable hostesses, and tested by talented volunteers. They warmly invite you to dine and celebrate as they do. Welcome to *New York Entertains*.

Contents

CONTENTS   9

Recipes are included for the starred items in each menu.

Spring

Formal Spring Dinner

for Eight

Kirs
*Terrine de Chagny Lameloise
White and Whole-wheat Toast
*Cream of Spinach Soup
*Poached Red Snapper with *Green Peppercorn Sauce
*Herbed Rack of Lamb
*New Potatoes (see Index)
Salad of Arugula, Romaine, and Radishes with *Mustard
Vinaigrette (see Basic Recipes)
*Pots de Crème à l'Orange
*Florentines

This elegant evening begins with cocktails and the justly famous terrine from the beautiful Burgundian inn of Lameloise in Chagny. If you are accustomed to a good deal of chopping and grinding when you prepare a terrine, you will be pleasantly surprised at how quickly this one is put together; yet the flavor has depth and integrity.

Since your guests have an important meal ahead of them, why not offer a selection of cassis apéritifs or kirs served in carafes instead of cocktails? Vermouth cassis, white wine cassis with a touch of cognac, and champagne cassis would make an interesting group from which to choose.

With the exception of the poached red snapper and the herbed rack of lamb, everything can be done a day or two in advance, allowing time on the day of the party for setting out your nicest things and polishing the silver. Serving a five-course meal smoothly, however, calls for intricate advance planning. In the absence of lots of hired help, you might have the purée of spinach soup waiting invitingly at the table when you call your guests to dinner. Ask your husband or a good friend to serve the fish, then carve the lamb, while you clear the table. In the meantime the salad can sit wiltlessly on the sideboard with the dressing at the bottom of the bowl and the greens piled on top, ready for a willing friend to toss and serve, before you bring out the light and luscious orange pots de crème and Florentines.

This is definitely a menu for a person who loves cooking to prepare for friends who love to eat.

TERRINE DE CHAGNY LAMELOISE

¾ pound chicken livers
4 tablespoons butter
2 eggs
⅓ to ½ cup cognac or bour-
    bon
1 onion, chopped
2 cloves garlic, finely
    chopped
½ teaspoon allspice
Freshly ground black pepper
½ pound sausage meat
    (homemade if possible, or
    any good brand without
    filler or excess preserva-
    tive)

2 to 3 tablespoons flour
½ teaspoon cooking oil
Salt
¾ pound fresh pork fat,
    thinly sliced
White or whole-wheat toast

Preheat oven to 350 degrees.

Sauté the livers in butter until just firm enough to handle. Purée in a blender with the eggs, cognac, onion, garlic, allspice, and a generous amount of pepper. Blend this mixture with the uncooked meat and flour. The mixture will be very liquid at this point. Cook a teaspoonful of the mixture in oil in a small frying pan and taste to check the seasoning. Add salt to taste.

Line a 6-cup earthenware terrine, bread tin, or mold with the strips of pork fat. Pour in the chicken liver and sausage mixture. Cover with aluminum foil and a lid. Bake at 350 degrees for 1½ to 2 hours, or until the liquid in the pan is clear. Remove lid, and cool for ½ hour or longer. Put a heavy weight of 3 pounds or more on the foil to press down the terrine. Refrigerate overnight, weighted. Either serve from the cooking vessel if it is attractive enough, or turn out onto a platter and remove salt pork. Serve with thin slices of white or whole-wheat toast. The terrine will keep at least 1 week, covered and refrigerated. Serves 10 to 12.

CREAM OF SPINACH SOUP

4 tablespoons butter
¾ cup sifted flour
2 quarts hot chicken broth,
    well degreased
3 shallots, coarsely chopped
2 stalks celery, chopped
2 leeks, chopped
2 or 3 sprigs parsley, chopped
1 pound spinach, tough stems
    removed, or 10-ounce
    package frozen spinach,
    thawed

2 egg yolks
1 cup light cream
Salt
Freshly ground nutmeg (op-
    tional)
2 hard-cooked eggs
2 tablespoons fresh, finely
    chopped chives

Melt the butter in a 3-quart saucepan, stir in the flour, and cook until thickened and pale yellow. Gradually add the hot chicken broth and whisk until smooth. Add the shallots, celery, leeks, and parsley and simmer for 30 minutes. Strain through a fine sieve into a mixing bowl and set aside.

Wash the fresh spinach and cook, with the water clinging to the leaves in a large pan, for 2 to 3 minutes, until dry. If using frozen spinach, thaw, drain, and sauté as for the fresh spinach. Either blend it with a small amount of the chicken base in a blender, or mince it fine. Add the spinach to the soup base, return to the 3-quart saucepan, and bring the soup very slowly and carefully to a boil so that it does not scorch. Blend the egg yolks with the cream and add ½ cup of the hot soup, a bit at a time. Mix this thoroughly and pour it into the hot soup, stirring constantly. Do not let the soup come to the boil after this point. Correct the seasoning if necessary, adding nutmeg if desired. Sieve egg yolks and chop the whites. Garnish with hard-cooked eggs and sprinkle with chives.

POACHED RED SNAPPER WITH GREEN PEPPERCORN SAUCE

4-pound red snapper,
  cleaned, with head and tail
  left on
1 quart Court Bouillon (see
  Index)
4 tablespoons unsalted butter
3 tablespoons green peppercorns, slightly crushed
  (available, canned, in most
  gourmet or food specialty
  stores)

2 cups heavy cream
Salt
3 tablespoons chopped parsley

Poach the snapper in cheesecloth in the court bouillon about 30 minutes, until it just flakes easily. Remove to a heated platter and reserve the court bouillon for future use, or freeze it. Melt the butter in a small, heavy-bottomed saucepan; blend in the green peppercorns, and cook gently 1 to 2 minutes. Stir in the heavy cream and bring to a simmer. Simmer 5 to 6 minutes, then season to taste with salt. Stir in the parsley just before serving. Serves 8 as a first course. For 8 as an entree, double the recipe.

HERBED RACK OF LAMB

2 8-chop racks of lamb (7½
  to 8 pounds)
2 tablespoons salt
Freshly ground black pepper
4 heaping tablespoons finely
  chopped fines herbes (1
  tablespoon each fresh tarragon, chives, parsley, and
  shallots, all finely chopped
  —if dried, use one half
  the amount)

1 cup fresh bread crumbs
2 heaping tablespoons minced
  parsley
4 cloves garlic, finely
  minced
Minced herbs

Preheat oven to 450 degrees.

If your butcher has not trimmed the fat from the ends of the chop bones, do so by cutting down each rib bone, halfway to the base, and removing the strip of fat.

Sprinkle and press in the salt and a generous amount of pepper over the surface of the meat. Score the fat with a sharp knife and rub the fines herbes into the meat. One very large baking sheet or pan might accommodate both racks, or the broiling tray from the oven may be used. Both racks of lamb, however, should be on the same level in the oven.

Roast in 450-degree oven for 25 to 30 minutes. While the lamb is roasting, combine the bread crumbs with the minced parsley and garlic. When the lamb has finished its initial roasting, remove from oven and sprinkle the outside of the meat thoroughly and carefully with this mixture. Return to the oven for 5 minutes for rare lamb, 10 minutes for medium-rare lamb, or 15 minutes for well done. Serve garnished with more minced herbs. Serves 8.

POTS DE CRÈME À L'ORANGE

3 cups heavy cream
6 egg yolks
6 tablespoons sugar

3 tablespoons Grand Marnier
1 heaping tablespoon freshly
   grated orange zest

Preheat oven to 325 degrees.

Heat the cream in a saucepan until almost scalded. Beat the yolks with the sugar until pale and thick, then add the hot cream in a steady thin stream—beating continually. Stir in the Grand Marnier and grated orange zest and pour into 8 individual pots-de-crème molds or small ramekins. Set the pots in a baking dish with sufficient boiling water to come halfway up the sides of the pots and cook in the bottom half of a 325-degree oven for 35 to 40 minutes. The custards are done when a knife, inserted, comes out clean. If pot lids are used, as with classic pots de crème, there will be no crust; if not, there will be a thin crust on top of the crème. Cool, then chill before serving. Serves 8.

FLORENTINES

½ cup sugar
⅓ cup heavy cream
⅓ cup honey
4 to 5 tablespoons butter
¼ cup Candied Orange Peel, chopped (see recipe below)
3 tablespoons sifted flour

½ cup ground blanched almonds
Butter for preparing baking sheets
8 ounces semi-sweet chocolate
1 tablespoon Grand Marnier
1 tablespoon butter

Preheat oven to 400 degrees.

Combine sugar, cream, honey, and butter in heavy saucepan. Stir over low heat until sugar is dissolved, then raise heat and boil without stirring until a soft ball forms when a small amount is dropped into cold water (238 degrees on a candy thermometer). Cool slightly, then stir in orange peel, flour, and ground almonds. Generously butter baking sheets and drop small rounds of batter from a teaspoon on the well-greased sheets, leaving at least 2 inches between cookies. They will spread while cooking. Bake 8 to 10 minutes, but be sure to check after 6 to 7 minutes, as they burn easily. They may be pulled into a round shape if desired by using a greased 3-inch cookie cutter.

While the cookies are still quite warm, remove them from pans with a spatula and cool on a rack. Prepare an icing by melting semi-sweet chocolate, Grand Marnier, and butter. Spread the bottom of each cookie and place cookies in refrigerator until chocolate has set.

Candied Orange Peel for Florentines

1 cup water
2 cups sugar
Zest of 3 oranges, cut into thin strips

1 teaspoon Grand Marnier

Bring water and sugar to a boil in a heavy saucepan, then add the strips of orange and the Grand Marnier. Cook 10 to 15 minutes, until the strips are tender. Cool, drain, and then chop for use in the cookies. Extra peel may be stored in a small, tightly covered jar in the refrigerator.

An Asparagus Feast Recalling

New York's Dutch Heritage for Eight

Chilled Genever (Dutch gin)
*Asparagus, Low Countries' Style
*Whole-wheat Bread
 Sweet Butter
 Edam and Gouda Cheeses
*Chocolate Fudge Pie

Manhattan was discovered by an Englishman employed by a Dutch company to find the Spice Islands. Instead, Henry Hudson found Manhattan Island and claimed it for the Low Countries. The Dutch settled the island, and much of lower Manhattan as we know it reflects their stamp. One can still walk below Wall Street on a quiet Sunday afternoon and contemplate New York's beginnings. Then Wall Street was just that: a wall indicating the northern end of the Dutch settlement, and the *bouwerij* was not the Bowery as we know it but the literal translation: farmland. Many Dutch settlers had townhouses south of Wall Street and farms in the *bouwerij*—weekend retreats even then.

As a tribute to New York's Dutch heritage, a simple Dutch meal is offered here. Perhaps it could serve as a supper after a tour of the sites of old New Amsterdam to celebrate the first asparagus of spring. This is a feast centered around fresh asparagus served with a sauce of butter, parsley, minced ham, boiled new potatoes, and hot hard-cooked eggs. The sauce is actually prepared by each guest at the table.

A simple supper such as this seems to call for simple table decor. You might serve it on a butcher-block table with muslin napkins. The centerpiece could be a large wire egg basket filled with eggs and parsley bouquets. Pottery and stainless steel extend the motif to one of practicality—since eggs and asparagus combine to blacken sterling silver in minutes. Precede the dinner with iced genever—the Dutch eau-de-vie—served "neat" in small chilled glasses. Serve hot loaves of whole-wheat bread to be sliced at the table accompanied by pottery mini-crocks of sweet butter for each person, and accompany the asparagus with chilled beer. After the Gouda and Edam cheeses, serve the rich chocolate fudge pie and toast Henry Hudson, not for finding the Spice Islands but for finding Manhattan Island instead.

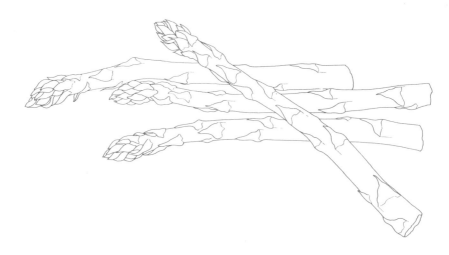

ASPARAGUS, LOW COUNTRIES' STYLE

¾ pound asparagus, about 10
   to 12 stalks
2 small new potatoes, peeled
2 eggs, at room temperature
4 to 6 tablespoons unsalted
   butter

¼ cup finely chopped best-
   quality ham
¼ cup chopped fresh pars-
   ley
Salt, freshly ground pepper

Wash the asparagus thoroughly, and trim bases. Peel each spear, starting about one third below the tip, taking care to remove all the fibrous peel at the base without damaging the fragile tip of the spear. Fill a very large enameled or stainless steel pot with water and bring to a boil. Drop in the new potatoes, the asparagus and the eggs in their shells and let boil vigorously uncovered for 10 to 12 minutes, or until the asparagus and the potatoes are tender and the eggs hard-cooked. Remove the eggs to a bowl and peel just before serving. Keep the asparagus, potatoes, and eggs warm.

While the asparagus, potatoes, and eggs are cooking, melt the butter and stir in the minced ham and parsley. Season to taste with salt and pepper.

At the table, offer platters of asparagus and potatoes with bowls of the warmed, peeled, hard-cooked eggs. Each diner prepares his own sauce by mashing potatoes and eggs together with a fork to the desired consistency, then blending in the butter, parsley, and ham.

If serving the asparagus for a first course, halve the above ingredients. Serves 1.

WHOLE-WHEAT BREAD

1 cup milk
¾ cup butter
½ cup honey
2 teaspoons salt
2 packages active dry yeast
¾ cup warm water (105 to
   110 degrees—check with
   meat thermometer)

3 eggs, lightly beaten
4 cups all-purpose flour
2 cups whole-wheat flour
Butter

Heat milk in small saucepan until boiling. Stir in butter, honey, and salt until butter is melted. Cool to lukewarm. Sprinkle yeast over warm water and stir until dissolved. Add milk mixture and eggs, stirring well. Combine the all-purpose and whole-wheat flours and add ⅔ of the flour to yeast mixture. Beat with electric mixer at low speed until blended. Then beat at medium speed until smooth, about 2 minutes. Gradually beat in the remaining flour with a wooden spoon, stretching the dough out with the spoon 20 to 30 times.

Cover with foil or wax paper and a towel and let rise in warm, draft-free place until doubled in bulk, about 1 hour. Lightly butter a 2½- or 3-quart soufflé dish or casserole or two 9 by 5 by 2¾-inch loaf pans. Punch down dough and beat with spoon until smooth. Turn into baking dish or loaf pans, cover, and let rise until doubled in bulk, about 30 minutes. Preheat oven to 375 degrees. Bake 45 to 50 minutes, until bread is nicely browned. Remove from baking dish or loaf pans to wire rack to cool. Brush 1 teaspoon butter over top and serve warm.

Note: If a less sweet bread is desired, reduce honey to ¼ cup.

CHOCOLATE FUDGE PIE

¼ pound butter
3 1-ounce squares unsweetened chocolate
4 eggs, well beaten
3 tablespoons light corn
 syrup
1½ cups sugar
¼ teaspoon salt

¼ cup milk
1 teaspoon vanilla, cognac, or
 dark rum
10-inch unbaked pastry shell
 (see Basic Recipes)
1 cup heavy cream, whipped
Shaved chocolate

Preheat oven to 450 degrees.

Melt butter and chocolate in top of a double boiler. Combine the eggs, corn syrup, sugar, salt, milk, and vanilla or cognac or rum. Add the chocolate and butter. Mix thoroughly and pour into the unbaked pastry shell.

Bake pie at 450 degrees for 10 minutes, lower heat to 350 degrees. Bake the pie for 30 to 35 minutes, until top is crusty and the filling set. Cool. Spread whipped cream over the pie before serving and sprinkle with shaved chocolate.

Serves 8.

A Festive Chinese Dinner for Good Friends

*Shredded Chicken in Many-flavored Sauce
*Cold Noodles with Sesame Paste
*Watercress and Meatball Soup
*Pork Broth
*Chinese Sea Bass with Black Beans
*Mo Shu Pork with *Chinese Pancakes
*Dry Sautéed Green Beans
*Szechuan Spiced Shrimp
*Hot Spiced Beef with Orange Flavor
*Oriental Rice
*Oranges in Red Wine
  Jasmine Tea

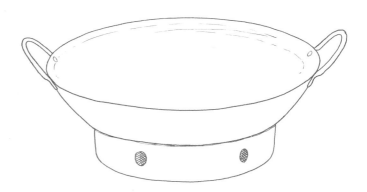

A truly authentic Chinese dinner is a spectacular way to entertain informally—informally because in order to ensure the freshness and quality of the hot dishes, they must be served the minute they are cooked, and the best way to do this is to serve each dish as a separate course, cooking it between courses. Good friends won't mind the pause. They'll be having fun learning to master the use of chopsticks. And you can invite them into the kitchen to watch your artistry at the wok.

Preparing good Chinese food, even though it must be cooked at the last minute, is not so difficult or complicated as it sounds, as long as the hostess is very carefully organized. In this menu, most of the preparation can be done several hours to a day in advance. Measure out and put the prepared ingredients in cups or little bowls and group them together so that during the actual cooking, everything for a particular dish is right at hand. The actual cooking time for each dish is no more than five to ten minutes. Chinese ingredients are available in oriental markets and in many gourmet food shops.

In planning a Chinese menu, the rule of thumb is one "dish" for every two people. Thus this menu, with eight "dishes," is for sixteen. If there are only to be eight guests, or twelve, or six, do not halve or otherwise divide recipes; rather, eliminate dishes altogether. A nice dinner for eight would be one of the cold dishes, the watercress and meatball soup, Chinese sea bass with black beans, and the dry sautéed green beans—a balanced menu of crisp and soft textures, spicy and subtle flavors, and color—appealing to all the senses. For four people, we do suggest serving three dishes to make the menu more interesting, perhaps the Szechuan spiced shrimp or shredded chicken in many-flavored sauce, then Mo Shu pork with Chinese pancakes, and finally hot spiced beef with orange flavor.

Set the table simply—napkins and chopsticks are all that are needed. Chinese soup bowls and porcelain spoons are nice to have and these and the chopsticks are inexpensively available at oriental import stores. The food itself is the centerpiece: serve dinner "family style"—put each platter in the center of the table and let the guests help themselves. Serve beer or a light rosé or white (not too dry) wine, and jasmine tea with the oranges. For those who really cannot manage chopsticks, have forks hidden nearby—but the fun is in trying.

SHREDDED CHICKEN
IN MANY-FLAVORED SAUCE

3 tablespoons sesame paste
3 tablespoons strong tea
½ tablespoon hot oil
⅛ teaspoon monosodium
  glutamate
1 teaspoon salt
2 teaspoons sugar
4 tablespoons very thinly
  sliced scallions (including
  green parts)
2½ tablespoons imported
  soy sauce
2½ teaspoons sesame oil

1 tablespoon coarsely
  chopped garlic
2 tablespoons vinegar
⅓ cup peanut oil
1 tablespoon Prepared Szechuan Peppercorns (see
  recipe below)
2 large whole chicken
  breasts, lightly poached
  and cooled in their cooking water
Chopped coriander or parsley (optional)

Make the sauce: put the sesame paste into a bowl and slowly blend in the tea. Add the hot oil, monosodium glutamate, salt, sugar, scallions, soy sauce, sesame oil, garlic, vinegar, peanut oil, and Szechuan peppercorns, and stir until well blended. Set aside.

Skin and bone the poached chicken breasts. Cut the chicken meat into thin strips or shred it with your fingers. Arrange the shredded chicken on a serving dish and pour the sauce over the chicken. Cover with plastic wrap and chill several hours. Garnish with chopped coriander or parsley if desired.

Preparation of Szechuan Peppercorns

Szechuan peppercorns are available at Chinese groceries or gourmet specialty shops. Prepared in the following manner, they will keep indefinitely if stored in an airtight jar.

To bring out their flavor, put the whole peppercorns in a small skillet over medium heat and cook, shaking and stirring until roasted, about 3 to 4 minutes. Then whirl the peppercorns in a blender until finely ground.

COLD NOODLES WITH SESAME PASTE

1 pound soft fresh noodles (lo mein)

2 tablespoons peanut oil

1 teaspoon finely chopped garlic

5 tablespoons plus 1 teaspoon finely chopped Szechuan mustard pickle

3 tablespoons preserved Chinese cabbage (tong choy)

2 scallions, including green tops, very thinly sliced

4 teaspoons sugar

2 teaspoons white vinegar

2 teaspoons sesame oil

⅛ teaspoon monosodium glutamate

4 teaspoons imported soy sauce

2 tablespoons plus 2 teaspoons Sesame Paste Mixture (see recipe below)

½ to 1 teaspoon hot bean sauce (the commercial Chili Paste with Garlic may be substituted)

Hot oil (optional)

Shredded chicken, pork, or cucumber; green peas; or bean sprouts (optional)

Cook the noodles in boiling water until they float, about 3 to 4 minutes. Drain, run under cold running water, then drain well again. Do not overcook: noodles become too soft and stick together. Toss immediately with peanut oil to prevent their sticking together.

When cool enough to handle, sprinkle garlic, mustard pickle, preserved Chinese cabbage, and scallions (see note) over noodles and toss with hands to mix well. Sprinkle sugar, vinegar, sesame oil, monosodium glutamate, soy sauce, sesame paste mixture, and hot bean sauce over noodles and toss to mix well, being particularly careful that sesame paste mixture is evenly distributed and mixed well. Taste for seasoning: if necessary, add vinegar, soy sauce, and hot bean sauce. If desired, flavor with hot oil and top with one of the optional ingredients. Cool in refrigerator; however, noodles should not be served too chilled.

Note: If preparing more than 2 or 3 hours in advance, do not stir in the scallions until just before serving.

Sesame Paste Mixture

7- or 8-ounce jar sesame paste

12-ounce jar peanut butter
6 tablespoons peanut oil.

Combine sesame paste, peanut butter, and peanut oil to make a smooth paste. If mixture is too thick, thin with a little more oil. Mixture must be at room temperature before adding to noodles, otherwise it is too firm to mix properly.

WATERCRESS AND MEATBALL SOUP

1 pound finely ground lean
   pork
1 tablespoon finely chopped
   fresh ginger
2 scallions, finely chopped
8 to 10 water chestnuts,
   finely chopped
Salt
1½ teaspoons imported soy
   sauce
Freshly ground white pepper

2 teaspoons cornstarch
2 2-ounce packages cello-
   phane noodles (bean
   thread or transparent
   noodles are other names)
10 cups pork or chicken
   broth or water
2 bunches fresh crisp watercress
⅛ teaspoon monosodium
   glutamate

ADVANCE PREPARATION

Combine pork, ginger, scallions, water chestnuts, 1 teaspoon salt, soy sauce, ¼ teaspoon pepper, and cornstarch. Mix well and form into small balls about the size of a quarter. These may be prepared well in advance and frozen. Makes about 55 meatballs.

Soak noodles in hot water until soft, about 30 minutes.

COOKING AND SERVING

Bring the broth or water to a slow boil and poach a few meatballs at a time until they float (this is the sign of doneness). Remove and set aside. Pick over the watercress, removing very tough stems and wilted bits. Wash in cold water and drain well.

Just before serving, bring broth or water to a boil and add noodles. Cook about 2 minutes, until tender, then add meatballs and season with monosodium glutamate and salt and pepper to taste. Add watercress and cook, uncovered, a few minutes until just wilted and bright green. Serve immediately.

PORK BROTH

4 to 6 pounds pork bones   Salt
Water to cover (about 12   4 or 5 slices fresh ginger
    cups)

Put pork bones in a large pan and cover with water. Bring to a boil and skim surface as scum rises. When skimming is no longer necessary add salt and sliced ginger.

Simmer 5 or more hours. Strain and cool. When broth is well cooled, degrease carefully. May be used immediately or frozen for later use.

Note: Bones from pork roasts may be frozen and accumulated to make broth. Bones may also be purchased from a Chinese butcher.

CHINESE SEA BASS WITH BLACK BEANS

6 tablespoons salted black   6-pound sea bass, cleaned,
    beans   with head on
3 slices fresh ginger   Flour
15 to 18 whole scallions   Cornstarch (optional)
6 to 9 tablespoons peanut oil

ADVANCE PREPARATION

Crush black beans in a mortar with a little water. Peel ginger slices and cut into thin, narrow strips. Cut the white parts of the scallions lengthwise into very thin shreds about 1 inch long and the green parts into 1-inch pieces.

COOKING AND SERVING

Heat oil in a wok or large skillet. Add the ginger and white part of scallions; stir-fry (a tossing and turning-folding motion) over high heat for 2 to 3 minutes. Dust bass with flour and fry over medium heat for 7 minutes on each side. Add the black beans and 1 cup water. Cover wok or skillet, lower heat, and simmer bass for 20 minutes. Add green tops of scallions after 10 minutes.

Serve fish with sauce as is, or mix 2 to 3 tablespoons cornstarch with ½ cup water, blend into sauce, and stir over medium heat until thickened. Pour over fish.

MO SHU PORK

3 tablespoons black fun-
  gus (a dried mushroom)
½-pound pork butt in 1
  piece, frozen
16-ounce can winter bamboo
  shoots
1 teaspoon salt
1 tablespoon cornstarch
6 eggs

4 scallions
⅛ teaspoon monosodium
  glutamate
3 tablespoons imported
  soy sauce
14 tablespoons peanut oil
16 to 20 Chinese pancakes
  (see recipe below)

ADVANCE PREPARATION

Pour boiling water over black fungus and soak at least ½ hour, until soft. Slice pork very thinly with a sharp cleaver or knife, then cut slices into thin shreds. Cut bamboo shoots into similarly sized shreds. Mix pork with salt, then cornstarch. Beat eggs until well mixed. Cut scallions on sharp diagonal into ½-inch pieces.

COOKING AND SERVING

Heat 10 tablespoons oil in a wok or large skillet and quickly scramble eggs. Do not overcook. Turn out onto a plate.

Heat 4 tablespoons oil in wok or skillet and stir-fry (a tossing and turning-folding motion) pork over high heat with a wide spatula until cooked, about 2 minutes, then add bamboo shoots and black fungus. Toss and stir together, then add eggs and mix well. Add monosodium glutamate, soy sauce, and scallions and mix. Serve immediately with Chinese pancakes. Each person should take a pancake, put a spoonful of the pork mixture on it, roll it up, and eat with hands. *Note:* Do halve this recipe to serve 8.

CHINESE PANCAKES

2 cups flour
¾ to 1 cup very hot water

1 tablespoon peanut oil
1 tablespoon sesame oil

Put flour in a bowl and stir in water a little at a time to make a smooth, soft dough. Flour hands and knead a few minutes. Dough should be soft and smooth, but if it is too sticky, add a little more flour. Cover and let dough rest 30 minutes.

Flour a board well. Pull off a chunk of dough and form it into a roll 1¼ inches in diameter. Roll dough in flour, then cut into 1-inch slices. Pat each piece into a round and flatten it so it is about 1¾ inches in diameter and ½ inch thick.

Combine peanut and sesame oils. Brush 1 side of each round with oil, being sure to coat the edges well. Put 2 rounds together, oiled sides in, and flatten with the hands so each piece is the same size. Put on a lightly floured board, roll once in one direction, turn over and rotate a quarter, and roll again in one direction. Repeat until pancake is about 6 inches in diameter.

Heat wok without oil and put in 1 pair of rolled-together pancakes. Reduce heat to medium-low. Cook until there is a very slight change of color on the underside (hardly any at all) and the pancake bubbles. Turn and cook until pancake bubbles on the other side. Remove from wok and carefully pull apart the 2 pancakes. If they are to be served immediately, fold in quarters and wrap in a linen towel to keep warm. Otherwise wrap well in foil and freeze. To serve, defrost, then steam on a rack over boiling water to heat. Makes about 30 6-inch pancakes.

DRY SAUTÉED GREEN BEANS

1½ cloves garlic, peeled
4 slices fresh ginger
2 scallions
1 pound green beans
Peanut oil
¼ pound ground pork
¼ cup finely chopped Szechuan mustard pickle
¼ cup preserved Chinese cabbage (tong choy)
Salt
⅛ teaspoon monosodium glutamate

ADVANCE PREPARATION

Chop garlic and ginger fine. Slice scallions very thin. Wash the beans and snap off the ends. If you are doing this well in advance, cover and set aside. Heat 5 tablespoons oil in wok or large skillet. Add pork and stir fry until well cooked, breaking it up with spatula or spoon. Add chopped ginger, garlic, mustard pickle, and preserved cabbage and mix thoroughly with pork. Set aside.

COOKING AND SERVING

Heat half a wok full of peanut oil, or 1½ to 2 inches oil in a large skillet. Add green beans and fry until they are a bright green, about 2 to 3 minutes. Drain off oil, then add pork mixture, salt to taste, monosodium glutamate, and scallions, and toss 1 to 2 minutes, until thoroughly mixed and heated. Serve immediately.

Note: The green beans must be cooked at the last minute; even a 5-minute wait will alter the texture and flavor.

SZECHUAN SPICED SHRIMP

- 2 pounds shrimp
- 2 egg whites, beaten lightly until frothy
- 2 tablespoons cornstarch
- ¼ cup finely chopped winter bamboo shoots
- ¼ cup finely chopped water chestnuts
- ¾ cup very thinly sliced scallions (white and green parts)
- 1 tablespoon Prepared Szechuan Peppercorns (see Index)
- 1 teaspoon commercial Chili Paste with Garlic
- 1½ tablespoons very finely chopped garlic
- 2 tablespoons very finely chopped fresh ginger root
- 1 cup chicken broth
- ½ cup catsup
- ⅛ teaspoon monosodium glutamate
- 1 teaspoon imported soy sauce
- ¼ cup rice wine or dry sherry
- 1 teaspoon sesame oil
- 3 cups peanut oil
- Salt

Shell and devein shrimp: cut straight along the back of the shell with a pair of scissors, peel off shell, and rinse out the vein under cold running water. Pat the shelled and deveined shrimp dry on paper towels.

Combine the egg whites with the cornstarch in a shallow pie plate. Add the shrimp and coat well with the egg white-cornstarch mixture. Cover with plastic wrap and refrigerate at least 5 hours.

Combine bamboo shoots, water chestnuts, scallions, prepared Szechuan peppercorns, Chili Paste with Garlic, garlic, and ginger root in a small bowl.

Combine chicken broth, catsup, monosodium glutamate, soy sauce, sherry, and sesame oil in another bowl.

COOKING AND SERVING

Put the shrimp in a sieve or strainer. Heat peanut oil to medium hot in a wok, small deep casserole, or deep-dish fryer large enough to accommodate the sieve. The oil should not be too hot.

Lower the shrimp into the hot peanut oil and cook for about 1 minute without browning. Remove the sieve from the oil.

Pour out all but 2 tablespoons of peanut oil from wok. Heat over a high flame. Add shrimp and the bamboo-shoot mixture and cook quickly, tossing and stirring constantly. Add the chicken broth mixture and continue to cook quickly until all the ingredients are well combined and piping hot. Add salt to taste.

HOT SPICED BEEF WITH ORANGE FLAVOR

2 tangerines	2 tablespoons imported soy
2-pound flank steak, frozen	sauce
7 dried red chilis, about 1½	1 tablespoon sugar
inches long	1 teaspoon sesame oil
4 slices fresh ginger	1 tablespoon rice wine or
3 to 4 scallions	sherry
1 teaspoon salt	1 teaspoon white vinegar
1 egg	⅛ teaspoon monosodium
2 tablespoons cornstarch	glutamate
Peanut oil	8 Szechuan peppercorns

ADVANCE PREPARATION

Peel tangerines. Tear peel into pieces and set out to dry thoroughly. (Fruit is not needed.)

Cut flank steak into thirds or half lengthwise with a sharp heavy cleaver or knife. Slice each piece on the diagonal very thinly, then cut slices into thin shreds.

Cut chilis in half and remove some of the seeds if a less spicy dish is preferred. Cut ginger into ¼-inch squares. Cut scallions diagonally into ¼-inch slices. Put all prepared ingredients, except drying peel, in containers and refrigerate.

COOKING AND SERVING

The day of cooking, mix beef well with salt, egg, 1 tablespoon corn-starch, and 1 tablespoon oil in that order, making sure mixture is well blended before next addition. Combine soy sauce, sugar, sesame oil, rice wine or sherry, vinegar, and monosodium glutamate to make sauce.

Heat 5 tablespoons oil in wok or large skillet. Stir-fry beef, tossing and turning-folding about 2 minutes, until color changes. Remove and set aside. Heat 2 tablespoons oil and add tangerine skins, chilis, and Szechuan peppercorns. Cook until blackened, stirring occasionally. Beware of strong chili fumes. Add ginger, scallions, and beef. Stir for 10 seconds, then add sauce mixture and stir vigorously for 1 minute. Serve immediately.

Note: This dish may also be prepared with chicken. Substitute 6 thighs and 6 legs for the beef. Bone and skin the meat, then lightly pound the inside (bone side) of the chicken pieces with cleaver or knife blade to tenderize meat a little. Cut into 1-inch squares and proceed with recipe as directed.

ORIENTAL RICE

3 cups extra-long-grain rice   5 cups water, approximately

Put rice in a sieve and wash carefully and thoroughly under cold running water until the water runs clear.

Put rinsed rice into a heavy enameled saucepan and add water: the rice should be covered by about 1 inch of water. Test by putting index fingertip on the surface of the rice. The water should be at the first knuckle.

Bring to a boil over high heat and cook about 10 minutes. Reduce heat to very low, cover pot tightly, and cook about 20 minutes longer, until rice is quite tender. Serve immediately. Serves 8.

Note: This rice will be sticky and lumpy and thus easier to eat with chopsticks than rice cooked in the Western fashion where separate grains are desirable.

ORANGES IN RED WINE

1 ½ cups sugar   4 cinnamon sticks
2 cups water   8 lemon slices
2 cups dry red wine   12 large navel oranges
10 cloves

Combine sugar, water, wine, cloves, cinnamon sticks, and lemon slices in a heavy saucepan and bring to a boil. Lower heat and simmer 10 minutes to make a light syrup.

While syrup is simmering, peel oranges and carefully remove all white pith. Cut into their natural sections, or slice crosswise into ½-inch slices and put in a large serving bowl. Pour hot syrup over orange sections and refrigerate until serving. Serves 16.

A Springtime Celebration for Eight

*Mushroom Caps Filled with Sausage
*Cold Purée of Asparagus Soup
*Sautéed Shad Roe
  Tiny Peas
*Steamed New Potatoes
*Crème de Menthe Pie with Fresh Strawberries

Synonymous with the springtime scene and reason enough to celebrate: tender shoots of asparagus, tiny red new potatoes, strawberries bursting with juice, and the first, the finest fresh shad roe. For many years, this fine fish was scarce in New York. The shad had deserted the Hudson River for cleaner waters. However, now that the river has been rejuvenated, so has the supply. Fishermen find a plentiful supply of shad to be had in the springtime. So why not welcome the season and welcome back the shad with a dinner designed both to delight your guests and capitalize on spring's early harvest.

Begin with cocktails and a canapé served hot from a chafing dish: mushroom caps stuffed with a spicy sausage. Then, at the dining table—banked with as many daffodils and tulips as space will allow—chilly bowls of asparagus soup sprinkled with chopped watercress.

Not to be tampered with is the delicate flavor of the shad roe. The late Lucius Beebe presented a paean of praise for this loveliest of fish many years ago. It claimed, "the fish of fish is shad." One could sing equal praises of its roe. The recipe offered here is the simplest of preparations, one that capitalizes on its natural flavors. The roe is simply sautéed in butter with a squeeze or two of fresh lemon juice and served immediately.

To top off this springtime celebration offer a rich yet refreshing mint-flavored pie topped with fresh strawberries. It's the perfect prelude to coffee and cordials.

MUSHROOM CAPS FILLED
WITH SAUSAGE

1 pound fresh mushrooms, 1
  to 1½ inches in diameter
Lemon juice, if needed

1 pound (approximately)
  hot or sweet Italian
  sausage
Salt

Preheat oven to 350 degrees.

Wash mushroom caps and remove the stems. (Reserve stems for another use.) If prepared in advance, rub caps with lemon juice to keep them white.

Squeeze the sausage from the casing and stuff each cap cavity with enough of the sausage meat to fill it completely, mounding it slightly. Salt to taste. Put in a large ovenproof baking dish and bake for 25 minutes.

Drain fat, and serve warm in a chafing dish. Serves 8.

COLD PURÉE OF ASPARAGUS SOUP

3 pounds fresh asparagus,
  washed, with tough ends
  removed
¼ pound butter
1 medium onion, chopped
2 quarts chicken broth

Salt, freshly ground black
  pepper
½ teaspoon nutmeg
2 tablespoons chopped parsley or watercress

Cut off asparagus tips and reserve. Peel the stalks and slice diagonally into ½-inch pieces.

Heat the butter in a 10- to 12-inch skillet. Add the onion and cook until transparent. Add the sliced stalks and cook 1 minute. Add 6 cups of broth, salt and pepper to taste, and nutmeg. Bring to a simmer and cook until stalks are tender, about 18 minutes. Add tips, and cook until tender, about 3 minutes. Reserve some cooked tips for garnish if desired.

Purée the cooked asparagus and liquid in a blender, 2 cups at a time. Chill for several hours. The mixture will be thick. Thin the asparagus mixture as desired with remaining chicken broth. Serve in chilled bowls garnished with chopped watercress or parsley and the reserved asparagus tips. Serves 8.

SAUTÉED SHAD ROE

1 small pair shad roe per person	2 tablespoons butter
Salt, freshly ground pepper	Lemon wedges, 2 or 3 per person
Flour	

Wipe shad roe with a damp cloth. Season with salt and pepper and dredge lightly in flour. Melt butter in a heavy sauté pan and, when sizzling, add the shad roe. Cook over medium heat about 7 minutes, until nicely browned, then turn and cook another 7 to 8 minutes. Shad roe can also be cooked in 2 to 3 tablespoons of bacon fat and garnished with crisp bacon slices, 2 for each pair of roe, and lemon wedges.

STEAMED NEW POTATOES

2 dozen small new red or white potatoes	Chopped parsley
Salt	¼ pound butter (optional)

Wash potatoes well and put in a vegetable steaming basket, then put the basket over water in a saucepan. Or use a colander that will fit into the bottom of the saucepan.

Cover the pan and bring water to a simmer. Begin testing for doneness after 15 to 20 minutes, rearranging potatoes if necessary, as those on the bottom may be cooking faster than those on top. Potatoes are done when they are tender all the way through but still hold their shape firmly.

They may be served plain, sprinkled only with salt and parsley. They may also be dressed with melted butter. For a particularly attractive and very French touch, peel a small strip around the center of each potato before cooking. Serves 8.

CRÈME DE MENTHE PIE
WITH FRESH STRAWBERRIES

1 envelope unflavored gelatin
½ cup cold water
3 eggs, separated
½ cup sugar
⅛ teaspoon salt
½ cup green crème de
   menthe
2 cups heavy cream, whipped

¼ cup confectioners' sugar
½ teaspoon vanilla
9-inch graham cracker crust,
   baked in a 350-degree
   oven for 10 minutes (follow directions on graham
   cracker package)
½ pint strawberries, washed
   and hulled

Sprinkle the gelatin over the cold water in a saucepan. Beat egg yolks
and add to gelatin with ¼ cup of the sugar and salt; stir to blend.

Heat the gelatin mixture over low heat, stirring, until the gelatin
dissolves and the mixture thickens. Do not boil.

Remove from the heat and stir in the crème de menthe. Pour into
a mixing bowl and chill until the mixture begins to set. Begin checking
after 30 minutes. Stir occasionally.

Beat the egg whites until stiff, gradually adding the remaining ¼ cup
sugar. Fold into the gelatin mixture along with ½ of the whipped
cream. Turn into the crust. Chill several hours or overnight.

Add the confectioners' sugar and vanilla to the remaining whipped
cream. Garnish the pie with the cream and the fresh strawberries. Serves
8.

A Lunch for

Weekend Guests for Eight

*Spring Onion Soup
*Pâté and Marrow with Artichoke Bottoms on Croutons
  Bibb Lettuce with *Lemon Vinaigrette (see Basic Recipes)
  Fresh Strawberries
*Lemon Squares

This is a lunch to linger over and savor. It's a wonderful, unrushed way to spend a carefree Saturday—with fine wine and food and close friends. The entree is an unusual one—a delicately flavored mélange of pâté, marrow, and artichoke bottoms, served on crisp toast rounds. Preceding the entree—a freshly different spring onion soup. And, later on, crisp Bibb lettuce with lemon vinaigrette, followed by plump strawberries and tart lemon squares.

The suggested table decor capitalizes on the brightest colors of spring: fresh green and sunny yellow. Use bright yellow napkins tied with green ribbons on a green tablecloth; the centerpiece might be a pyramid of lemons sprigged with greenery.

To construct the lemon pyramid, build a triangular base of lemons proportionate to the size of your table. Secure the lemons to each other with toothpicks, and continue to top the base with successively smaller triangles of lemons, and, finally, top it off with a single lemon. The stems of the greens—or, fancier yet—tiny bows tied on florist's wire—can be inserted between the lemons for a really lovely effect. With such attention to detail and atmosphere, you may start a new trend of leisurely Saturday lunches—and enjoy the reputation of entertaining with flair.

SPRING ONION SOUP

3 cups chopped green onions (including green part)
2 small cloves garlic, minced
4½ tablespoons butter
3 tablespoons flour
6 cups hot chicken stock, homemade or canned
2 egg yolks
¾ cup heavy cream
Minced chives or parsley

Sauté onions and garlic in butter over low heat in a heavy 2½-quart saucepan until tender but not browned. Stir in flour, and gradually add the chicken stock, stirring constantly, until thickened. Simmer over low heat for 30 minutes, then strain through a fine sieve. This may be done the morning of the lunch or the day before. Just before serving, heat soup, and beat the egg yolks into ½ cup of cream. Slowly stir mixture into hot soup and heat until very warm, but do not boil. Whip remaining cream and garnish each portion with a spoonful. Sprinkle with chives or parsley. Serves 6.

Note: When adding egg yolk and cream to a warm mixture as in this soup, always stir the yolk-cream mixture into just a small amount of the warm mixture, then add this to the remaining soup, sauce, or whatever you are enriching in this way.

PÂTÉ AND MARROW WITH ARTICHOKE BOTTOMS ON CROUTONS

2 generous-size marrowbones
1 bay leaf
¼ teaspoon thyme
3 sprigs parsley
3 black peppercorns
2 bread rounds cut to size of artichoke bottoms
Unsalted butter
2 artichoke bottoms, cooked and trimmed
2 slices of pâté de foie (the tunnel-shaped cans of imported pâté are the best)
Salt, freshly ground pepper
Watercress

Gently poach the marrowbones in water to cover with the thyme, parsley, bay leaf, and peppercorns, for 1 hour or until center is tender. Carefully extract marrow and keep warm until serving time. (A vegetable peeler is perfect for extracting the marrow.) Sauté bread rounds in butter until browned. Heat artichoke bottoms. Put a slice of pâté on the bread round, and the hot artichoke bottom, cup side up, on top. Fill with 1 to 2 tablespoons marrow. Dribble a tablespoon of melted butter over all and season to taste with salt and pepper. Garnish generously with watercress and serve. Serves 1.

Note: The reserved cooked artichoke leaves left over from preparing the bottoms may be served with drinks with a mustard sauce for dipping.

LEMON SQUARES

2 ¼ cups flour
½ pound butter
½ cup plus 2 teaspoons confectioners' sugar
4 eggs

2 cups granulated sugar
½ teaspoon salt
6 tablespoons lemon juice
Grated zest of 2 lemons
Confectioners' sugar

Preheat oven to 350 degrees.

Cream together 2 cups flour, butter, and ½ cup confectioners' sugar. Press into a 9 by 13-inch pan. Bake in a 350-degree oven for 15 minutes, until pale gold at edges.

Mix eggs, granulated sugar, and salt, then blend in lemon juice and grated zest. Sift remaining flour and confectioners' sugar onto egg mixture and fold in. Pour egg mixture over crust and return to oven for 30 minutes. Sift confectioners' sugar over top and loosen edges with a spatula. Cool, then cut into squares. Makes about 48 1 ½-inch squares.

St. Patrick's Day Party
for Eight

Black Velvets
*Toasted Nuts
*Glazed Corned Beef
*Casserole of Cabbage, Potatoes, and Apples
*Julienne of Carrots and Parsnips
Crocks of Mustards
*Irish Soda Bread I
*Irish Soda Bread II
*Tipsy Squire

In New York, everyone is Irish on St. Patrick's Day. It's a glorious excuse for the wearing of the green and a toast at a neighborhood pub. And there's the parade up Fifth Avenue. There was even a time when the traffic lines were painted green for the day. The parade is noisy and crowded. Brass bands blare "Macnamara's Band" and people wear green carnations.

The dinner suggested here features some authentic Irish dishes, starting with an Irish drink—black velvet. It's a mixture of stout and champagne that is surprisingly hearty and good. The meal itself begins with its main course: corned beef studded with cloves, spiced with chili powder, and glazed with brown sugar and beer. It is served with crocks of mustard, and accompanied by a casserole of sliced and layered cabbage, potatoes, and apples, and a julienne of buttered parsnips and carrots. For dessert, serve Tipsy Squire, a true Irish version of the classic trifle.

Extend the "wearing of the green" to the table. Make it a riot of green and white—mixed checks, stripes, plaids, and polka dots. Set place cards in miniature pots of shamrock, and use green ferns for your centerpiece. This meal and its setting are a wonderful way to celebrate St. Patrick's Day—even if it's the only day you're Irish.

TOASTED NUTS

4 cups assorted nuts, shelled
  (pecans, almonds, and
  walnuts are a good
  combination)
¼ pound unsalted butter,
  melted

4 to 6 tablespoons peanut oil
Coarse salt, either sea salt or
  kosher salt
Seasonings such as curry
  powder, chili powder, or
  ground cumin

Preheat oven to 350 degrees.

Spread the nuts evenly in a large flat baking dish or jelly roll pan. Lightly dribble the butter and peanut oil over all. Roast in 350-degree oven for 20 to 25 minutes, shaking pan several times to coat all of the nuts evenly. Turn the nuts onto absorbent paper toweling, then flavor as desired, either altogether with the coarse salt or in separate batches, each flavored to taste with curry powder, chili powder, or ground cumin. Serves 12.

GLAZED CORNED BEEF

1 4-pound piece corned beef
20 cloves or more, as desired
½ cup brown sugar
1 ½ teaspoons chili powder

½ cup beer
3 to 4 tablespoons additional
  brown sugar

Preheat oven to 425 degrees.

Parboil corned beef according to package directions and proceed as follows: stud corned beef evenly with cloves. Prepare a paste of brown sugar, chili powder, and enough beer to make a spreadable paste. Spread paste over corned beef and put in oven. Reduce heat at once to 350 degrees and bake 20 minutes. Sprinkle with additional brown sugar and cook 20 minutes longer or until you have an attractive, shiny glaze. Serves 8 to 10.

CASSEROLE OF CABBAGE, POTATOES, AND APPLES

1 medium head of green cabbage, thinly sliced
3 baking potatoes, peeled and
   thinly sliced
3 cooking apples (preferably
   Greenings), peeled, cored,
   and thinly sliced

1 onion, finely chopped
Butter
Salt, freshly ground pepper
1 cup heavy cream
¼ cup fine bread crumbs
¼ cup finely grated Swiss
   cheese

Preheat oven to 350 degrees.

Arrange ⅓ of the cabbage, potatoes, apples, and onion in layers in a large ovenproof casserole. Dot heavily with butter, and sprinkle with salt and pepper. Repeat with the next ⅓ of the vegetables, and again dot with butter and season. Layer the remaining ⅓ of the vegetables, piling it high in the center of the casserole; dot with butter and season. The dish will now be quite full, but it will cook down. Pour in the heavy cream, cover the casserole, and bake in a 350-degree oven for about 45 minutes, or until just tender. Sprinkle with the bread crumbs and cheese, and return to oven, uncovered, until the top becomes browned and forms a nice crust. Serves 8.

JULIENNE OF CARROTS AND PARSNIPS

4 or 5 young medium parsnips
4 or 5 medium carrots
¼ pound unsalted butter
2 teaspoons light brown
   sugar

Salt, freshly ground pepper
Minced parsley

Choose parsnips that are not too wide at the top or they will be woody. Peel and slice the carrots and parsnips in julienne strips. Melt the butter in a saucepan and add carrots and parsnips and enough water almost to cover. Sprinkle on sugar, salt, and pepper. Cover partially and simmer until tender, about 20 minutes. Boil rapidly to evaporate liquid if necessary. Sprinkle with parsley. Serves 8.

IRISH SODA BREAD I

4 cups flour, sifted
3 ½ teaspoons baking pow-
    der
½ teaspoon baking soda
½ teaspoon salt
1 cup sugar
¼ cup butter

2 to 3 teaspoons caraway
    seeds
1 ¼ to 2 cups seedless raisins
1 ½ cups milk or as needed
Butter or oil for preparing
    skillet

Preheat oven to 300 degrees.

Mix flour, baking powder, baking soda, salt, and sugar. Blend in butter, caraway seeds, and raisins, then mix in milk to make a stiff dough. Butter or oil a 10-inch iron skillet, and fill with bread dough. (Make deep crossed incisions through center of loaf.) Bake 1 hour in a 300-degree oven. Serves 8 to 10.

IRISH SODA BREAD II

3 cups flour
Salt
½ teaspoon baking soda
1 teaspoon baking powder
1 to 2 tablespoons sugar
1 teaspoon caraway seeds

6 tablespoons butter
1 ¼ cups raisins
1 egg, beaten
1 to 2 cups buttermilk
Butter or oil for loaf pan

Preheat oven to 300 degrees.

Sift flour, a dash of salt, soda, and baking powder together. Add sugar and caraway seeds. Cut butter into small pieces and work into flour mixture with fingertips. Add raisins and beaten egg, and as much buttermilk as needed to make the batter "too soft to handle, but too thick to pour." Butter or oil a 9 by 5 by 2¾-inch loaf pan and fill with batter. Cut a crisscross in center at the top and bake in a 300-degree oven for 45 minutes. Serves 8 to 10.

TIPSY SQUIRE

12 ladyfingers, split, or a 7 by 11-inch Spongecake (recipe below), cut into squares and split horizontally

⅓ cup seedless black raspberry jam

½ cup white wine

1½ cups milk

3 tablespoons sugar

¼ teaspoon salt

4 egg yolks

1 cup heavy cream, whipped

1 tablespoon sugar

1 teaspoon vanilla

¼ cup toasted slivered almonds

Spread ladyfingers or spongecake with jam, cover with a top layer, and put in a rectangular 7 by 11-inch glass dish. Pour wine over the top and refrigerate about 4 hours.

Cook the milk, sugar, salt, and yolks over low heat, stirring constantly, until thickened. Do not allow to come near the boiling point. Whip cream, sugar, and vanilla until stiff. Add the custard to the cake in the dish and top with whipped cream and toasted almonds just before serving. Serves 8 to 10.

Spongecake

4 eggs

¾ cup sugar

Grated zest of 1 lemon

1¼ cups sifted cake flour

Butter for cake pan

Preheat oven to 350 degrees.

Beat eggs and sugar in the top of a double boiler over simmering water until thick and creamy. Remove from heat and beat 5 minutes longer. Add the lemon zest and fold in the flour. Butter a 7 by 11-inch pan and pour in batter. Bake for 20 minutes in a 350-degree oven, until a toothpick inserted in center comes out clean.

An Academy Awards
Event for Twelve

*Ham Paste with Green Peppercorns
  Thinly Sliced French Bread or Tiny Hot Biscuits
*Red Snapper Salad
*Veal Birds with Oysters
*Buttered Rice (see Index)
*Baked Cherry Tomatoes
*Unmolded Chocolate Pouding

An elegant, at-home Oscar evening when your dinner guests not only can watch (via television) but win the awards? Even Oscar himself would applaud such a delicious idea. And to add to the glitter and glamour—a show-stopping buffet menu. It blends unusual flavors in dazzling new ways.

In the opening scene you'll sip cocktails and sample canapés spread with a ham paste spiked with green peppercorns. The appetizing plot moves on to the buffet, set with a salad of red snapper tossed with endive and served on a bed of romaine. The climactic main course features plump oysters tucked into wine-simmered veal birds, served with herbed baked cherry tomatoes. And for the finale, a devastating dessert —equally as eye-filling as the Academy Awards to follow.

To enhance the excitement of the Academy Awards televiewing— prepare a posterboard listing all the individual award categories along the top, and the names of the guests down the side. The more categories listed—the greater the element of chance and suspense.

Pre-dinner, each guest is asked to predict a winner in each category on his own personal score sheet. He or she would then bet a set amount of money on his predictions ($1–$5–$10—you set the pot!). The host or hostess would pool the stakes and tally the individual predictions on the posterboard. When the televised Oscar festivities begin, the poster should be placed in a prominent spot so that everyone can keep track of his or her predictions as the Oscars are awarded. At the end of the evening, the pot would be divided up among three winners. Money prizes would be given to the guests who came closest and second in guessing the Oscar winners. And for the worst guesser—a funny consolation prize.

HAM PASTE WITH GREEN PEPPERCORNS

1 tablespoon green peppercorns
4 or 5 slivers garlic
1 teaspoon cinnamon
6 tablespoons unsalted butter, softened
Salt
4 to 5 cups (about 2 to 2 ½
   pounds) minced baked
   ham

4 tablespoons Dijon mustard
2 tablespoons cognac
Mayonnaise, preferably
   homemade (see Basic
   Recipes)
French bread, biscuits, or
   lettuce leaves with
   cornichons

Mash the green peppercorns with the garlic and cinnamon in a mortar and pestle. Work in the butter until thoroughly blended. Taste for salt and add if necessary, depending on the saltiness of the ham.

Blend the green peppercorns, butter, ham, mustard, cognac, and just enough mayonnaise to bind the mixture—not so much that mixture becomes too moist. Chill just until firm. Serve with thinly sliced French bread or tiny hot biscuits for cocktails, or as a first course on lettuce leaves with cornichons. Makes 5 to 6 cups.

RED SNAPPER SALAD

16 to 24 endives, cut crosswise in small crescents
3 cups mild olive oil
1 cup vinegar or lemon juice
12 tablespoons mustard
Salt, freshly ground pepper
9 tablespoons milk
2 3- to 4-pound baked or
   poached red snappers,

cooled, skinned, and flaked
   in good-sized pieces (see
   directions for poaching
   fish in Index)
Romaine leaves for bed of
   salad

Put endive into a bowl. Mix oil, vinegar, mustard, salt, and pepper, and milk, and pour over the endive. Toss. Add snapper pieces and mix gently. Line salad bowl with romaine leaves and turn dressed snapper and endive into it. Chill 30 minutes and serve. Serves 12.

Note: This is a salad that should not be prepared too far in advance. Prepare the snapper ahead of time, and combine with the endive and dressing just before chilling and serving.

VEAL BIRDS WITH OYSTERS

3 cups fine, freshly made bread crumbs (see Basic Recipes)
1 scant teaspoon sage
2 eggs, lightly beaten
2 tablespoons minced parsley
½ pound butter, melted
Salt, freshly ground pepper

2 dozen oysters, drained (reserve the liquor for sauce)
12 thin scaloppines of veal, 6 by 3 inches when pounded out
4 tablespoons flour
2 tablespoons minced shallots
½ cup dry white wine
¾ cup chicken broth

Prepare the stuffing: mix together bread crumbs, sage, eggs, parsley, 8 tablespoons melted butter, and salt and pepper to taste. Encase the oysters, 2 per serving, in the stuffing and put at narrow end of each slice of veal. Roll up the slice and tie with string in 2 places to secure. Dust the veal rolls lightly with flour seasoned with salt and pepper. Melt the remaining butter in a skillet and brown the veal on all sides. Add the shallots and cook several more minutes; add the wine, ½ the reserved oyster liquor, and the chicken broth and bring to a boil. Cover and simmer about 20 to 25 minutes. Add more oyster liquor if desired. The birds may also be served with green noodles. Serves 12.

BAKED CHERRY TOMATOES

3 pint-size baskets cherry tomatoes
⅓ cup or more olive oil
Salt, freshly ground pepper

Chopped fresh parsley
Chopped basil
Butter

Preheat oven to 350 degrees.

Put the tomatoes in 1 layer in a rectangular cake pan or a roasting pan. Brush with olive oil, shake pan, and brush the uncoated sides until the tomatoes are lightly but completely coated with oil. Sprinkle with salt and pepper and bake for about 10 minutes. Begin checking at 8 minutes. Tomatoes should cook long enough to warm through and soften a bit, but do not bake until the skins begin to split. Put in a warm, buttered serving dish and sprinkle with herbs. Serves 12.

UNMOLDED CHOCOLATE POUDING

Butter
Sugar
1½ cups milk
5 ounces extra bittersweet
    chocolate (Swiss, *not* do-
    mestic)
1½ tablespoons water or
    coffee

5 egg yolks
½ cup sugar
3 tablespoons flour
1 tablespoon vanilla
5 egg whites
1 cup heavy cream, whipped
Vanilla, rum, or cognac

Preheat oven to 375 degrees.

Butter well a 3- to 4-cup soufflé dish or charlotte mold, and dust thoroughly with sugar. Scald milk and melt the chocolate with the water or coffee.

Mix yolks, sugar, and flour until pale yellow and thickened. Add half of the scalded milk to this mixture gradually, beat well, and then return this to the remaining milk in saucepan. Continue to stir and cook until boiling for several minutes. Pour into large bowl, and stir in the melted chocolate and vanilla.

Beat egg whites until stiff, fold them gently and thoroughly into the yolk-milk mixture, and pour into the prepared mold. Put in a *bain-marie* containing boiling water and put this in a 375-degree oven for 15 minutes. Turn down to 350 degrees and bake 45 to 50 minutes.

The pouding will rise exactly like a soufflé during the cooking. Then push pouding back into its mold or dish, gently but firmly. Unmold to serve, blot excess butter from the pouding with a paper towel, and decorate with whipped cream flavored with vanilla, rum, or cognac. When serving 12, as in this menu, prepare the recipe twice rather than doubling the ingredients. Since it is not a conventional risen soufflé, it may wait successfully. Serves 6.

An Easter

Luncheon for Six

*Fonds d'Artichauts Forestière
*Bass Stuffed with Shrimp and Oysters
*Buttered Rice
 Salad of Bibb Lettuce and Watercress, with
    *White Wine Vinaigrette (see Basic Recipes)
*Fresh Pineapple with Kirsch and Mint
*Macaroons

Perhaps it is that spring has come or is coming to the city, but New Yorkers from all five boroughs traditionally celebrate Easter by donning their finest garb—hats, too—and parading on Fifth Avenue in the Fifties, near St. Patrick's Cathedral. The mayor strolls with the throngs, cheerfully being greeted by and greeting the crowds. Joy and spring are in the air. It's a scene from a film spectacular with casts of thousands: the thin, young, and trendy; the older, portly, and orchid-corsaged; the chic, and the would-be chic. All the day needs is Gene Kelly, Fred Astaire, Judy Garland, *Easter Parade*, and a carefully rehearsed "impromptu" dance or two.

New Yorkers have many and various Easter rituals but they always seem to include the parade, whether it's church in the Bronx and the long trip to Fifth Avenue, or brunch at the Plaza and then the parade, or church, the parade, and a late festive luncheon. The menu offered here is for the last tradition—celebrating with an elegant but light luncheon after church and a walk to see and be seen. It does require some attention, but Easter is special.

A well-known and talented New York decorator blows eggs, then carefully and beautifully decorates or paints them, hangs them on branches as a centerpiece, and then gives each quest an egg to take home. An alternative requiring less patience and talent might be a large crystal bowl filled with greens and colored alabaster and marble eggs. They are pretty and inexpensive. Use fresh spring colors for your table, and the air of spring will be in the menu and the mood.

FONDS D'ARTICHAUTS FORESTIÈRE

12 large or 18 medium mushrooms
½ lemon
6 Boston lettuce leaves
6 cooked fresh artichoke bottoms (reserve leaves for
   hors d'oeuvres, see Index)

1 ½ cups Mustard Sauce (see
   recipe below)
3 tablespoons chopped parsley

Wipe mushrooms with a damp towel and cut off stem even with cap (reserve stems for soups, stuffings, flavorings for stock). Rub caps with lemon juice to prevent their discoloring.

Just before serving, arrange lettuce leaves on a serving platter or individual plates. Put an artichoke bottom on each. Fill with 1 or 2 spoon-fuls of mustard sauce. Slice mushrooms thinly and arrange the slices, overlapping, on or around the artichoke bottoms. Coat lightly with sauce. Sprinkle with chopped parsley. Serves 6.

Mustard Sauce

4 tablespoons Dijon mustard
4 tablespoon heavy cream or
   Crème Fraîche (see In-
   dex), at room temperature
4 tablespoons boiling water
¾ cup olive oil

Lemon juice
Salt, freshly ground pepper
1 tablespoon minced shallots,
   green onions, or chives
1 tablespoon chopped parsley

Warm a small mixing bowl with hot water. Put in the mustard and cream and blend well. Add the water drop by drop, beating with a whisk. Then add the oil drop by drop, beating as for a mayonnaise, until sauce is thick and creamy. Season to taste with lemon juice, salt, and pepper, and fold in the herbs. Makes about 1 ½ cups.

BASS STUFFED WITH SHRIMP
AND OYSTERS

4½- to 5-pound striped bass, cleaned, with head and tail left on
Salt, freshly ground black pepper
5 to 6 tablespoons butter
2 tablespoons flour
1 cup oysters
1 cup fresh shrimp, peeled and deveined
1 cup dry bread crumbs
1 cup chopped scallions, green tops included
½ cup chopped celery
1 heaping tablespoon minced parsley
Butter for baking dish
6 to 8 shrimp, sautéed (optional)
6 to 8 oysters, sautéed (optional)
½ pound sliced mushrooms, sautéed (optional)
Sliced lemons
Chopped parsley or watercress

Preheat oven to 350 degrees.

Season the bass with salt and pepper, inside and out, and rub generously with 2 tablespoons butter and sprinkle with flour. Coarsely chop the oysters and shrimp, and combine with the bread crumbs, scallions, celery, and parsley, and season to taste with salt and pepper. Melt 2 to 3 tablespoons butter, and blend into the oyster mixture to bind. Stuff the fish with oyster mixture, skewer or sew the opening closed, and put the fish in a well-buttered baking dish. Butter the top of the fish thoroughly, and bake in a 350-degree oven for about 45 minutes, basting frequently with pan juices. The fish may be garnished with additional shrimp and oysters, cooked, and sautéed mushrooms, or, more simply, with lemon slices and parsley or watercress. Serves 6.

BUTTERED RICE

1½ cups rice
3 cups cold water
4 tablespoons butter
Salt, freshly ground pepper

Combine rice, water, 1 tablespoon butter, and 1½ teaspoons salt in a heavy saucepan. Bring to a boil, stir carefully with a fork, then cover tightly and lower heat. Cook over low heat 15 to 18 minutes, until rice is just tender. Meanwhile, melt remaining butter. When rice is cooked, gently toss in melted butter with a fork and season to taste with salt and pepper. Serves 6.

Variation: Herbed Rice

A green-flecked rice is most attractive. Add ⅓ cup minced parsley or watercress to the rice with the butter, or to complement further other dishes in the menu, an herb such as dill or tarragon (for fish or chicken dishes), basil, or thyme. If fresh herbs are available, use 1 to 2 tablespoons minced; if not, use ½ teaspoon dried plus ¼ cup minced parsley.

FRESH PINEAPPLE WITH KIRSCH AND MINT

1 large or 2 small fresh ripe pineapples	2 tablespoons shredded mint leaves
¼ cup kirsch	

To judge the ripeness of a pineapple, you should be able to smell its fragrant scent *before* cutting into it, and the lower quarter to half should be bright orange. Leave at room temperature until fruit reaches desired ripeness.

Cut pineapple in half lengthwise. Cut out fruit in neat wedges, using a sharp knife or grapefruit knife, leaving a shell. Cut out and discard core, and slice pineapple. Combine pineapple with kirsch and put into shells. Sprinkle with mint. If mint is not available, use 1 to 2 tablespoons finely shredded orange zest. Serves 6.

MACAROONS

8-ounce can almond paste	⅓ cup pine nuts
2 egg whites	Butter
1 cup sugar	

Preheat oven to 375 degrees.

Grate almond paste, or push through a coarse sieve, then combine with egg whites, sugar, and pine nuts until mixture is a smooth paste.

Heavily butter two cookie sheets, then cover them with parchment, typewriting paper, or buttered wax paper. Put the mixture by heaping teaspoonfuls on the paper, about 1½ to 2 inches apart. Bake about 15 minutes, watching carefully, until macaroons are lightly colored. To remove macaroons from paper, press a damp sponge on back of paper. Makes about 30.

A Delightful

Spring Dinner for Eight

*Cream of Lettuce Soup
*Sweetbreads Princesse
*Artichoke Bottoms with Tiny Asparagus Tips
  Salad of Endive, Watercress, and Scallions with
      *White Wine Vinaigrette (see Basic Recipes)
*Hazelnut Bavarian Cream

All the soft, pale colors that mark the arrival of spring are the inspiration for this charming dinner. To create the mood (and honor the season and your guests), tuck the invitations into tiny bouquets of tiger or parrot tulips—those beautiful hybrids that create the illusion of one delicate pastel color melting into another, and deliver personally.

The table should reflect the ambiance of spring. For your tablecloth, use a length of pale moiré fabric (or dye an old white damask cloth a pastel color) and napkins in complementary tones. Carry out the tulip theme in the centerpiece, and arrange tulip-shaped place cards in tiny pots of moss and fern. Lighting should be soft so that your finest silver and crystal will reflect the pale colors effectively.

The menu also offers an unusual array of delicate tastes and colors, starting with a cream of lettuce soup that echoes that special pale green of the first tiny leaves of spring. The rich, smooth soup can be made well in advance and garnished at the last moment with shredded lettuce.

The main course, sweetbreads princesse, is one of the most elegant and savory dishes in any hostess's repertory—although sweetbreads may take some courage to prepare the first time. Even professed sweetbread-haters have succumbed to them prepared in this way—crisp medallions in a fragrant lemon, cognac and cream sauce, garnished with poached mushrooms and served with artichoke bottoms and asparagus tips.

Like spring, the salad is very fresh and green: endive and watercress sprinkled with thinly sliced scallions. The hazelnut Bavarian cream pleasingly contrasts the textures of smooth cream and crunchy pralin. Serve it surrounded by fresh flowers as a final tribute to spring.

CREAM OF LETTUCE SOUP

2 pounds romaine
Salt
¼ cup green peas, fresh or
    frozen
6 tablespoons butter
½ cup minced green onions
Freshly ground pepper

4 tablespoons flour
1 quart best chicken stock,
    heated (see Basic Recipes)
Chervil
½ to ¾ cup heavy cream
Shredded lettuce or salted
    whipped cream (optional)

Wash, trim, chop roughly, and blanch the lettuce in a large amount of boiling salted water for about 10 minutes, or until wilted. Toward the end of the cooking, toss in the peas. Drain and chop again. Melt butter in a large, heavy 2½-quart saucepan, sauté green onions until soft; add lettuce, peas, and salt and pepper to taste, and sauté, stirring, for 2 to 3 minutes. Add flour and blend in well, cooking for a minute or two. Add the hot chicken stock, stirring. Taste for seasoning, then whirl in a blender 2 to 3 cups at a time to desired smoothness. Some prefer the soup with a bit of texture, others prefer it perfectly smooth. Add a generous pinch of chervil. Return to saucepan and add cream to desired thickness. This may be served hot or cold with a bit of shredded lettuce or a dollop of whipped cream on top. Makes 8 servings.

Note: The stock should be of the very best quality or this particular soup will have little personality. If you are using canned broth, simmer it for 20 minutes with ½ cup each thinly sliced carrots and onions, 4 sprigs parsley, a big pinch of thyme, and ¼ cup or more white wine.

SWEETBREADS PRINCESSE

4 pairs sweetbreads (fresh
   if possible)
Juice and rind of 2 lemons
2 pounds mushrooms, stems
   trimmed and thinly sliced
½ cup fresh lemon juice
¼ pound butter
⅔ cup water or chicken or
   veal stock

½ teaspoon salt
Flour seasoned with salt and
   freshly ground pepper
¼ to ½ pound butter
¼ to ½ cup cognac
6 tablespoons lemon juice
1 to 1½ cups heavy cream
Salt, freshly ground pepper

Buy sweetbreads with little or no odor. Prepare by soaking them in cold water several hours or overnight, changing the water 2 or 3 times. In a large pan bring to a brisk boil the juice and rind of 1 lemon plus enough water to cover the sweetbreads. Reduce heat so that water is simmering, add sweetbreads, and blanch for 6 minutes. Plunge the sweetbreads immediately into iced water to stop the cooking. When cool enough to handle, remove the membrane and trim the sweetbreads. Put on a flat plate, cover with another flat plate and a heavy weight. Put the weighted sweetbreads in the refrigerator for at least 4 hours. When ready to prepare the dish, proceed as follows:

Poach the mushrooms in lemon juice, butter, and water or stock for 3 minutes. Drain, reserving the liquid for another use, and set aside. Keep warm. Cut each sweetbread in half crosswise, and carefully cut in half again horizontally to make 4 thin medallions or scallops. Dust each medallion with seasoned flour, and sauté in ¼ pound melted butter in a heavy-bottomed sauté pan over medium to high heat, until crisp. Remove to a platter and keep warm.

To make the sauce pour ¼ cup cognac into the pan in which the sweetbreads were sautéed, and scrape brown bits from the bottom of the pan. Flambé the cognac. When the alcohol has burned off, add remaining 3 tablespoons lemon juice and heavy cream. Heat through but do not boil. Correct seasoning. Cover medallions with poached mushrooms, and mask with the sauce. Serves 8.

ARTICHOKE BOTTOMS
WITH TINY ASPARAGUS TIPS

16 artichoke bottoms
12 tablespoons butter, melted
Salt, freshly ground pepper
3 to 4 asparagus tips, 2 to 2½
    inches long, cooked

(amount depends on size
    of artichoke bottoms),
    per artichoke bottom
Chopped parsley

Before serving, sauté artichoke bottoms lightly in 6 tablespoons butter. Sprinkle with salt and pepper. Warm asparagus tips in the remaining 6 tablespoons butter and season to taste. Put asparagus tips on each artichoke bottom, and sprinkle with parsley. Put on a flat-bottomed serving platter. Serves 8.

HAZELNUT BAVARIAN CREAM

6 large eggs, separated
1 cup sugar
1 cup milk, boiling
1½ tablespoons gelatin dis-
    solved in ½ cup water
    with ½ teaspoon instant
    coffee already dissolved in
    it

Heaping ½ cup Hazelnut
    Pralin (see below)
1 cup heavy cream, lightly
    whipped
1 tablespoon vanilla
Stiffly whipped cream and
    Pralin for garnish

Put yolks in a heavy 2½-quart saucepan and (off the heat) beat 1 to 2 minutes. Gradually begin adding sugar and continue beating until the mixture is very thick and a pale yellow, nearly white. Add hot milk gradually, and put over medium heat, stirring constantly until thickened or the mixture coats a wooden spoon, but not too thickly. Stir in gelatin and continue to stir until dissolved. Beat egg whites until stiff peaks form and fold in with the pralin. Beat over a bowl of ice cubes if you are in a hurry, or set in the refrigerator until the mixture begins to set. Fold in whipped cream and add vanilla.

Rinse an 8-cup mold with cold water and shake out excess water.

Pour in cream mixture. Put in refrigerator until completely set. This can be done a day in advance. Unmold and decorate with piped, stiffly whipped, cream rosettes. This can be done shortly before the guests arrive and returned to refrigerator. Just before serving, sprinkle with pralin. Serves 8.

Hazelnut Pralin

1 cup hazelnuts (filberts)   ¼ cup water
1 cup sugar

Preheat oven to 300 degrees.

Put nuts on a tray (a jelly-roll pan is perfect) and toast in a 300-degree oven for 15 to 20 minutes, shaking and tossing occasionally. Use blanched hazelnuts if you can get them, otherwise, after toasting, rub those with skins between your hands, a few at a time, until as much skin as possible is rubbed off. Grind in the blender. Run ground nuts through a fine mesh sieve. Put those pieces which are too big to go through the sieve into a ½-cup measure and fill to ½ cup with finer ground, if necessary. Then make up another ½ cup of the finely ground nuts. Caramelize ½ cup of sugar with 2 tablespoons water and add the finely ground nuts. Pour immediately onto a clean, oiled section of your countertop (or a marble slab if you have one). Repeat this process with the other ½ cup of more coarsely ground nuts. Grind the fine pralin once again in the blender; whack up the coarse with a mallet. The finely ground nut pralin is best for the Bavarian cream and the coarser grind best for the garnish, as it is crunchier.

Derby Day

Luncheon for Sixteen

*Parmesan Onion Rounds
*Stuffed Cherry Tomatoes
*Okra Salad
*Country Ham with *Mustard Sauce
*Baked Hominy Grits
*Southern-style Green Beans
*Whiskey Cake
*Pecan Pie
*Curried Baked Fruit (to go with leftover ham)

If you can't be in Kentucky on Derby Day, you can capture the color, the excitement, and the mood of the first of the season's three big thoroughbred races in your own home with traditional drinks, southern dishes, and a dashing table decor.

Plan to start your Derby Day celebration well before the race itself begins. The casually elegant look of the table settings will set the pace for the party. Each table is covered with a black and white checkerboard cloth and sparked with sunny yellow napkins encircled by toy horseshoe napkin rings. As a centerpiece, a derby hat turned upside down is filled with yellow black-eyed Susans. Each guest's name is printed on a place card—a miniature version of the racing derby hat, and the bill of fare is featured on a racing form.

Get quickly into the spirit with traditional mint juleps served in tall frosty glasses and served with bubbly Parmesan toast rounds and cherry tomatoes stuffed with an herbed mixture. Get quickly into the action by setting up a betting game based on the odds of the Derby.

Your sumptuous spread, preferably served from a sideboard, starts with a flavorful okra salad and is followed by a southern ham, cooked in wine. As accompaniments to the ham—dishes with a Deep South accent —baked grits, and fresh, garnished green beans. For dessert, guests choose from two sweets—an intoxicating whiskey cake, and a tempting, whipped-cream-garnished pecan pie. What better way to celebrate Derby Day than with a flavorful dose of southern hospitality?

PARMESAN ONION ROUNDS

48 2-inch bread rounds
1 cup Mayonnaise (see Basic
Recipes)
¾ cup freshly grated im-
ported Parmesan cheese

1 cup very thin white onion
slices

Preheat oven to 375 degrees.

Toast bread rounds on one side. Blend the mayonnaise and grated Parmesan cheese. Put a thin slice of onion on the untoasted side, and top with a generous spoonful of mayonnaise-Parmesan cheese mixture. Bake in 375-degree oven 10 to 12 minutes, until puffed and golden. Watch carefully, for they burn easily.

STUFFED CHERRY TOMATOES

1 tablespoon minced fresh
tarragon
6 tablespoons finely minced
sour pickles
1 heaping tablespoon finely
minced shallots
1 tablespoon finely chopped
parsley
1 tablespoon Dijon mustard
1 clove garlic, finely chopped
(optional)

1 hard-cooked egg, finely
chopped (optional)
2 cups Mayonnaise, preferably homemade (see Basic
Recipes)
Salt, freshly ground pepper
4 pints cherry tomatoes
½ pound shrimp, cooked
and cut into small pieces

Combine tarragon, pickles, shallots, parsley, mustard, garlic, and hard-cooked egg, if desired, with mayonnaise. Season to taste with salt and pepper.

Cut tops from cherry tomatoes and scoop out insides with a demitasse spoon, leaving a shell. Fill with mayonnaise mixture. Garnish each with a piece of shrimp. A very thin slice can be cut off the bottom of any tomato that will not stand up easily.

OKRA SALAD

3 pounds fresh okra (or 4 10-
    ounce packages frozen)
Salt
2 medium onions, finely
    chopped
1 green pepper, seeded and
    finely chopped
6 tablespoons olive oil
4 medium tomatoes, peeled,
    seeded, and chopped

1 cup tart Vinaigrette Sauce
    (see Basic Recipes)
Tabasco sauce
½ cup each of chopped
    parsley and basil
3 scallions, chopped
Freshly ground pepper

Slice okra ¼ inch thick and cook in boiling, salted water until just tender. Drain.

Sauté the onions and green pepper in olive oil until tender. Add tomatoes and continue to cook, stirring occasionally, until tomatoes have rendered their juices, about 10 minutes.

Toss the hot, cooked okra in the vinaigrette sauce. Add a few dashes of Tabasco. Fold in tomato, onion, and pepper mixture, and refrigerate. The salad may be prepared well in advance and refrigerated until ready to serve.

Before serving, sprinkle generously with parsley and basil mixture, and scallions. Season very well with salt and pepper. Serves 16.

COUNTRY HAM

14-pound Smithfield ham,
    pepper-coated

½ gallon domestic red wine
Brown sugar (optional)

Scrub the ham thoroughly with a stiff brush, and soak 24 to 36 hours in cool water to cover, changing the water several times. Soaking removes the strong saltiness.

In a pan large enough to hold the ham, put red wine, the ham, and cool water to cover. Cover and simmer the ham over low heat for about 20 minutes per pound, or 4½ hours. Remove the ham to a large platter. When cool enough to handle, carefully cut away the skin on the fat side of the ham.

Preheat the oven to 350 degrees. Score the fat with a sharp knife, cutting diagonally across the surface one way, and then the opposite way to form diamond shapes. At this point, the ham may be glazed with brown sugar, if desired. It is served unadorned, since it is accompanied by the pungent mustard sauce.

Bake the ham in a 350-degree oven for about ½ hour, until nicely browned. Serves 16.

Mustard Sauce

1 2-ounce can English dry   3 eggs
  mustard   1 cup granulated sugar
1 cup cider vinegar

Combine mustard and vinegar in a bowl and allow to stand overnight. Break eggs into a heavy saucepan and blend in sugar. Stir over low heat until smooth. Add the mustard and vinegar mixture. Cook slowly, stirring constantly, over medium heat until thick. Cool and store in jar in refrigerator. Keeps well indefinitely and makes nice gifts in small crocks. Makes 2 to 3 cups.

BAKED HOMINY GRITS

1 quart milk   1 teaspoon salt
13 tablespoons plus 1 tea-   1 cup grated Swiss cheese
  spoon butter   ⅓ cup freshly grated Parme-
1 cup quick-cooking hominy   san cheese
  grits

Preheat oven to 350 degrees.

Put milk in a heavy enameled saucepan and bring to a boil over medium heat. Add 8 tablespoons butter and stir until melted; then gradually stir in grits and return to the boil, stirring until thickened (about the consistency of thin cream of wheat).

Remove from the heat and season with salt. Beat hard with an electric beater for 5 minutes. Pour into a 1½-quart casserole. Melt remaining butter. Combine cheeses and sprinkle over top of grits, then dribble with butter. Bake in a 350-degree oven for about 1 hour, until top is browned and crusty. Serves 8.

Note: The dish can be assembled well in advance and refrigerated until ready to bake. Make two casseroles to serve 16.

SOUTHERN-STYLE GREEN BEANS

4 pounds green beans
12 slices raw bacon
1 tablespoon cooking oil

2 medium onions, chopped
Salt, freshly ground pepper
Butter

Snap ends off beans and string if necessary. Leave the beans whole. Add beans and bacon to a large pot of boiling water and cook until beans are just tender, about 15 minutes. Drain and remove bacon slices. Run cold water over beans to stop cooking. Pat bacon dry and sauté in the oil until crisp. Crumble and set aside. Add chopped onion to pan and cook in rendered bacon fat until soft. Drain off excess fat. Add beans to pan and mix well with onions. Season with salt and pepper to taste. Before serving, reheat the beans, butter a serving dish, and turn the beans into it. Sprinkle with crumbled bacon. Serves 16.

WHISKEY CAKE

½ cup butter
1 cup sugar
1 cup bourbon, cognac, or
   rum

9-inch freshly baked single-
   layer white or yellow
   cake, cooled
¾ cup confectioners' sugar

Heat butter and sugar until bubbling and stir in bourbon, cognac, or rum. Punch large holes with a 2-prong fork in the top of cake. Pour topping over sides and top of cake. Just before serving, sieve confectioners' sugar generously over the cake.

PECAN PIE

1 cup light corn syrup
¾ cup sugar
½ teaspoon salt
1 tablespoon butter, melted
  and cooled
1 teaspoon vanilla
2 tablespoons dark rum
4 eggs, lightly beaten

1 cup pecans, halved
9-inch Pastry shell, partially
  baked (see Basic Recipes)
1 cup heavy cream, whipped
  and flavored with 2 to 3
  tablespoons dark rum and
  2 tablespoons sugar *or* 1
  pint vanilla ice cream

Preheat oven to 400 degrees.

Combine corn syrup, sugar, salt, butter, vanilla, and rum with the eggs and stir to mix thoroughly. Spread pecans over the pastry shell, and cover with the egg mixture. Put in the oven and immediately reduce heat to 350 degrees. Bake about 50 minutes, until the filling is firm. The pecans will rise to the top. Cool before serving, and serve with rum-flavored whipped cream or vanilla ice cream. Serves 8, so make 2 pies to serve 16.

CURRIED BAKED FRUIT
(FOR LEFTOVER HAM)

½ cup butter
¾ cup packed brown sugar
4 teaspoons curry powder
1-pound 13-ounce can pear
  halves
1-pound 13-ounce can cling
  peaches or apricot halves

20-ounce can pineapple slices
  or chunks
8-ounce jar maraschino cherries with stems

Preheat oven to 325 degrees.

Melt butter, add sugar and curry powder, and stir until blended. Drain fruit and arrange in a 1½- to 2-quart baking dish. Pour butter mixture over fruit and bake for 1 hour in a 325-degree oven. This can be prepared the day before and reheated in a 325-degree oven until heated through. Serves 12.

June Anniversary

Dinner for Four

*Toasted Sardine Rolls
*Baked Clams René Verdon
*Cornish Game Hens with Triple Sec
  Tiny Green Peas
*Mushrooms Gruyère
*Wine Jelly with Nectarines or Peaches

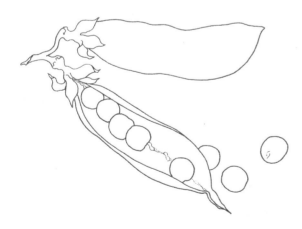

A wedding anniversary should always be a gay and romantic occasion—one on which a couple can recall the past with affection and toast the future with anticipation. The celebration suggested here is a very personal and private evening designed to create that mood of romance—one that should be shared with only the best of friends. The best man or maid of honor maybe?

This June anniversary dinner for four starts spinning its spell in a shade of soft pink—a table covered in delicate pink, sparkling crystal, and gleaming silver to set off a mirage of reflected light from the unique centerpiece. The centerpiece is made of pieces of mirror cut and glued together in solid geometrical shapes to create three-dimensional sculptures. You can make these sculptures yourself from mirror obtained from a local glass cutter. Placed in the center of the table surrounded by candles, the mirrored surfaces will reflect a warm glittering glow. Silver picture frames showcase the menu at each place setting, along with silver cups filled with tiny pink roses and baby's breath.

Start the evening with cocktails and canapés—toasted sardine rolls tart with lemon. The meal itself is unusual and special enough for the occasion. It begins with baked herbed clams topped with dots of Gruyère cheese. The main course, Cornish game hens stuffed with wild rice lightly flavored with orange peel and thyme, is basted in Triple Sec sauce and accompanied by tiny peas and mushrooms Gruyère. All of this, of course, is served with plenty of champagne to toast the happy couple.

For dessert, a delicate wine jelly encircled by fresh sliced nectarines or peaches is served with a sauce boat of brandied whipped cream—and best wishes for many happy returns.

TOASTED SARDINE ROLLS

1 tablespoon Mayonnaise
(see Basic Recipes)
1 tablespoon Worcestershire
sauce
Juice of ½ a lemon, or more,
to taste

4-ounce can boneless, skin-
less sardines, partially
drained and mashed
6 slices spongy sandwich
bread, crusts removed

Preheat oven to 350 degrees.

Blend the mayonnaise, Worcestershire sauce, and lemon juice with
the mashed sardines to make an easily spreadable paste. Roll each slice of
bread with a rolling pin to compress and flatten it. Spread with sardine
spread and roll up, jelly-roll fashion. Cut in half and secure with toothpicks. When ready to serve, bake in a 350-degree oven, turning once, for
12 to 15 minutes, or until nicely browned. Serve immediately. Serves 4.

BAKED CLAMS RENÉ VERDON

32 cherrystone clams on half
shell
½ cup finely chopped shallots or scallions
4 tablespoons dry white wine
1 tablespoon minced parsley
2 teaspoons minced fresh tarragon or ½ teaspoon dried
(optional)

4 cloves garlic, finely
chopped
2 to 3 tablespoons fresh bread
crumbs
6 tablespoons softened butter
Salt, freshly ground pepper
32 small squares of Gruyère
cheese

Preheat oven to 400 degrees.

Arrange the clams on a large baking dish or cookie sheet covered with
foil to contain any excess liquid. Heat the shallots or scallions with the
wine in a small saucepan until most of the wine has evaporated. Combine
the shallots, parsley, tarragon if desired, garlic, and bread crumbs with
the butter and salt and pepper to taste to make a paste. Spread a little of
this paste, pushing it off the tip of a spoon, on each clam until all of the

mixture is used. Top each clam with a square of cheese and bake 8 to 10 minutes until heated through and the cheese is melted.

These are most easily served if cooked in individual au gratin dishes, though they are not messy or difficult to serve from a baking dish or pan. Serves 4.

CORNISH GAME HENS
WITH TRIPLE SEC

2 large Cornish game hens
   (1½ to 2 pounds) or 4
   small (¾ to 1 pound)

2 teaspoons salt

Stuffing

½ cup wild rice
1 cup chicken stock
2 tablespoons butter
¼ cup chopped scallions
1 cup finely chopped celery

½ teaspoon grated orange
   zest
¼ teaspoon thyme
1 teaspoon Triple Sec

Orange-butter baste

4 tablespoons melted butter
2 tablespoons Triple Sec

½ teaspoon grated orange
   zest

Triple Sec Sauce

1 cup chicken stock
⅛ teaspoon thyme
¼ teaspoon salt

1 tablespoon cornstarch
2 tablespoons Triple Sec

Preheat oven to 325 degrees.
Wash hens and pat dry with paper towels. Sprinkle interiors with salt

and set aside. Prepare stuffing: cook wild rice in chicken stock until all liquid has been absorbed, about 30 minutes. Melt butter in a heavy skillet and sauté scallions and celery until soft but not browned. Remove from heat and stir in orange zest and thyme. Add rice and toss lightly, then add Triple Sec. Stuff the hens with this mixture and truss. Put in baking pan, breasts down. Prepare baste: melt butter and combine with Triple Sec and zest. Baste birds well with orange-butter mix and roast in a 325-degree oven for 15 to 20 minutes. Turn hens onto their backs, baste again, and roast 30 to 40 minutes longer (20 to 30 minutes for smaller birds), or until leg joint moves easily, or juices run clear when leg is pricked with a fork.

Remove to a heated serving dish, reserving pan juices for Triple Sec sauce. Add the chicken stock to pan in which the hens were roasted, scraping up brown bits from bottom, and blend until rich brown. Stir in thyme and salt. Blend cornstarch and Triple Sec in a measuring cup. Add to the pan juices and stir until sauce thickens and boils. Pour a few spoonfuls over the hens and serve the remaining sauce in a sauceboat. Serves 4.

MUSHROOMS GRUYÈRE

⅓ cup butter
1 clove garlic, finely chopped
1 shallot, finely chopped
1 pound mushrooms (quartered or sliced if large)
2 teaspoons lemon juice
½ cup finely chopped celery
Salt, freshly ground pepper
2 tablespoons finely grated Gruyère cheese
2 tablespoons finely chopped parsley

Melt butter in medium-size skillet. Sauté garlic and shallot until tender. Add mushrooms and lemon juice, and cook, stirring for 3 minutes. Add celery and season to taste with salt and pepper. Cook 1 minute longer. Remove from heat. Stir in cheese and parsley and continue stirring until cheese is just melted. Serve immediately. Serves 4.

WINE JELLY WITH NECTARINES OR PEACHES

2 packages unflavored gelatin
½ cup cold water
1 ½ cups boiling water
1 cup sugar
3 tablespoons lemon juice

2 tablespoons orange juice
1 cup sherry
3 fresh peaches or nectarines
1 cup heavy cream, whipped
Sugar

Soften gelatin in cold water. Stir into the boiling water with sugar. Stir until completely dissolved, add the orange and lemon juices and sherry, and stir until well blended. Rinse a 4-cup mold with cold water and shake out excess. Pour in gelatin mixture, and refrigerate until firm.

Peel and slice 2 peaches or nectarines. Unmold jelly onto an attractive plate and surround with the cut fresh fruit. Refrigerate. Dice remaining peach or nectarine, and fold into the whipped cream with sugar to taste. Serve as a sauce with the jelly. Serves 4 to 6.

Morning-after

Brunch for Twelve

*Bloody Marys
*Salty Dogs
*Mimosas
*French Toast with Grand Marnier
*Oyster Casserole
*Apple Muffins
  Sausage Cakes
  Hot Croissants and Rolls
*Grapefruit and Pineapple Compote

The next time it's your turn to have a party in connection with a wedding weekend or to assist a friend with house guests, the brunch suggested here might be just the thing. The menu is geared to the over-enthusiastic drinkers of the night before, but it will be just as welcome to the most moderate of people.

On the theory that the hair of the dog is a good cure, three classic eyeopeners are suggested. Gin fizzes or a good milk punch would be fine choices, too. Have the drinks in pitchers ready for self-service pouring as the guests arrive. And don't forget to dip the wet rims of some of the glasses into coarse salt for the Salty Dogs.

The menu is a snappy blend of flavors and textures. Dessert really isn't necessary. However, a large bowl of minted fresh grapefruit and pineapple sections macerated in kirsch would be delicious after the sweet french toast marinated in Grand Marnier and zippy enough to restore a feeling of well-being to the victims of the night before.

If you want to emphasize the morning-after theme for this party, you might send out invitations on pink construction paper elephants. An amusing centerpiece would be a branch potted in a large tomato juice can and hung with packets of Alka-Seltzer set against the backdrop of a blue denim cloth and gaily printed napkins. This ultra-casual brunch might just come as a clever change of pace during a long weekend of more formal activities.

NEW YORK JUNIOR LEAGUE
BLOODY MARYS

1 cup vodka
3 cups tomato juice
2 teaspoons Worcestershire
   sauce
8 dashes Tabasco sauce

6 generous grindings of black
   pepper
Ice cubes
1 large lime cut into 8 wedges

Combine vodka, tomato juice, Worcestershire, Tabasco, and pepper in a pitcher over ice cubes. Pass limes separately to be squeezed into the drinks. Makes 8 4-ounce drinks.

SALTY DOGS

1 ½ cups vodka
4 cups grapefruit juice

Coarse salt

Combine vodka and juice in a pitcher of ice. Dip the rims of 8 glasses in water and then in coarse salt, and shake off excess, so that the glasses are attractively frosted. If using regular table salt, sprinkle the salt around the rims with your fingers. Makes 8 5-ounce drinks.

MIMOSAS

1 quart orange juice

1 bottle chilled champagne

Mimosas may be made to taste. Half orange juice and half champagne is a good way to start. You may prefer to increase the amount of champagne. Serve the champagne from its bottle and the juice from a pretty pitcher. Makes 8 8-ounce servings (4 ounces champagne and 4 ounces orange juice).

FRENCH TOAST
WITH GRAND MARNIER

24 slices best-quality sandwich bread
12 eggs
3 cups milk
¾ cup Grand Marnier
1 tablespoon finely grated
   orange zest

3 tablespoons sugar
1 ½ teaspoons vanilla
¾ teaspoon salt
12 tablespoons butter
Confectioners' sugar

Arrange bread in single layer in three 12 by 8 by 2-inch baking dishes. Beat eggs with milk, add Grand Marnier, orange zest, sugar, vanilla, and salt, and blend. Pour over bread, turning slices to coat both sides. Cover and refrigerate overnight. Heat butter in skillet and sauté until golden brown, about 4 minutes per side. Dust generously with confectioners' sugar, and pass additional sugar at the table. Serves 12.

OYSTER CASSEROLE

3 dozen oysters, cut up
   finely with scissors
3 onions, finely chopped
3 stalks celery, finely
   chopped
½ pound butter
¼ cup lemon juice
Grated zest of 2 lemons

2 tablespoons Worcester-
   shire sauce
Dash of Tabasco sauce
5 slices bread, crusts removed and cubed
2 eggs, lightly beaten
Cracker crumbs

Drain oysters in a colander and set aside in a large bowl. (Reserve liquor to freeze for soup.) Sauté onions and celery in 12 tablespoons butter until soft. Add lemon juice and zest, Worcestershire sauce, and Tabasco to oysters. Stir in the onions and celery, and add the bread and eggs. Butter an 8 by 12-inch casserole dish and pour in oyster mixture. Melt the remaining 4 tablespoons of butter. Sprinkle cracker crumbs on top of the casserole and dribble with the melted butter. Bake in a 350-degree oven 20 to 25 minutes until bubbly. This recipe serves 4 to 6. To serve 12, as for this menu, prepare 2 to 3 casseroles.

APPLE MUFFINS

Butter for muffin tins
1 ¼ cups bran
⅔ cup milk
2 eggs
1 ¼ cups sugar
¼ cup liquid shortening
1 cup flour
2 ½ teaspoons baking pow-
    der

½ teaspoon salt
1 teaspoon cinnamon
½ teaspoon ground cloves
4 large apples, peeled,
    cored, and cut into
    chunks
1 cup raisins

Preheat the oven to 400 degrees.
Butter large muffin pans (for 12 muffins).
Soak the bran in the milk until liquid is almost totally absorbed. Add eggs, sugar, and shortening. Sift flour, baking powder, salt, cinnamon, and cloves into the mixture. Fold in apples and raisins quickly. Pour batter into prepared muffin pans and bake in a 400-degree oven for 25 to 30 minutes or until well browned. Makes 12 large muffins.
Note: Whenever muffins or cakes are being prepared, the faster the mixture is put into the oven after the liquid ingredients have been added to the dry ingredients often spells the difference between having it rise or not rise, owing to the presence of baking powder.

GRAPEFRUIT AND PINEAPPLE COMPOTE

2 medium, ripe pineapples
4 medium grapefruit
½ cup kirsch

2 tablespoons sugar
Fresh mint

Pare, core, and dice pineapple. Peel and seed grapefruit and cut into sections. Combine fruits with kirsch. Sprinkle with sugar and refrigerate until ready to serve. The compote may be prepared a day in advance. Before serving, finely snip about a tablespoonful of mint leaves and mix into the fruit, and decorate with sprigs of fresh mint. Serves 12.

Dinner Honoring

a Foreign Friend for Eight

*Fresh Crabmeat Soup
*Quail Braised in White Wine
*Wild and Brown Rice
*Asparagus with *Sauce Maltaise
*Fresh Strawberry Ice

Any book on entertaining is bound to state the basic rule that the liveliest conversations around a dinner table most often occur when the guests are both lively themselves and of different professions. To that rule add the corollary that one or two couples of different nationalities also make an evening sparkle. The menu that follows is especially designed to show off American culinary know-how to those foreign friends.

Naturally, foreign visitors are interested in our typical native foods and customs, but you don't want to do Thanksgiving dinner more than once a year. Instead, begin with a creamy crab soup using the fine lump crabmeat from Maryland or the slightly different but equally delicious Dungeness variety available on the West Coast. Follow the soup with another popular American bird—the quail. Here the quail are carefully braised in white wine to preserve their juices and their tenderness. Accompany them with one of our finest gifts to the table, wild rice. A recipe for stretching wild rice with natural brown rice is included. The asparagus with a marvelous orange-flavored hollandaise is not uniquely American, but it is perfect for this menu; and finally a homemade, fresh strawberry ice.

This menu is a sophisticated way to use some of our own indigenous ingredients, and will surely provide the starting point of a grand evening for your foreign friends and other guests as well.

FRESH CRABMEAT SOUP

1 pound fresh lump crabmeat
3 tablespoons unsalted butter
1 ½ tablespoons flour
Basil
Rosemary
Salt, freshly ground white
  pepper

3 cups milk
2 cups heavy cream
1 teaspoon Gentleman's Relish, an English anchovy
  paste, or a good-quality
  domestic anchovy paste

Carefully pick over crabmeat to remove bits of shell and cartilage. Set aside any particularly large, beautiful lumps. Melt butter in a heavy saucepan and stir in crabmeat. Sprinkle over flour, blend well, and season with pinches of basil, rosemary, salt, and pepper. Cook this paste 10 minutes over very low heat, stirring carefully.

Heat milk and cream and blend gradually into crab mixture. Stir in Gentleman's Relish or anchovy paste. Taste for seasoning: if it seems to need salt, add Gentleman's Relish or anchovy paste instead. Stir in large crabmeat lumps and heat through. Serves 8.

Note: This soup can be a delicious stew: increase amount of crabmeat to 1 ½ pounds, and serve with toasted Boston brown bread for a supper.

QUAIL BRAISED IN WHITE WINE

8 quail
Flour
Salt, freshly ground pepper
8 to 12 tablespoons unsalted
  butter
5 to 6 shallots, minced
2 cups dry white wine
4 to 6 cups chicken stock, or

more, depending on size of
  quail
Bouquet garni: parsley, bay
  leaf, thyme
1 to 2 tablespoons arrowroot
Madeira
Lemon juice

Preheat oven to 350 degrees.

Dust quail with flour and sprinkle with salt and pepper. Heat 8 tablespoons butter in a heavy ovenproof casserole and lightly brown quail on all sides. Remove the quail and set aside. Add shallots, and a little butter if necessary, and cook gently until soft. Add white wine, raise heat, and cook, stirring to scrape up brown bits, until reduced by half. Return quail to casserole and add enough chicken stock so quail are barely covered. Cover and braise in a 350-degree oven about 20 to 30 minutes, until quail are tender.

The sauce probably needs to be thickened: remove quail and set aside in a warm place, covered. Cook sauce rapidly to reduce a little and intensify flavor. Blend arrowroot with a little Madeira to make a paste and stir this into the sauce off the heat. Cook, stirring, until thickened. Taste and season if necessary with salt, pepper, and a few drops of lemon juice. Return quail to casserole, heat through, and serve. Serves 8.

WILD AND BROWN RICE

¾ cup wild rice
¾ cup brown rice
4½ cups chicken broth or
   water

1½ teaspoons salt
Butter
1 tablespoon chopped parsley

Follow the preliminary preparation of wild rice (see Index) or as follows: rinse wild rice under cool running water. Put in a saucepan and add water to cover. Bring slowly to a simmer. When water reaches a simmer, cook 2 to 3 minutes, drain rice, and proceed with recipe.

Bring the stock or water to a boil, add combined rices and salt. Cover, reduce heat to a simmer, and cook 45 minutes, or until brown rice is tender, and the wild rice is well opened and curled back. Both rices have a nuttier, chewier quality when done than white rice. Butter a serving dish, put in rice, and sprinkle with parsley. Serves 8.

ASPARAGUS WITH SAUCE MALTAISE

6 to 8 asparagus per person
Boiling water

Salt

Rinse asparagus under running water. Cut off tough, woody ends, then peel the stalks up to the tips. The asparagus are then ready to be cooked in either of the following ways:

STEAMING METHOD: Arrange the asparagus on a rack, put the rack over 1 to 2 inches boiling water, depending on the height of the rack, cover, and steam 5 to 8 minutes, until just tender when pierced with the tip of a knife. The cooking time depends on the thickness of the asparagus. (Rectangular vegetable steamers with racks are available and are perfect for cooking any vegetable in this manner.)

BOILING METHOD: Tie the asparagus in bundles about 3 inches in diameter. Bring a large pot of water to a boil, add 1 to 2 tablespoons salt, then put in the asparagus bundles. Boil 6 to 8 minutes, until just tender when pierced with the tip of a knife.

Sauce Maltaise

2 cups Hollandaise Sauce
   (see Basic Recipes)
4 to 6 tablespoons strained
   fresh orange juice

Grated zest of 2 oranges
Lemon juice, if needed

Prepare basic hollandaise sauce, using only 1 tablespoon lemon juice and omitting Tabasco. When the sauce is ready to be served, stir in the orange juice and grated orange zest. Taste and correct the seasoning by adding ½ teaspoon lemon juice if desired.

FRESH STRAWBERRY ICE

3 pints ripe strawberries
½ to ¾ cup sugar (depend-
   ing on sweetness of strawberries)

½ cup water
Juice of 1 orange
Juice of 1 lemon
Kirsch, rum, or cognac

Wash and hull strawberries. Purée in blender. Combine sugar with the water, and heat until sugar has dissolved. Combine with strawberry purée, orange juice, and lemon juice. Flavor with 2 to 3 tablespoons kirsch, rum, or cognac. Freeze in electric or manual ice cream freezer as directed. Makes about 1½ quarts. Serves 8.

Summer

The Bicyclers'

Back-pack Picnic for Four

*Cold Lemon Soup
*Salade Niçoise
  Buttered Sesame Bread Sticks Wrapped in Prosciutto
  Radishes and Carrot Sticks
  Fresh Fruit
  Canadian Cheddar Cheese

What's cooking? Not these chilled picnic dishes. They're prepared in advance to travel with ease. This is a totally portable menu that includes tangy lemon soup—icy and refreshing—a salad that won't wilt, crunchy breadsticks wrapped in prosciutto, crudités, cheese, fruit, and a chilled bottle of wine. (Don't forget the corkscrew!)

Everything can be packed in regular or wide-mouthed Thermos bottles, large or individual serving-sized plastic containers, and served on plastic or paper. Furthermore, it all fits in the space available in a back pack or a bicycle basket.

Everyone is biking now, more than ever. What a nice way to celebrate a beautiful summer day with friends: take a long and leisurely bicycle ride, spread a wildly patterned no-iron sheet for a brightly different picnic cloth, relax, and enjoy the food and the day.

COLD LEMON SOUP

3 cups rich chicken stock,
   fresh or canned
1 ½ tablespoons small tapioca
2 egg yolks
1 ½ tablespoons freshly
   squeezed lemon juice
¾ tablespoon grated lemon
   zest

Salt
Tabasco sauce
¾ cup heavy cream
Light cream
Lemon juice

Bring the stock to a boil in the top of a double boiler. Add the tapioca slowly. Cook quickly for 3 to 4 minutes, then lower the heat to a simmer, and cook, partially covered, for 5 minutes more.

Combine egg yolks, lemon juice and zest, salt to taste, and a dash of Tabasco in a small bowl. Add the heavy cream. Remove the hot stock

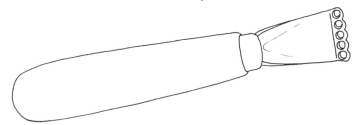

from the heat. Add 1 tablespoon simmering stock to cream mixture and stir well. Add another tablespoon and stir. Continue to add stock to cream mixture by the tablespoon until you have added about a dozen tablespoons.

Return the stock to the double boiler. Pour heated cream mixture into the stock, and stir continuously with a wooden spoon until the soup has thickened enough to coat the back of a spoon.

Pour the soup into a chilled bowl and cool to room temperature. Cover tightly and refrigerate until the soup is icy cold. Serve thinned with a little light cream and more lemon juice if desired. Serves 4.

Note: You can speed up the cooking process by stirring carefully and constantly over direct heat rather than over a double boiler. There is a chance the soup will curdle, however, if you are not extremely careful.

SALADE NIÇOISE

1 ½ cups sliced cooked new potatoes

1 ½ cups cooked fresh green beans

½ cup red onion rings

7-ounce can oil-packed tuna fish, broken up with fork into chunks

1 tablespoon small capers

Salt, freshly ground pepper

⅔ cup olive oil

¼ cup wine vinegar

1 teaspoon Dijon mustard

¼ teaspoon sugar

8 anchovy fillets (optional)

8 cherry tomatoes

2 hard-cooked eggs, quartered

8 pitted black olives

Toss potatoes, green beans, onion rings, tuna fish, capers, and salt and pepper to taste. Combine oil, vinegar, mustard, sugar, salt and pepper to taste in blender container, with anchovies, if desired, and whirl until smooth. Toss this dressing with the tuna mixture until well moistened. Chill. Serve in individual containers (or on a bed of Boston lettuce if not picnicking) with tomatoes, eggs, and olives. Garnish with anchovies if they are not in dressing. Serves 4.

A Mediterranean

Summer Feast for Eight

*Curry Garlic Dip for Crudités
*Gazpacho with Cumin
*Gigot à la Grecque
*Salsa Fria for Leftover Lamb
*Spanakopita
*Lime Mousse
*Almond Cookies

Nowhere in the world do they know how to cope with heat better than in the Mediterranean area. The following menu consists of different dishes from that region and follows the techniques for lightness and simplicity so welcome during the searing summer months.

This Mediterranean mélange includes Spanish gazpacho, marinated lamb, and a spinach pie from Greece, all of which can be prepared ahead. The lamb and the spinach pie need about 1½ hours in a moderate oven, the only last-minute cooking required. Prepare the gazpacho the day before your dinner. Early the day of the party, put the lamb in the marinade and assemble the spanakopita. The tart lime mousse—or pie if you prefer, since it serves nicely in a graham cracker shell—may also be prepared in the cool of the morning.

Included, too, is a Middle Eastern-type sandwich idea for any left-over lamb. A crunchy, zesty raw relish, salsa fria, which can be prepared in quantities and keeps well, is delicious served with the leftover lamb in steamed pita or Middle Eastern bread. It might also serve as a simple prepare-ahead lunch for weekend guests. The lamb can be roasted and cooled the day before.

In keeping with the Mediterranean menu, consider tablecloths of un-bleached muslin and bright-colored napkins tied with Greek key-patterned ribbon for your table setting. An effective, imaginative, and inexpensive centerpiece might be a glossy, hollowed-out eggplant filled with bright garden poppies. White china provides a cool note. Set a carafe of hearty red wine between every two guests. Before dinner offer ouzo, the Greek anise-flavored apéritif, with crushed ice and water and serve light hors d'oeuvres: bowls of Greek olives and platters of crudités with a zesty curry garlic dip.

Enjoy this unusual menu—a blend of Mediterranean culinary traditions—and the time it provides you to be cool and fresh for your guests.

CURRY GARLIC DIP FOR CRUDITÉS

¾ cup mayonnaise
¾ cup sour cream
1 or 2 cloves garlic, put through a press
1 to 2 teaspoons good-quality imported curry powder

Salt, freshly ground pepper
Lemon juice
2 to 3 teaspoons dark rum

Combine mayonnaise, sour cream, garlic, curry powder, and salt and pepper to taste. Flavor with lemon juice and rum. Let stand at room temperature about 1 hour to develop flavors, then refrigerate. Correct seasoning if necessary. Makes 1½ cups, enough for 8.

Note: A crudités tray might include: cauliflower flowerets, carrot sticks, cherry tomatoes, celery ribs, sliced zucchini, sliced cucumber, and sliced green pepper.

GAZPACHO WITH CUMIN

4 cloves garlic, crushed
2 slices fresh white bread, crusts cut off
5 to 6 tablespoons red wine vinegar
6 tablespoons olive oil
1 teaspoon ground cumin or more, to taste

6 cups V-8 juice
3 cups peeled, seeded, and finely chopped cucumber
1 cup finely chopped green pepper
1 cup finely chopped onion
Salt, freshly ground pepper
Toasted croutons (optional)

In a mortar and pestle, or a blender, make a paste of the garlic, bread, vinegar, oil, and cumin. Scrape into a large bowl and add the V-8 juice, mixing well. Stir in the chopped cucumber, green pepper, and onion, and season to taste. Chill thoroughly. This actually improves on sitting 24 hours or more before serving. The soup may be garnished with toasted croutons, but they are not necessary since it is crunchy. Serves 8.

GIGOT À LA GRECQUE

½ cup freshly squeezed
   lemon juice
Grated zest of 1 lemon
3 cloves garlic, put through a
   press
2 tablespoons dried orégano
¼ cup finely chopped parsley

1 tablespoon coarse salt
1 teaspoon coarsely ground
   pepper
¾ cup olive oil
6- to 7-pound leg of lamb

Preheat oven to 350 degrees.

Combine the lemon juice, zest, and garlic. Crush the dried orégano in your hand or a mortar and pestle and add to the lemon juice mixture. Stir well with fork. Stir in the parsley, salt, and pepper. Beat the olive oil in with a fork until marinade is thick and well blended. Score the lamb all over and put it, fat side up, in a large pan. Marinate at room temperature for several hours, basting frequently.

Roast the lamb, basting frequently with marinade, until just done but still quite pink, about 1¼ to 1½ hours (12 to 14 minutes per pound). If roasting the lamb over charcoal, use a meat thermometer and check after 1 hour—internal temperature should be 145 to 150 degrees. Serves 8.

LEFTOVERS: The leftover lamb is delicious served sliced in steamed Middle Eastern bread (pita), split, and filled with Salsa Fria (see recipe below).

SALSA FRIA

4 tomatoes, peeled, seeded,
   and finely chopped
2 onions, finely chopped
1 green pepper, finely
   chopped
2 or 3 cloves garlic, finely
   chopped
4-ounce can Mexican green
   chilies, finely chopped
1½ tablespoons olive oil

1½ tablespoons red wine
   vinegar
½ teaspoon coarse salt
¼ teaspoon coarsely ground
   black pepper
2 or 3 dried red chilies,
   crushed
Ground cumin to taste
Pinch of ground coriander

Mix all ingredients together well. Makes 1 quart of relish. This relish, refrigerated, keeps well for several weeks. Salsa fria is an excellent cold accompaniment for most cold meats. It is also excellent heated until liquid has evaporated and used as a spicy omelet filling or as a bed for poached eggs.

SPANAKOPITA (GREEK SPINACH PIE)

3 pounds fresh spinach (or 3 10-ounce boxes frozen)
8 scallions, finely chopped
⅓ cup olive oil
¾ cup pine nuts
1 pound feta cheese, crumbled
Salt, freshly ground pepper
Grated nutmeg
8 sheets of phyllo or strudel pastry (available in Greek specialty or gourmet shops)
½ cup melted unsalted butter

Preheat oven to 350 degrees.

Wash the spinach thoroughly and steam in the water clinging to its leaves in a large, covered pot until wilted, about 5 minutes. Drain the spinach thoroughly, squeeze dry, and chop coarsely. (If using frozen spinach, defrost completely, squeeze dry, and chop coarsely. Do not cook.) Sauté the scallions in the olive oil, in a large skillet, until soft and translucent but not browned. Add the spinach and continue cooking until all moisture has evaporated. Add pine nuts, crumbled feta, and salt, pepper, and grated nutmeg to taste, and toss lightly to mix.

Butter a shallow baking dish, about 8 by 12 inches, line with a phyllo sheet, and brush the sheet with melted butter (see Note below). Cover the first sheet with 3 more phyllo sheets, brushing each with melted butter. Fill with the spinach mixture, and cover the mixture with the remaining sheets of phyllo, buttering each well. Fold overlapping pastry over to close and seal the pie, and brush top with butter. The pie may be prepared ahead to this point and refrigerated until ready to cook. Bake the spanakopita at 350 degrees 35 to 45 minutes, until the pastry is a golden brown. If the pie has been refrigerated, adjust the cooking time to about 1 hour. Serves 8.

Note: See directions for working with phyllo or strudel pastry (see Index).

LIME MOUSSE

6 eggs, separated
¾ cup sugar
¾ cup freshly squeezed lime
    juice
1 ½ tablespoons butter

1 tablespoon grated lime zest
1 ½ teaspoons unflavored
    gelatin
½ teaspoon vanilla

Grate lime rind for zest before squeezing for juice.

Combine egg yolks, sugar, ½ cup lime juice, butter, and 1 ½ teaspoons grated lime zest in the top of a double boiler. Cook over simmering water, stirring, until the mixture is thick. Remove from heat. Soften gelatin in remaining lime juice and dissolve over a pan of hot water. Stir into egg yolk mixture. Set aside to cool.

Beat egg whites until stiff. Stir vanilla into yolk mixture, then fold in egg whites. Pour into 8 parfait or coupe champagne glasses and sprinkle with remaining lime zest. Chill for several hours before serving. Serves 8.

ALMOND COOKIES

Butter and flour for preparing cookie sheets
¼ pound unsalted butter
¾ cup almonds
½ cup sugar

1 teaspoon flour
2 tablespoons milk
2 tablespoons heavy cream
Finely slivered almonds

Preheat oven to 375 degrees.

Butter cookie sheets with unsalted butter, and flour them. Melt the butter over low heat. Cool. Pulverize almonds in a blender and mix with sugar, flour, melted butter, milk, and cream. Using small end of melon ball scoop, drop batter, well spaced, on cookie sheets. The batter will be quite liquid. Top each raw cookie with slivered almonds. Bake 5 to 6 minutes, watching constantly. Cool a moment and remove from cookie sheets. They quickly become too brittle to handle. If this occurs, return to oven for a moment. Makes 3 ½ dozen cookies.

A Christening

Lunch for Twelve

*Cheese-filled Turnovers (see Index)
*Tiny Quiches Louisiane (see Index)
  Melons, Pears, and Figs with Prosciutto
*Spinach and Chicken Crêpes
  Salad of Mixed Greens with *Lemon Vinaigrette
    (see Basic Recipes)
  Brioches
*Lime Pots de Crème

With advance planning and a little careful thought, this christening celebration can be put smoothly into motion the minute you arrive home from the church. Guests walk in the door to the inviting sight of small tables covered with pink or blue tablecloths. Apropos of the occasion, the centerpieces might be tiny wooden cribs heaped with almonds iced with pink, blue, or white sugar. Or, you might simply mass tiny pale rosebuds and baby's breath in low, water-filled containers which will be invisible in the cribs. As a tribute to the newly christened child, menus can be printed on photostated copies of the birth certificate and set at each place as a memento of the occasion.

Juice and drink makings can be set up on trays in advance—with ice in bags in the freezer ready to put into buckets. The mouth-watering canapés need no further preparation and the first course is ready to serve. This—refreshing melons, figs, pears, and prosciutto garnished with wedges of lime—can be presented as soon as you have put the crêpes, prepared beforehand, into the preheated oven.

Now is the time to relax with your family and guests and let someone else bounce the baby. Twenty minutes later you simply toss the salad. It can be arranged early in the morning by putting the dressing in the bottom of the bowl, crossing the servers over it, and placing the greens on top. This effectively separates the greens from the dressing and prevents them from wilting. Cover and refrigerate until ready to serve. At the last moment, garnish the bubbling hot crêpes with parsley, and invite your guests to join you. With luck, the guest of honor will co-operate by napping.

SPINACH AND CHICKEN CRÊPES

¼ pound butter
1 pound mushrooms, finely
  chopped
2 large onions, finely
  chopped
2 pounds fresh or 2 10-ounce
  boxes frozen spinach,
  cooked, well drained, and
  finely chopped

4 cups diced cooked chicken
½ cup sour cream
¼ cup dry sherry
1 teaspoon salt
Cayenne pepper
24 Crêpes (see recipe below)
Butter
Sherry Cheese Sauce (see
  recipe below)

Preheat oven to 350 degrees.

Melt butter in a heavy skillet and sauté mushrooms and onions until soft; if mushrooms exude a great deal of liquid, raise heat for a minute to evaporate. Add spinach, chicken, sour cream, sherry, salt, and a pinch of cayenne.

Put 1 to 2 tablespoons of filling on each crêpe, and roll. Arrange in a buttered shallow ovenproof serving dish. Spoon sauce over crêpes and heat at 350 degrees until sauce is bubbling and lightly browned, about 30 to 45 minutes. Serves 6.

Note: The rolled filled crêpes may be refrigerated or frozen at that point. When ready to finish cooking, defrost, pour sauce over, and bake as directed.

Crêpes

4 eggs
2 cups milk
4 tablespoons melted butter,
  cooled slightly
1 teaspoon salt

¼ teaspoon freshly grated
  nutmeg
1 cup sifted flour
Butter for pan

Combine eggs, milk, melted butter, salt, nutmeg, and flour in blender container and whirl until smooth. Refrigerate for 2 hours before making crêpes.

Heat a 6- or 7-inch crêpe pan and brush lightly with softened butter. Ladle in about 2 tablespoons batter and quickly tilt pan to spread batter evenly; pour out any excess. Cook until lightly browned, about 1 minute, then turn and cook until browned on the other side. Makes about 24 6- or 7-inch crêpes.

Note: Crêpes may be made in advance, stacked with waxed paper between every 3 or 4, and refrigerated or frozen.

Sherry Cheese Sauce

¼ pound butter
½ cup flour
4 cups chicken stock, fresh
    or canned (see Basic
    Recipes)

2 cups milk
1 cup each freshly grated
    Parmesan and Swiss cheese
1 cup dry sherry
Salt, cayenne pepper

Melt butter, stir in flour, and cook gently for 2 minutes. Blend in chicken stock and milk and cook over low heat, stirring, until smooth and thickened. Add cheese, sherry, and salt and cayenne to taste. Stir until cheese is melted.

LIME POTS DE CRÈME

4 eggs, separated
2 14-ounce cans condensed
    milk
1 cup fresh lime juice
1 tablespoon grated lime zest

Several drops green food coloring (optional)
Butter cookies
Whipped cream

Beat yolks in a large bowl, adding the condensed milk and lime juice gradually, then adding the grated zest and coloring, if desired. Beat the whites until stiff and then fold them into the lime mixture—the color should be that of lime sherbet. Pour into pots de crème and chill. When ready to serve, crumble cookies over each cup and top with a dollop of freshly whipped cream.

Note: Select the brand of condensed milk that is the least sweet, as indicated by the label.

A Summer City Lover's

Supper for Six

*Spinach Vicomtesse
*Cold Poached Bass with Cucumber Sauce
*Rice Salad
*Janie's Blueberry Pie

Some people escape—but others stay because they like New York in the summertime. Shops are less crowded, restaurants less busy. It's actually possible to get theater tickets for a hit. Everything moves at a more leisurely pace. So it's a time when one can fuss and get fancy about food because there's simply more time for it. And since few people entertain—a supper with a menu such as the one suggested here will be much more than mere refreshment to even the most confirmed summer city dweller.

A cool way to start the evening would be with frosty gin and tonics accompanied by plump, iced cherry tomatoes and coarse salt to dip them in. Since the menu concentrates largely on light, cool dishes and an almost no-cook dessert, the appetizer—spinach vicomtesse—is appropriately presented bubbling hot. This lovely adaptation of a Parisian recipe swathes delicately poached eggs nestled on a bed of spinach in a cheese-rich Mornay sauce.

The main course, poached bass, is served cold with a creamy, lemon-accented cucumber sauce and complemented by a lovely cold rice salad garnished with peas and pimientos. For dessert, take advantage of one of summer's blessings—blueberries—non-baked but beautiful with almonds and Cointreau in this perfection of a pie.

Think cool, too, in the color schemes for your table settings and consider understated lighting after the glare of the day. Green, white and pale blue are soothing colors. Spark them with a pot of hot pink field flowers. Subdue them with soft candlelight. Like the city itself in summer, pace your dinner leisurely, serve it with the sort of relaxed conversation that will make your guests glad they're city dwellers too.

SPINACH VICOMTESSE

Butter for preparing dish
4 pounds fresh spinach,
    washed and stems re-
    moved or 6 10-ounce
    boxes frozen leaf spinach,
    stems removed after cook-
    ing
Salt
2 or 3 cloves garlic, halved

3 tablespoons butter
Freshly ground pepper
6 eggs
⅔ cup grated Monterey Jack
    cheese
⅓ cup grated Gruyère
    cheese
2 cups Béchamel Sauce (see
    Basic Recipes)

Preheat oven to 350 degrees.

Butter a 10-inch shallow ovenproof dish. Cook spinach in boiling salted water until tender. Drain well and chop finely. Sauté spinach with garlic in the butter for about 5 minutes, remove garlic, and spread spinach evenly in buttered dish. Season with salt and pepper to taste. Poach the eggs lightly, then lift them carefully from the pan, drain on a paper towel and arrange them evenly spaced on the bed of spinach. Stir the cheeses into the béchamel sauce with a whisk over low heat. Cool, so as not to cook the eggs further, and pour over the tops of the eggs. Bake in 350-degree oven until bubbly (about 15 minutes). Eggs should still be runny when served. Serves 6.

COLD POACHED BASS

2 ½ quarts water
1 bottle good, white wine
4 carrots, sliced
2 medium onions, sliced
2 small bay leaves
¼ teaspoon thyme
12 peppercorns
8-pound striped bass, or
    other firm white fish such
    as red snapper, cleaned
    with head and tail left on

Cucumber Sauce (see
    below)
Cucumbers (optional)
Parsley (optional)
Cherry tomatoes (optional)

Put water, wine, carrots, onions, bay leaves, thyme, and peppercorns in a fish poacher and simmer, covered, for 10 to 15 minutes. Wrap the fish in cheesecloth and lower into hot court bouillon. The fish should be barely covered by liquid. Return court bouillon to a simmer, and sim-

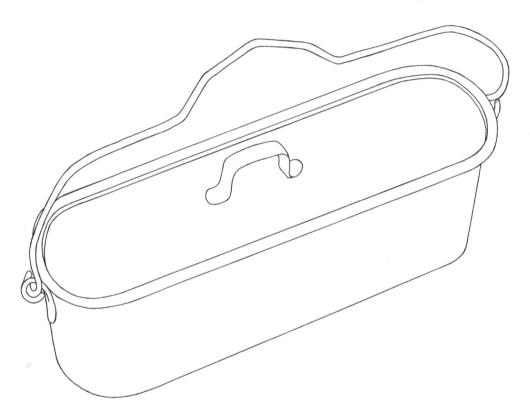

mer 8 minutes per pound over very low heat. The water should barely be bubbling. Allow the fish to cool 1 or 2 hours in the stock, then remove to a serving platter and take out as many loose bones as you neatly can. Refrigerate the fish.

Reduce the stock to about 2 cups. Then refrigerate until it is thickened. Spoon some over the fish for a shiny glaze. If you are ambitious, you might continue to cover the fish in a fancy aspic coating, instead of the simple glaze. You might also make an attractive design with notched cucumbers and surround the fish with parsley and cherry tomatoes. The fish will need about 4 hours to cool thoroughly before serving, but keeps for as long as 8 hours without losing flavor or texture. Serve with cucumber sauce. Serves 6.

Note: A large roasting pan can be used just as well as a fish poacher, but you must increase the amount of court bouillon by increasing proportions of the recipe listed above. Don't increase amount of liquid by just adding water, please.

Cucumber Sauce

2 large cucumbers, peeled, seeded, and grated
2 cups sour cream

2 teaspoons lemon juice
4 tablespoons red caviar
½ cup heavy cream, whipped

Add cucumber to the sour cream. Mix in lemon juice and caviar, and fold in whipped cream. Serve with the bass or any cold fish. Serves 6.

RICE SALAD

2 cups uncooked rice
1 cup olive oil (very best imported available)
¼ cup white wine vinegar
½ teaspoon dry mustard
¾ to 1 cup closely packed watercress leaves and tender stems
2 teaspoons dried basil (or 3 tablespoons of fresh chopped)

Salt, freshly ground pepper
1 cup cooked peas
2 or 3 chopped scallions
6 parsley sprigs
Cherry tomatoes or pimientos and parsley

Cook rice according to package directions. When done stir several times to release steam. While rice is cooking, prepare a vinaigrette dressing as follows. Put olive oil, vinegar, mustard, and the green herbs with salt and pepper to taste in a blender container and blend until herbs are finely chopped.

When rice is cooked, toss immediately with the vinaigrette, season to taste, and refrigerate overnight. It may appear a bit oily at first, but the oil will all be absorbed.

Before serving toss in peas and scallions and garnish with cherry tomatoes or pimientos and parsley. Serves 6.

Note: This makes a very generous amount, but it will keep a couple of days and is nice to have on hand.

JANIE'S BLUEBERRY PIE

4 cups blueberries, washed
  and drained
¾ cup sugar
½ cup water
2 tablespoons cornstarch dissolved in ¼ cup cold water
¼ teaspoon cinnamon
1 tablespoon butter
1 tablespoon Cointreau
¼ cup slivered toasted almonds

9-inch baked Pastry shell
  (see Basic Recipes)
1 cup heavy cream, whipped
  and flavored with 2 tablespoons sugar, ¼ teaspoon
  almond extract
2 to 4 tablespoons toasted
  slivered almonds

Cook 1 cup blueberries with sugar and water for 10 minutes, until blueberries are cooked. Purée, then add cornstarch and cinnamon and cook until thickened. Blend in butter and Cointreau and cool.

Add almonds to blueberry mixture and fold in remaining blueberries. Pour into pastry shell and just before serving top with flavored whipped cream. Decorate with toasted slivered almonds. Serves 6 to 8.

The Galley Slave's

Reprieve for Six

*Marinated Mushrooms
*Curried Chicken and Green Pea Soup
*Fresh-caught Fish Baked in Foil
*Spliced Carrots
*Avocado Salad with *Tequila-Lime Dressing
*Melon Compote
*Chocolate Coconut Pecan Squares

After a day of fresh air and fishing offshore on a boat—dinner aboard shouldn't be a hassle for the hostess. And it isn't with this menu. If the galley is outfitted with a cooker and a cooler you can enjoy your catch—these simply prepared fresh fillets of fish—with a maximum of 25 minutes of preparation. As it cooks you can relax and enjoy a frosty drink with your family and guests on the deck.

The logistics of dining aboard successfully requires careful advance planning—everything that can be should be accomplished at home, where space and equipment are less limited. The soup, for instance, can be prepared in your kitchen, toted in Thermoses, and served hot or cold. The dishes and eating utensils should be simple, unbreakable, and rust-proof. Paper plates and stainless steel or even plastic knives and forks make for minimum maintenance and cleanup.

The main course suggested here and its accompanying spliced carrots can be wrapped in heavy foil and cooked simultaneously at the same oven temperature or over a grill or set on a rack above a covered pot of simmering water. Or, you might even cook the fish by a method a fisherman friend developed for the shoreside chef: simply place the foil-wrapped packs of fresh fish fillets on the top shelf of the dishwasher and run the washer through one full cycle—no detergent please! The fisherman swears this ingenious method not only works—it's the most delicious way to eat fresh fish at home. But you will have the benefit of the sunset and sea breezes, which makes dining at anchor so special.

MARINATED MUSHROOMS

2 pounds fresh mushrooms	Salt
½ cup chopped onion	¼ teaspoon tarragon
1 clove garlic, minced	1 cup white wine
¼ cup chopped parsley	½ cup white vinegar
2 bay leaves	¼ cup olive oil
⅛ teaspoon freshly ground pepper	1 tablespoon lemon juice

Trim ends of mushroom stems and wipe clean with a damp towel. Combine in a large heavy saucepan with onions, garlic, parsley, bay leaves, pepper, salt to taste, tarragon, white wine, vinegar, olive oil, and lemon juice, and bring to a boil. Reduce heat and simmer 8 to 10 minutes, or until tender, stirring several times. Refrigerate and serve on toothpicks with drinks. Will keep two weeks under refrigeration. Serves 6.

CURRIED CHICKEN AND GREEN PEA SOUP

1 tablespoon butter	2 tablespoons flour
2 tablespoons vegetable oil	2 cups chicken broth
1 onion, finely chopped	¾ to 1 cup light cream
1 clove garlic	1 cup finely chopped cooked chicken meat
2 cups shelled fresh green peas or 10-ounce box of frozen	Salt, freshly ground pepper
2 teaspoons imported curry powder	Milk

Heat the butter and vegetable oil in a deep saucepan. Add the onion and garlic and cook slowly for 3 minutes. Add the peas. Reduce heat, cover, and continue cooking very slowly until peas are soft. Add curry powder and cook 1 minute longer. Remove from heat and stir in flour. Add chicken broth and return to heat. Cook, stirring, until the mixture boils. Remove from heat and rub through a fine strainer. Return soup to pan and add cream, chicken, and salt and pepper to taste.

May be served hot or cold. If served cold, thin with a little milk. Serves 6.

FRESH-CAUGHT FISH BAKED IN FOIL

1 medium onion, chopped
2 tablespoons chopped pars-
    ley
½ teaspoon thyme
3 tablespoons white wine or
    vinegar
6 tablespoons olive oil
Salt, freshly ground pepper

3 pounds firm white fish
    (such as flounder, bluefish,
    tropical dolphin, or
    swordfish) cut into 6 fillets
2 large tomatoes, sliced
1 bay leaf, crushed
Juice of ½ lemon
6 lemon wedges

Preheat oven to 350 degrees.

Combine the onion, parsley, thyme, wine or vinegar, oil, and salt and pepper to taste. Line a pan with sufficient foil to cover and seal in the fillets tightly. Pour half the mixture onto the foil. Lay the fillets in the pan; cover them with tomato slices and sprinkle with the crushed bay leaf and lemon juice. Pour over the remaining wine and oil mixture. Wrap and seal the fish in the foil and bake in a 350-degree oven or over a charcoal grill about 30 to 45 minutes, until the fish flakes easily. Check toward the end to prevent overcooking. Carefully remove from the foil to prevent fillets from breaking, and serve with lemon wedges. Serves 6.

If an oven or grill isn't available, the fish may be steamed over a burner on a rack placed within a 12-inch skillet, filled with boiling water to cover the bottom of the pan.

SPLICED CARROTS

18 medium carrots, peeled,
    cut in half lengthwise, and
    sliced
3 tablespoons butter

1 tablespoon chopped fresh
    dill, or 1 teaspoon dried
Salt, freshly ground pepper

Preheat oven to 350 degrees.

Arrange the carrots so that they overlap each other in the middle of a sheet of aluminum foil. Add the butter, dill, and salt and pepper to taste. Seal the carrots in the foil tightly. Cook in a 350-degree oven or over a charcoal grill for about 45 minutes or until tender. Serves 6.

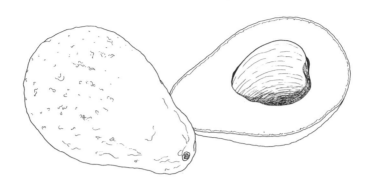

AVOCADO SALAD
WITH TEQUILA-LIME DRESSING

3 avocados, halved, peeled,
  and pitted
1 head Boston lettuce
¼ cup tequila

¼ cup fresh lime juice
2 teaspoons coarse salt
Freshly ground pepper

Arrange 6 avocado halves on 6 beds of lettuce. Combine the tequila, lime juice, coarse salt, and pepper to taste. Pour over the avocados. Taste and correct seasoning if necessary: dressing should be salty. Serves 6.

Note: Do not peel and pit the avocado halves ahead of time, as they darken quickly.

MELON COMPOTE

Fresh melons
Lemon juice or kirsch

Sugar to taste

Choose an assortment of various fresh melons (cantaloupe, casaba, Cranshaw, watermelon, or honeydew) to serve 6 and cut with a melon baller. Chill well and sprinkle with lemon juice or kirsch and sugar to taste.

CHOCOLATE COCONUT PECAN SQUARES

¼ pound butter
1 cup graham cracker crumbs
1 cup chocolate bits
1 cup chopped pecans

1 cup shredded coconut
1 can sweetened condensed
 milk

Preheat oven to 350 degrees.

Melt butter in 9 by 11-inch pan. Sprinkle graham cracker crumbs evenly over melted butter, then sprinkle remaining ingredients *in order listed* over the butter-crumb mixture, ending by pouring the condensed milk evenly over the top. Bake in a 350-degree oven for 30 minutes. Cool thoroughly and refrigerate awhile before cutting into bars or squares. Makes 30 small squares.

Picnic

at Home for Eight

*Frannie's Fried Chicken
*Golden Corn Pudding
*Green Beans with Water Chestnuts and Bacon
*Baked Chutnied Peach Halves
  Buttermilk Biscuits
*Carrot Cake

Maybe all the inspiration needed for this repast is an upcoming televised sporting event. Whether your at-home party revolves around the Golf Classic, a big match at Forest Hills, the Super Bowl, the Olympics— you'll be grateful for these fork-and-finger foods that are simple to create, simple to serve, and wonderful to eat.

The supper is planned in a casual vein—so insist your guests dress likewise. You might decorate your table in a shade-of-the-event motif: a bright cloth centered with a group of sand-filled plastic pails holding gaily colored Japanese paper umbrellas, for a summer spectacular. Indian or African-print handkerchiefs or scarves from the five-and-ten will do nicely as napkins. And you might serve the chicken and piping hot biscuits in baskets and let everyone help himself.

Offer frosty pitchers of sangria, tankards of iced tea, or bottled beer nestled in crushed ice. After all, what better way to relax and enjoy an afternoon TV special and a special feast?

FRANNIE'S FRIED CHICKEN

½ cup salt
4 quarts water
2 3½-pound chickens, cut
   in serving pieces
1 to 2 pounds lard
1 cup milk
2 eggs

2 cups flour
1 teaspoon sugar
1 teaspoon salt
½ teaspoon cinnamon or
   thyme, tarragon, poultry
   seasoning, or chili powder

Combine the salt with the water in a pot or bowl large enough to accommodate all the chicken. Drop in the chicken pieces and let them soak in the solution for ½ hour. Remove and pat dry on paper towels.

Melt 1 pound lard in a large frying pan. (If you wish to have 2 skillets cooking simultaneously—you will need another pound of lard.) Meanwhile, mix milk and eggs in a pie plate. Combine flour, sugar, salt, and cinnamon or other seasoning in a paper bag.

Bring lard to very high heat. Coat each piece of chicken in the egg-milk batter, then shake it in the flour mixture in a paper bag. Make sure it is well coated. Put the chicken pieces in the heated lard—but do not let them touch each other. Lower the heat immediately to low/moderate and cover the frying pan. In about 15 minutes, lift a sample piece of chicken from the pan with tongs. If the crust is not yet golden, return it to the frying pan in its original position. It is important that the chicken pieces be turned only once. When the crust on one side has reached the desired degree of doneness, turn the chicken pieces completely over and recover the pan, letting them cook for an additional 12 to 15 minutes or longer. Breasts and wings cook faster than legs and thighs.

Remove chicken pieces from pan when crust is golden on both sides and drain on paper towels. Continue cooking chicken pieces, skimming any floating material from the lard as it accumulates.

When all the chicken is fried, sprinkle it with additional salt to taste. Do not refrigerate. Serve at room temperature. Serves 8.

GOLDEN CORN PUDDING

Butter for preparing dish
4 cups freshly cooked corn,
    cut from the cob *or* 2 cups
    drained, canned, whole
    kernel corn
2 teaspoons salt
4 eggs, well beaten

2 tablespoons butter, melted
2 teaspoons sugar
½ teaspoon freshly ground
    pepper
Tabasco sauce
2 cups milk
4 tablespoons cracker crumbs

Preheat oven to 350 degrees.

Butter a 2-quart baking dish. Mix together corn, salt, eggs, butter, sugar, pepper, a few drops of Tabasco, and milk. Pour into the prepared baking dish. Top with crumbs, and set dish into a shallow pan of hot water. Bake for 60 to 70 minutes or until a knife inserted in the center of the pudding comes out clean. Serve immediately. Serves 8.

GREEN BEANS WITH WATER CHESTNUTS AND BACON

2 pounds green beans,
    washed and tips removed
5 slices bacon

1 8½-ounce can water chest-
    nuts, drained and sliced
    very thinly

Cook beans in boiling water for 8–10 minutes and cool by plunging immediately into cold water to stop cooking. The beans should be tender but slightly crunchy. Pierce with a fork to test. Cook the bacon until crisp. Drain the bacon thoroughly and crumble. Discard fat from frying pan. Return the crumbled bacon, sliced water chestnuts, and cooked green beans to the frying pan, toss together, and heat thoroughly. Serve immediately. Serves 8.

BAKED CHUTNIED PEACH HALVES

8 peach halves   Imported curry powder
8 tablespoons chutney

Preheat oven to 350 degrees.

Put peach halves in a muffin tin, and put 1 tablespoon of chutney in each. Sprinkle lightly with curry powder to taste. Bake for 20 minutes or until heated through. Serve immediately. Serves 8.

CARROT CAKE

4 eggs   2 teaspoons cinnamon
2 cups sugar   3 cups grated carrots
1 ½ cups corn oil   ½ cup chopped nuts
2 cups flour   (pecans or walnuts)
2 teaspoons baking soda   Oil and flour for preparing
1 teaspoon salt   baking pan

Preheat oven to 350 degrees.

Beat eggs until fluffy. Add sugar and oil gradually. Sift flour, baking soda, salt, and cinnamon together, and add the grated carrots and chopped nuts. Combine thoroughly with eggs, sugar, and oil.

Oil and lightly flour a 9 by 13-inch cake pan. Pour in the batter, and bake in a 350-degree oven for 30 to 35 minutes. Serve plain or dusted with powdered sugar. Serves 8.

An Inspired
Dinner for Six

*Potted Shrimp
*Crisp Melba Toast (see Basic Recipes)
*Herb Baked Chicken
*Indiana Baked Corn
  Romaine Salad with *Lemon Vinaigrette (see Basic Recipes)
*White Grape Mousse

Some summer afternoon you'll be in such fine fettle that you're ready to leave the barbecue grill behind, get back into the kitchen, and produce a really smashing dinner. This is the menu for that afternoon. It is grand enough to satisfy that burst of creative inspiration, yet retains the feel and the flavor of summer.

Potted shrimp served with crisp Melba toast are suggested here for a first course. They are an old favorite presented with new glamour in hollowed-out, scalloped lemon shells which are perched very effectively in inexpensive white egg cups purchased at an oriental import store. The chicken is uncomplicated but enticing with herbs and butter. It is served with fresh corn prepared in an authentic Indiana manner which enhances its flavor. And, of course—a fresh green salad.

The cooling dessert is bound to draw praise. It's a delicious combination of grapes and whipped cream, brown sugar, and sour cream, a tart-sweet complement to the meal.

A summery way to set off your dinner would be to put tiny flower pots filled with fresh summer blossoms and vegetable leaves at each place. Sheer inspiration!

POTTED SHRIMP

¼ pound unsalted butter
2 cups small raw shrimp,
    shelled and deveined
Mace, nutmeg, cayenne
1 or 2 slices fresh ginger,
    peeled and put through a
    garlic press (optional)

2 tablespoons lemon juice
Hollowed, scalloped lemon
    shells (optional)
Butter, melted

Melt unsalted butter and cook shrimp very gently 10 to 15 minutes —they must not brown. Flavor lightly with mace, nutmeg, cayenne, ginger if desired, and lemon juice. Pour into small pots or lemon shells, adding more melted butter to cover and seal. Refrigerate. Serve hollowed-out lemon shells in egg cups with fresh hot Melba toast. Serves 6.

Shrimp Pâté

For pâté: prepare the recipe as above, but put a little at a time in blender and whirl to chop coarsely. Pour into small pots and seal with additional butter.

HERB BAKED CHICKEN

4 tablespoons flour
½ teaspoon salt
¼ pound unsalted butter,
    softened
2 tablespoons lemon juice
2 or 3 cloves garlic, put
    through a press
Fresh or dried herbs, such as
    thyme, chives, dill, or

tarragon (2 or 3 table-
    spoons fresh or 1 table-
    spoon dried)
2 tablespoons finely chopped
    parsley
2 3½-pound chickens, cut
    in serving pieces

Preheat oven to 350 degrees.

Mix flour, salt, butter, lemon juice, garlic, and herbs. Spread on 1 side of chicken pieces. Bake in a 350-degree oven for about 1 hour until tender and golden, basting occasionally. Raise heat to 400 degrees for a few minutes at end of baking for increased browning if desired. Serve hot or just warm (let cool at room temperature, not in refrigerator). Serves 6 to 8.

INDIANA BAKED CORN

2 dozen ears of fresh corn
¾ cup milk (less if corn is
   young, more if old)
½ pound unsalted butter

4 tablespoons salt
1 ½ tablespoons pepper,
   fresh-ground

Preheat oven to 350 degrees.

Butter a large shallow baking dish. Scrape the corn with a corn scraper into the dish, pressing all liquid from kernels, add milk, dot generously with butter, and season with salt and pepper. Bake at 350 degrees for 35 to 45 minutes, stirring halfway through cooking time; it will be golden brown on top when done. Very young corn will require less cooking time. Serves 6.

This may also be done in individual ramekins for an unusual first course, in which case the cooking time should be reduced.

WHITE GRAPE MOUSSE

1 ½ pounds white seedless
   grapes, halved
¼ cup brown sugar, or more,
   to taste

3 to 4 tablespoons light rum
1 ½ cups sour cream
1 ½ cups heavy cream

Mix together grapes, sugar, rum, and sour cream. Chill well. Whip the heavy cream until stiff and fold it carefully into the grape mixture. Chill again before serving. Serves 6.

A Deli Brunch

for Summer

Bagels and Bialys

Rye Bread

Platters of Lox, Corned Beef, Salami, Roast Beef, and Other
Cold Meats Selected at the Delicatessen

Crocks of Mustards

Cream Cheese

Butter

Sliced Onions

*Borscht

Bowl of Cherries and Peaches

How often have you entertained guests on a summer weekend and fervently wished Sunday morning that breakfast would somehow prepare itself—that you wouldn't have to be the first one up, busy preparing food that you just hope will hold for late risers. Here is a brunch idea borrowed from many a New Yorker whose idea of Sunday morning is late rising, leisurely breakfasting, and the New York *Times*.

The breakfast fare is provided by your friendly neighborhood delicatessen: bagels and bialys (both delicious rolls when split, toasted, and spread generously with cream cheese or sweet butter), platters of lox—smoked salmon—and corned beef and other cold meats, bowls of cream cheese and butter, a plate heaped with sliced sweet onions, and crocks of mustard. A highpoint might be a tureen of refreshing cold borscht, traditionally served in glasses.

Arrange the platters of meats and lox the night before, covering well with plastic wrap. They'll keep in the refrigerator until morning, as will the bagels, bialys, cream cheese, sweet butter, sliced onions, borscht, and fruit. Set the table with plates, cups, saucers, knives, forks, spoons, napkins, and glasses for the borscht. Put out the electric coffee pot, ready to go, the toaster, breadboard and sharp knife for splitting the rolls, and ask only that the first one up plug in the coffee pot, and take the food from the refrigerator. Then it is each to his own: a split bagel spread with cream cheese, lox, and topped with a hearty onion slice; or a bialy (an onion-flavored bagel), toasted and piled high with corned beef and mustard, accompanied by head-clearing glasses of borscht and/or cup after cup of fragrant coffee. A perfect touch might be a Sunday paper for each of the guests, providing a relaxed and guilt-free summer Sunday.

BORSCHT

1 cup coarsely grated cabbage
1 cup boiling water
2 tablespoons butter
½ medium onion, finely
  chopped
1-pound can whole or julienne beets
2 cups chicken stock

½ teaspoon sugar
Salt, freshly ground pepper
1 to 1½ tablespoons fresh
  lemon juice
¼ cup dry white wine
Sour cream, snipped fresh
  dill (optional)

Cook the cabbage in the boiling water for 10 minutes. Melt the butter in a 3-quart heavy-bottomed saucepan, and cook the onion over low heat until translucent but not browned. Drain the beets, reserving the juice, and shred finely if using whole beets. There should be 2 cups of shredded beets. Add the chicken stock to the onion, and bring to a boil. Add the cabbage and the water in which it was cooked. Add the shredded beets, ½ cup reserved beet juice, sugar, salt and pepper to taste, and simmer over low heat for 10 minutes, skimming occasionally. Remove the pan from the heat, and add the lemon juice and wine. Return to the stove and bring just to the boiling point. Remove and chill thoroughly. Serve with bowls of sour cream and snipped dill, if desired. Serves 4.

Note: This borscht is equally delicious served hot, immediately after the final heating.

A Buffet of Summer's
Bounty for Eight

*Pesto Soufflé
*Grilled Hot and Sweet Italian Sausages
*Grilled Pepper Salad
*Poached Peaches with *Sabayon Sauce
*Lace Cookies

A summer outdoor buffet for eight celebrates summer's bounty of fresh vegetables, fruits, and herbs in a handsome display of vivid colors, varied textures, and garden-fresh flavors. Served in a rustic setting with baskets of zucchini, summer squash, green and red peppers as a center-piece—it seems to call for the simplest of tablerie: earthenware and an assortment of bold, colorful plaid buffet-size napkins.

The pesto soufflé served here as a first course is a unique recipe developed for this book. It has a cheese soufflé base enhanced with lightly sautéed tomatoes and a richly flavored pesto made from fresh basil, pine nuts, olive oil, garlic, and Parmesan cheese. Baked and served in a clear soufflé dish, it is certain to be the culinary triumph of the evening. Pesto is traditionally teamed with pasta, and if any is left over, it may be used to sauce any variety of spaghetti, or try a dollop in a bowl of hot bean soup.

The salad is a refreshing combination of grilled red, yellow, and green peppers, peeled and macerated in a tart vinaigrette. With the exception of the sabayon sauce, the dinner may be completed well in advance of the guests' arrival. The salad, peaches, and cookies can be cooked the day before, the sausages, onions, and mushrooms skewered, brushed with oil, and ready for last-minute charcoal broiling, and the soufflé, contrary to most cookbook instructions, can be completed an hour in advance of cooking if it is completely covered by a large bowl before it is set aside. Chilled red or rosé "jug" wines, decanted in carafes, would be a fine accompaniment.

PESTO SOUFFLÉ

Unsalted butter
¾ cup freshly grated im-
    ported Parmesan cheese
6 tablespoons flour
1½ cups milk, at room tem-
    perature
Salt, freshly ground pepper
Nutmeg

8 large eggs, separated, plus
    2 extra egg whites
4 to 6 scallions, finely chopped
8 medium tomatoes, peeled,
    seeded, and diced
¾ to 1 cup Pesto (see
    recipe below)

Preheat oven to 400 degrees.

Butter generously 2 6-cup soufflé dishes and sprinkle the inside of each with about 1 tablespoon grated cheese. Melt 6 tablespoons butter and when foam has subsided, blend in flour. Cook over low heat 2 minutes, stirring. Off the heat, blend in the milk with a whisk, then return to the heat and cook until thickened and smooth. Season to taste with salt, pepper, and nutmeg. Add the egg yolks one at a time, beating after each addition to blend well.

Sauté the scallions in 2 tablespoons butter until soft, then add tomatoes, raise heat, and cook rapidly until liquid has evaporated. Blend into sauce base with pesto and all but 2 tablespoons of the remaining cheese. Correct seasoning if necessary.

Beat egg whites (preferably in a copper bowl) with a pinch of salt until stiff peaks form. Stir a quarter of them into the sauce base to lighten it, then gently fold the remaining whites into sauce. Pour the mixture into the prepared soufflé dishes, smooth the tops with a spatula, and sprinkle with remaining cheese. Put into a 400-degree oven, immediately lower heat to 375 degrees, and bake soufflés 30 to 35 minutes, until well puffed and browned. Serve immediately. Serves 8.

Pesto

4 cups fresh basil leaves
4 or 5 cloves garlic
⅔ cup freshly grated im-
    ported Parmesan, Romano,
    or Sardo cheese

½ cup pine nuts
1 cup olive oil
Salt

Put half the basil in blender container with garlic, cheese, pine nuts, olive oil, and 1 teaspoon salt. Whirl until smooth, stopping to push down basil when necessary. Add remaining basil and whirl until fairly smooth —it may be necessary to add a little oil, but pesto should be thick. Taste for seasoning and add salt if necessary. Makes about 2 cups, enough for about 3 pounds of pasta.

Note: Pesto keeps well in refrigerator, or it may be frozen. It may be necessary to add garlic after defrosting, as garlic loses its flavor after having been frozen.

GRILLED HOT AND SWEET ITALIAN SAUSAGES

2 or 3 Italian sausages per person, hot and sweet
White wine or dry vermouth
4 to 6 mushroom caps, per person

4 to 6 small white onions, par-boiled for 10 minutes, per person
Olive oil

Poach sausages for 10 minutes in wine or vermouth. Arrange sausages on skewers alternately with mushroom caps and white onions. Brush with oil and cook over charcoal fire 10 to 12 minutes, turning 2 or 3 times.

GRILLED PEPPER SALAD

8 peppers, preferably a mélange of yellow, red, and green peppers
Olive oil sufficient to coat each pepper lightly as it is grilled (about ¼ cup)

½ cup Vinaigrette Sauce (see Basic Recipes)
Scallions, thinly sliced (optional)
Chopped parsley

Halve and seed the peppers. Brush skins lightly with olive oil and grill under the broiler or over a bed of hot charcoal. Put them under the

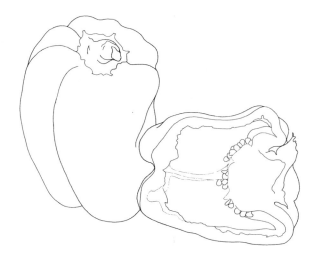

broiler (skin side up), or above the grill (skin side down) until skins are lightly blistered and charred. They are best done the day before serving. Peel the peppers, slice thinly, then chill and mix lightly with vinaigrette just before serving. Arrange attractively, alternating colors, on a flat plate. If desired, garnish with thinly sliced scallions. Sprinkle with chopped parsley. Serves 8.

POACHED PEACHES

8 large ripe peaches	1 cup water
2⅔ cups sugar	Sabayon Sauce (see recipe
1½ pieces vanilla bean	below)

Slide the peaches, one at a time, into a large pan of boiling water for 1 minute. Cool briefly and peel. Combine the sugar and vanilla bean with water and bring to the boil, then simmer for 10 minutes. Poach the peaches in the syrup for 15 minutes. Remove the peaches, cool, halve the peaches, and remove the pits, then chill. Serve with sabayon sauce. Serves 8.

Note: Two teaspoons of vanilla may be substituted for the vanilla bean. Add to the syrup with peaches.

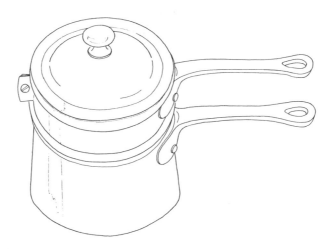

Sabayon Sauce

6 egg yolks
⅔ cup sugar, preferably superfine
1 cup dry white wine, a good
  varietal, imported or domestic

1 tablespoon kirsch
1 tablespoon Cointreau or
  Curaçao

Whisk the egg yolks and sugar in the top of a double boiler. Gradually add the white wine, beating constantly until the mixture is pale, thickened, and of a creamy consistency. Stir in the liqueurs and serve immediately.

LACE COOKIES

Butter for cookie sheets
3 tablespoons unsalted butter,
  softened
1 cup brown sugar
4 tablespoons flour

1 egg, beaten
1 cup blanched, ground almonds
1 teaspoon vanilla
1 teaspoon brandy or cognac

Preheat oven to 350 degrees.
Butter cookie sheets. Cream the butter and brown sugar, and then

blend in the flour, egg, ground almonds, vanilla, and the brandy or cognac. Drop the batter by half-teaspoons or demitasse spoons onto the prepared cookie sheets, spacing them well apart. Bake at 350 degrees for 8 to 10 minutes, checking after 7 to 8 minutes. The cookies should be crisp and removed quickly from the baking sheets and cooled on a wire rack. These cookies keep well. Makes approximately 3 dozen cookies.

A Gala Dinner Honoring

a Special Birthday for Eight

*Caviar Tarte

*Curried Zucchini Soup

*Suprêmes de Volaille with *Sauce Suprême

*Risotto

   Salad of Bibb Lettuce with *White Wine Vinaigrette
      (see Basic Recipes)

*Crêpes Framboises, with *Sauce Anglaise

What better way to welcome another year, be it the thirtieth or the thirty-ninth, than with the following festive fare! This birthday dinner is a delight to the eyes and delicious as well, from the luxurious gray-black caviar tarte framed with gold and white, through the pale green, quietly curried soup and the savory suprêmes and risotto to the fabulous finale of lightly sauced crêpes filled with summer raspberries.

Luscious and lovely, raspberries are a most memorable summer fruit. The taste, the smell, the delicious juiciness evoke memories—conjure up fantasies—of summers past and other raspberry dishes, sun, golden fields, mouths rosy with raspberry juice.

The table setting should be your finest china, silver, crystal, and heavy linen in pretty pastels. The centerpiece might be a gift for the honored guest, something to take home. You might buy a flat-surfaced round Styrofoam ice bucket, and glue photographs of the honored guest or magazine cutouts reflecting his or her hobbies and interests. Cover the entire surface, then spray the bucket with a clear plastic finish or paint it with polyurethane to protect the photographs and cutouts. Fill it with fresh garden flowers, echoing the pastels of the linens. Focus on the centerpiece by using classic white candles.

The prospect of an evening such as this makes the rest of us look forward to that landmark birthday and an unforgettable celebration.

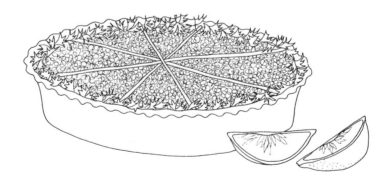

CAVIAR TARTE

3 hard-cooked eggs
2 lemons
8-inch pastry shell, fully baked in flan ring (see Basic Recipes)
Sufficient quantity of minced shallots or white part of

scallions to cover bottom of the tart (thin layer), about ½ to ¾ cup
½ pound pressed fresh caviar
1 to 2 tablespoons minced parsley

Separate the egg whites and yolks and put through a sieve. Cut the lemons into wedges. Line the bottom of the pastry shell with the minced scallions or shallots, then carefully spread the caviar over the shell. Use a cone made of foil or wax paper to hold the yolks and whites and decorate the top with alternating rows of each to suggest 8 slices. See illustration. The minced parsley may be distributed around the inside of the tarte and the lemon wedges served on the side. Serves 8.

CURRIED ZUCCHINI SOUP

3 tablespoons butter
2 or 3 medium onions, thinly sliced
1 large clove garlic, thinly sliced (optional)
1 tablespoon good-quality imported curry powder
8 medium or 6 large unpeeled zucchini, scrubbed and sliced ¼ inch thick

Salt, freshly ground pepper
3 cups chicken stock
Lemon juice
Cayenne pepper
1½ cups heavy cream
1½ tablespoons dark rum

Melt butter in a large heavy saucepan and add onions and garlic, if desired. Cook over low heat until soft but not browned. Stir in curry powder and cook very slowly for 2 minutes, then add zucchini, cover, and cook over low heat for 6 minutes, until zucchini is just beginning to become tender. Season with 2 to 3 teaspoons salt, and pepper to taste, then add chicken stock, cover, raise heat slightly, and simmer about 8 minutes, until zucchini is tender but still retains some crisp texture.

Purée in blender, using an off-on technique, constantly checking to avoid too smooth a purée. The crisp bits add a pleasant texture. Season to taste with salt, pepper, a few drops of lemon juice, and a dash of cayenne. Chill.

Just before serving, stir in cream and rum. Correct seasoning, if necessary. Serves 8.

SUPRÊMES DE VOLAILLE

4 whole chicken breasts, halved, skinned, and boned
Salt, freshly ground pepper
6 tablespoons unsalted butter, melted
Juice of ½ lemon
¾ cup dry white wine

Butter for aluminum foil or waxed paper
Sauce Suprême (see recipe below)
8 artichoke bottoms, sautéed lightly in butter and fresh lemon juice

Preheat oven to 450 degrees.

Season the chicken breasts with salt and pepper, then roll and tie them with string and brush well with melted butter. Butter a 10 by 12-inch ovenproof dish and arrange the breasts in it. Sprinkle them with lemon juice, salt and pepper to taste, and half of the white wine. Cover with parchment paper or lightly buttered foil or wax paper and bake in a 450-degree oven for 12 to 15 minutes, until just lightly colored, not browned. After 5 minutes, lift the paper and baste with the pan juices and the remaining wine, then recover.

Remove the string and arrange the breasts with artichoke bottoms on top on a warm serving platter. Reserve the braising juices for the sauce suprême. Warm this well, and then pour the sauce over the prepared chicken and artichoke bottoms. Serves 8.

Sauce Suprême

2 ½ cups rich Chicken Stock, homemade or good-quality canned (see Basic Recipes)
8 mushrooms, sliced
1 ½ cups Velouté Sauce (see Basic Recipes)
2 egg yolks

1 ½ cups light cream
Salt, freshly ground white pepper
Juices from cooking Suprêmes
1 cup Duxelles (see Basic Recipes)

Simmer the stock with the sliced mushrooms over medium heat until it is reduced by half. Combine with the velouté sauce and simmer gently, uncovered, until it is reduced to 1 ½ cups. Mix egg yolks and cream, stir in a little hot sauce, and add the mixture, whisking continuously, to the sauce, stirring until it is thickened and well mixed. Season with salt and pepper to taste and strain through a fine sieve.

Add the braising juices from the chicken and the duxelles and blend well.

RISOTTO

4 tablespoons unsalted butter
1 small onion, finely chopped
2 cups long-grain rice
4 cups chicken stock

Salt, freshly ground pepper
3 tablespoons minced fresh parsley

Preheat oven to 350 degrees.

Melt butter in ovenproof saucepan and sauté onion until soft and transparent, about 4 to 5 minutes. Stir in rice and cook for 2 to 3 minutes, until opaque and well-coated with butter. Add chicken stock, bring to a boil, cover saucepan, and set in lower third of oven. Cook 18 to 20 minutes, until stock is absorbed. Fluff rice with a fork, season to taste with salt and pepper and stir in parsley. Serves 8.

CRÊPES FRAMBOISES

1 ¾ cups milk
2 eggs plus 2 egg yolks
⅔ cup sifted flour
1 tablespoon sugar
Salt
2 tablespoons unsalted butter, melted
1 tablespoon cognac
Butter for preparing crêpes

Oil or butter for baking dish
2 pints fresh raspberries, rinsed and drained
Sugar
Kirsch or framboise
2 cups warm Sauce Anglaise flavored with framboise, cognac, or kirsch (see recipe below)

Put the milk and eggs in blender container, add the flour, sugar, a pinch of salt, butter, and cognac, and whirl at top speed for 1 minute. If any flour sticks to the sides of the blender, push it down with a rubber spatula and blend again for 1 or 2 seconds. Cover blender and refrigerate for at least 2 hours. Brush a 4- or 6-inch crêpe pan with melted butter and set it over medium heat. Ladle a generous spoonful of batter and quickly tilt pan to coat bottom evenly. Return the pan to heat for 1 minute or until the crêpe is brown on the bottom, then turn it with either your fingers or a spatula. Brown lightly on the other side for about ½ minute and slide onto a plate. Proceed with the rest of the batter. Set aside covered if not using immediately. Crêpes may be rewarmed by covering with foil and setting them in a slow oven. Makes 18 to 20 crêpes.

When ready to serve, oil or butter 1 or 2 shallow ovenproof baking dishes large enough to hold crêpes in 1 layer. Sprinkle the raspberries with sugar and kirsch or framboise to taste. Enclose as many berries as each crêpe will hold, roll them up, and arrange in prepared baking dish. Sprinkle again with sugar and bake in a 350-degree oven for 15 minutes or until warmed through. If a chafing dish is used, heat the crêpes in an oiled pan over boiling water until thoroughly warmed, then flambé with the desired liqueur. When serving the crêpes from a baking dish, follow the same procedure.

To flambé, heat the liqueur in a small saucepan over how heat until heated through. Ignite with a match and pour the flaming liqueur over the crêpes, turning and basting until all alcohol has cooked away and flame is extinguished. Coat the crêpes lightly with warm sauce anglaise, and pass the remaining sauce. Serves 8.

Sauce Anglaise

1 cup milk
1 cup heavy cream
3-inch-piece vanilla bean (or
   1 ½ teaspoons vanilla)
4 egg yolks

⅓ cup sugar
¼ cup framboise, cognac, or
   kirsch, or to taste for a
   richly aromatic sauce

Scald the milk and cream in a saucepan with the vanilla bean. Beat the yolks with the sugar in heavy saucepan until pale yellow and thick, then add the milk mixture in a thin stream, beating constantly. Cook over medium heat, stirring frequently, until the mixture thickens and coats a spoon. Do not boil. Add vanilla (if not using bean) and liqueur.

Sans Souci

Lunch for Two

*Caviar Soufflé
*Melba English Muffins
 Salad of Bibb Lettuce with *White Wine Vinaigrette (see
  Basic Recipes)
*Crêpes Gravetye Manor

When you're plotting a lunch to impress that very special someone, nothing could be more elegant and enticing than the rich caviar soufflé suggested in this menu. It is accompanied by a lovely, crisp, garden-fresh salad, crunchy Melba English muffins, a light, chilled sauternes, and the final sweet seduction—a smooth, chocolate-filled crêpe.

This is a simple but chic lunch. The only last-minute work required is beating and folding the egg whites into the soufflé base. The secret of an impressive soufflé is beating the whites at room temperature in an unlined copper bowl with a balloon whisk. And this soufflé has yet another secret: select good quality caviar rather than the less expensive lump-fish variety. The lumpfish caviar will not affect the height of the soufflé—but it could affect the color and turn it gray. With real caviar the end result will be a glamorous pale puff flecked with those delectable black caviar eggs. Equally delicious and pretty is a red caviar soufflé.

Since it's just the two of you, for added intimacy you might use individual trays with gay embroidered mats and matching napkins. Accent each tray with beautiful china, gleaming silverware, delicate wine-glasses and a porcelain minivase containing a small bouquet of flowers or rosebuds. *Voilà!* You've created the perfect atmosphere—*sans souci*—and impressed that special someone with a lovingly thought-out lunch.

CAVIAR SOUFFLÉ

4 tablespoons butter
2 tablespoons flour
½ teaspoon salt
Cayenne
1 cup milk, scalded
1 cup grated very mild
    cheese (such as Münster
    or Monterey Jack)

4 eggs, separated, plus 1 egg
    white
Butter
4 ounces black or red good-
    quality caviar

Preheat oven to 325 or 350 degrees, as desired.

Melt butter. Add flour, salt, and a pinch of cayenne, and cook gently for 2 minutes over moderate heat. Add milk, and stir until smooth. Add cheese and cook until blended, then cool slightly. Beat egg yolks, then blend into sauce. Beat egg whites until stiff peaks form, stir ¼ into sauce base, then fold remaining into sauce base. Butter a 2-quart soufflé dish and pour in half of soufflé mixture. Put half the caviar in the center. Fold remaining caviar gently into remaining soufflé mixture and pour into dish. Bake in a 325-degree oven for 25 minutes for a soft (French) soufflé, or in a 350-degree oven for 40 minutes for a firm soufflé. Serves 2.

MELBA ENGLISH MUFFINS

Frozen English muffins   Butter

Preheat oven to 200 degrees.

Press muffin firmly onto board with palm of hand, and carefully slice horizontally into 3 or 4 pieces with a sharp serrated knife. Put on a baking sheet and bake in a 200-degree oven until crisp and lightly browned, about 20 minutes, then butter lightly and return to oven for an additional 10 to 20 minutes. Do the muffins ahead of time and keep them warm in a toaster oven or bun warmer.

CRÊPES GRAVETYE MANOR

1 tart cooking apple (such   3-ounce bar Swiss extra
  as a Greening)   bittersweet chocolate
2 tablespoons butter   1 cup heavy cream, whipped
Sugar   8 6- or 7-inch Crêpes (see
Dark rum, cognac, or vanilla   Index)

Preheat oven to 450 or 500 degrees.

Peel apple, core, and chop finely. Melt butter in a small skillet and sauté apple until just tender. Sweeten to taste with sugar, and flavor with rum, cognac, or vanilla.

Melt chocolate over hot water, cool, and fold gently but thoroughly into whipped cream. Spread each crêpe with a bit of the apple mixture, then spread a large spoonful of the chocolate cream across the center of each and roll up. Arrange side by side in a shallow ovenproof serving dish, then spread remaining chocolate cream along the center. Put in a 450- to 500-degree oven for about 5 minutes, until heated through. Cream will begin to melt. Serve immediately. Serves 4.

Note: Recipe may be halved to serve 2.

A Wine Shower

Dinner for Twelve

*Céleri Rémoulade with *Moules Vinaigrette
*Roast Beef
*Popovers
*Brussels Sprouts with Water Chestnuts
*Horseradish Ring
  Spinach Salad with *Mustard Vinaigrette (see Basic Recipes)
  Chocolate Ice Cream with *Mocha Mousseline Sauce

A wine shower dinner in honor of a lucky-in-love couple is a happy and sophisticated way to celebrate their engagement. It's a gift-giving occasion that appeals to male and female alike. Guests are invited to bring something relating to wine: a book, a year's subscription to a wine magazine, a wine opener or cooler, a selection of young wines, or perhaps an estate-bottled rare vintage.

You might make the centerpiece incorporate your present. Six or more wineglasses each filled with a bunch of grapes chosen with an eye for their color would be effective. Or small, individual grape de-canters filled with wine and heaped in a big crystal bowl could serve as decoration as well as favors for the guests. For the table, capitalize on grape colors, shades of purple, deep red, and green—an iris-colored cloth, perhaps, with pale green napkins and predominantly white china. If you are clever at découpage—you might make place cards decorated with selected clippings from wine labels.

The menu itself is a gem and, with the exception of the roast beef, can be ready to serve before the guests arrive. This allows you time to enjoy the opening of the presents during the cocktail hour, rather than exile in the kitchen. The first course, for instance—a tart beginning—crunchy celery root rémoulade and mussels vinaigrette, is served cold. At the last minute all that's required is that the roast be carved, the Brussels sprouts warmed, the salad tossed. Then you, too, can sit down with your company and raise a toast to the honored two.

CÉLERI RÉMOULADE

3 pounds celery root
Juice of 1 lemon
Salt
3 egg yolks
1 tablespoon white wine
   vinegar
2 ¼ cups olive oil

6 tablespoons Dijon mustard
Freshly ground pepper
Lettuce leaves
Mussels Vinaigrette (see rec-
   ipe below)
Chopped parsley

Peel the celery root and cut into the thinnest julienne strips possible. Toss with the lemon juice and 1 ½ teaspoons salt and set aside.

Prepare the sauce: warm a medium-size mixing bowl with hot water and dry. Put the egg yolks in it with a large pinch of salt and beat with a whisk until thick and sticky (when you can see the bottom of the bowl between strokes). And the vinegar and beat well. Begin adding the olive oil by droplets, beating all the while, until the sauce thickens and "takes," then beat in oil in a thin, steady stream until all is added and mayonnaise is thick and creamy. Blend in the mustard and season to taste with pepper.

Drain celery root. Mix with mustard mayonnaise, then season with additional salt and lemon juice, if necessary. Serve a small mound on a lettuce leaf with a small mound of Mussels Vinaigrette next to it. Garnish with chopped parsley. Serves 12.

Note: Céleri Rémoulade is also good served with a slice of Westphalian ham, attractively rolled up.

MOULES VINAIGRETTE

2 ¼ cups dry white wine
9 quarts mussels, well
   scrubbed with a stiff brush
   and the beards pulled out
½ cup olive oil
2 tablespoons lemon juice, or
   more, as desired

3 to 4 tablespoons minced
   shallots
4 to 5 tablespoons freshly
   chopped parsley
Salt, freshly ground pepper

Bring the white wine to a boil in a large pot; boil 1 to 2 minutes. Add the mussels, cover tightly, and steam until the shells open, about 5 minutes.

Once or twice during the cooking time grasp the pot firmly and shake it hard up and down to redistribute mussels for even steaming. When the shells are opened, remove the mussels from them. Discard any that have not opened. Strain the liquid through cheesecloth and reserve.

Combine the olive oil, lemon juice, shallots, parsley, and 3 to 4 tablespoons of the reserved liquid. (Freeze remaining liquid for sauce or soup.) Mix gently with the mussels and season to taste with salt and pepper, adding more lemon juice if desired. Marinate at least 30 to 60 minutes before serving. Serves 12.

ROAST BEEF

1 tablespoon dry mustard	6-pound boneless sirloin roast
¼ cup flour	or a 4-rib roast
Salt, freshly ground pepper	1 cup red wine

Preheat oven to 450 degrees.

Mix together the mustard, flour, and salt and pepper to taste and rub the mixture over the fat and ends of the roast. Put roast on a rack in a large pan in the center of the oven and roast for 10 minutes at 450, then turn the oven down to 350 degrees and (including the first 10 minutes) cook the roast 15 minutes per pound to produce a rare roast. About ½ hour before the roast will be done, pour red wine over it to make good *jus*. Serves 12.

POPOVERS

3 eggs	½ teaspoon salt
1 ½ cups flour	Butter
1 ½ cups milk	

Preheat oven to 450 degrees.

Mix well eggs, flour, milk, and salt. Batter should be very smooth. It may be whirled in the blender. Butter 12 large muffin cups and fill each halfway full. Bake in a 450-degree oven for about 30 minutes, until well puffed and browned.

Note: These can be made in about 3 minutes and are a nice change from dinner rolls.

BRUSSELS SPROUTS
WITH WATER CHESTNUTS

1 ½ quarts Brussels sprouts   6 tablespoons butter, melted
1 quart chicken broth
3 8 ½ -ounce cans water
    chestnuts

Preheat oven to 350 degrees.

Cut off the ends of the sprouts and trim as necessary. Cut a cross in the base of each sprout with the tip of a sharp knife. Bring chicken broth to a boil in a large saucepan and cook the sprouts in the broth, uncovered, for 5 to 7 minutes, until just tender. Drain in a colander and then on paper towels.

Butter a 2-quart casserole. Put the sprouts and the water chestnuts in the casserole and pour the butter oven them. Bake uncovered until thoroughly heated, 20 to 30 minutes. This recipe may be prepared ahead to the baking stage. Serves 12.

HORSERADISH RING

1 envelope unflavored gelatin   ¼ cup prepared horseradish
¼ cup cold water   1 ½ cups sieved small-curd
1 ¼ cups boiling water   cottage cheese
¼ cup lime juice   1 tablespoon mayonnaise
1 teaspoon grated lime zest   1 teaspoon minced onion
1 teaspoon salt   Vegetable oil
⅛ teaspoon paprika   Chopped parsley

Soften gelatin in cold water. Add boiling water and stir gelatin until dissolved. Cool. Add the lime juice and zest, salt, paprika, horseradish, cottage cheese, mayonnaise, and onion, and beat until smooth. Put in refrigerator until the mixture begins to jell, about 15 to 20 minutes. Oil a 4-cup mold, pour in gelatin mixture, and chill until firm. Unmold and garnish with chopped parsley.

MOCHA MOUSSELINE SAUCE

6 egg yolks	Salt
3 tablespoons very strong coffee (may be made with instant coffee)	6 tablespoons brandy
	1 cup sugar
	2 cups heavy cream, whipped

Beat the egg yolks until light, then beat in the strong coffee, a pinch of salt, and the brandy. Gradually beat in the sugar, blending well. Cook in top of double boiler over hot water for about 5 minutes, stirring constantly. Remove from fire, cool completely, and fold in whipped cream. Chill. Serve as cold as possible. Spoon over chocolate ice cream. Serves 12.

A Seafood

Celebration for Four

*Moules Farcies Provençale
*Grilled Swordfish Steak with *Anchovy-Lemon Butter
*Grated Zucchini
*Vermicelli Soufflé
  Lemon Sherbet with Tangerines and Curaçao

Any New York cookbook would be incomplete without a salute to the abundant variety of fresh fish available here. Since the 1820s New Yorkers have been supplied all year round by the seafood markets in the Fulton Street area. Wholesale and retail fish markets still operate on Fulton Street in cramped but colorful old buildings not far from Wall Street. Local shellfish of many varieties are available and high on the list for both flavor and reasonable price are mussels.

The seafood celebration then begins at the table with mussels with a pungent garlic butter. Next comes a perfectly grilled swordfish steak with a savory compound butter. For an accompaniment, vermicelli soufflé is suggested. This is a delectable dish to use with any simply prepared entree. It is basically a noodle pudding turned into a soufflé by separating the eggs, whipping up the whites, and folding them into a mixture of vermicelli, sour cream, Parmesan, and egg yolks. The refreshing dessert is easily done by tossing tangerine sections with a bit of sugar and spooning them around lemon sherbet. Offer Curaçao as a topping.

This menu has definite male appeal and might be a good one to choose next time your husband asks you to entertain visiting businessmen. If you or your children are shell collectors, a pile or basket of your treasures would be attractive and easy to use as a centerpiece.

Appropriate at cocktails might be oysters and clams on the half shell, served simply with lemon and freshly ground pepper. Or shrimp with a curry garlic dip (see Index).

MOULES FARCIES PROVENÇALE

4 dozen mussels, scrubbed
  clean and debearded
1 cup boiling water
½ cup dry vermouth
¼ pound butter, softened
1 tablespoon finely chopped
  parsley

2 cloves garlic, put through a
  press
1 shallot, minced
1 tablespoon cognac

Put the mussels in a large pot with boiling water and vermouth. Cover and steam the mussels until they just open, about 5 minutes. Discard half of each shell.

Cream together the butter, parsley, garlic, shallot, and cognac. Put a dab of the flavored butter on each mussel. Just before serving run the mussels under the broiler for about 3 to 4 minutes, until bubbling. Serves 4.

GRILLED SWORDFISH STEAK WITH ANCHOVY-LEMON BUTTER

2 1- to 1½-inch-thick
  swordfish steaks, about
  2½ pounds
¼ pound unsalted butter

¼ cup lemon juice
2 tablespoons anchovy paste
Salt, freshly ground pepper
Lemon wedges

Wipe the swordfish steaks with a damp paper towel and pat dry. Combine the butter, lemon juice, anchovy paste, and salt and pepper to taste in a small heavy saucepan and heat over medium heat, stirring until well blended. Put the swordfish steaks on a broiling pan and spoon ¼ cup of seasoned butter over each steak. Broil 8 to 10 minutes on each side, basting every 5 minutes. Serve with lemon wedges. Serves 4.

GRATED ZUCCHINI

2 pounds zucchini
Salt
½ small onion, finely
    chopped (optional)
4 tablespoons unsalted but-
    ter

Freshly ground pepper
1 lemon
2 to 3 tablespoons chopped
    parsley

Scrub the zucchini and cut off the ends. Grate and put into a colander.
Toss with 2 to 3 teaspoons salt and leave to drain at least ½ hour (put
colander over a pan to catch juices). When ready to cook, just before
serving, squeeze the zucchini in a potato ricer to extract all the liquid
(reserve to use in soup). Melt the butter in a large heavy skillet and
sauté the onion, if desired, over low heat until soft. Add zucchini and
cook over medium-high heat, stirring and tossing constantly, for 3 to
4 minutes, until cooked but still crisp. Season with salt if necessary,
pepper, the juice of ½ to 1 lemon, and the parsley. Serve immediately.
Serves 4.

VERMICELLI SOUFFLÉ

3 large eggs, separated
1 pint sour cream
1 cup freshly grated im-
    ported Parmesan cheese
1 tablespoon finely chopped
    parsley
2 tablespoons finely chopped
    onion

Salt, freshly ground pepper
2 cups cooked vermicelli,
    brown a little before
    cooking
Butter

Preheat oven to 350 degrees.
Combine egg yolks and sour cream, and blend well. Add cheese,
parsley, onion, salt and pepper to taste, and vermicelli. Beat egg whites
until stiff but not dry and gently fold into the vermicelli mixture.
Butter a 6-cup soufflé dish and fill with soufflé mixture. Set in a pan
with hot water and bake in a 350-degree oven for 45 minutes until
puffed and browned. Serves 4 to 6.

A Movie Buff's
Buffet for Twelve

Calamata Olives
Stuffed Grape Leaves
*Tiropites (see Index)
*Greek Beef Stew
*Greek Salad
*Hot Herb Bread
*Olympian Cake
Popcorn

If you're an incurable romantic who can't hear Bogey utter, "Here's looking at you, kid," often enough—and you love informal entertaining, this is *your* kind of party. It's a dinner designed to please and entertain both Grecophiles and flick fans—a buffet that's easy on the hostess—followed by a movie that's easy on the eyes.

The strategy includes clever invitations: large, hand-lettered replicas of movie tickets admitting one (or two) to the film feature you've selected. "Canned" movies are available free through many public libraries. You might write the nearest one and request a list of what's available. But be sure to reserve the film far enough in advance so that you can be certain it will be available on the date of your party. Films may also be rented, as may film projectors and screens from private firms listed in the telephone directory yellow pages under "motion picture film libraries."

The real feature attraction, however, is the Greek buffet which might be presented against a collage backdrop or centerpiece you create of cut-out movie-star pictures or posters. The meal begins with tiropites —mini-cheese pies—calamata olives, and stuffed grape leaves. The satisfying, earthy beef stew—Greek, accented with cinnamon, cloves, and currants, is accompanied by Greek salad and herb bread. To drink with everything—a hearty domestic red wine—passed and poured from large carafes.

The interval between the main course and the ultra-rich dessert might be the perfect point to screen the movie. If chairs are insufficient— throw pillows do nicely for relaxed seating and plenty of hot buttered popcorn adds just the right touch to add to the amusement of the film. Lights . . . camera . . . pass the popcorn.

GREEK BEEF STEW

6 pounds trimmed lean beef,
    cut into 1-inch cubes
Salt, freshly ground pepper
½ pound butter
4 pounds small white onions,
    peeled
2 6-ounce cans tomato paste
⅔ cup red wine
4 tablespoons red wine vine-
    gar

2 tablespoons brown sugar
2 garlic cloves, minced
2 bay leaves
2 cinnamon sticks
1 teaspoon whole cloves
½ teaspoon cumin
    (optional)
1 cup currants or ½ cup
    raisins

Season meat with salt and pepper. Melt butter in heavy casserole or Dutch oven, add meat and mix; do not brown. Arrange onions over meat. Mix tomato paste, wine, vinegar, sugar, and garlic, and pour over meat and onions. Add bay leaves, cinnamon sticks, cloves, cumin, if desired, and currants or raisins. Cover with pottery plate, then cover pot and simmer over low heat for 3 hours or until meat is very tender. Do not stir during cooking. Skim off fat, and stir sauce gently just before serving. Serves 12.

GREEK SALAD

3 heads Boston lettuce, or
   romaine
8 tomatoes, quartered
½ pound feta cheese, crumbled
24 anchovy fillets
24 Greek olives
24 tiny hot peppers
24 tiny stuffed grape leaves,
   available in jars

4 onions, preferably red,
   thinly sliced
6 cucumbers, peeled and
   thinly sliced
1 ½ cups Vinaigrette Sauce
   (see Basic Recipes)
1 tablespoon dried orégano
Salt, freshly ground pepper

Tear the lettuce into bite-size pieces. Arrange the lettuce attractively in a large salad bowl with the tomatoes, feta cheese, anchovy fillets, olives, peppers, grape leaves, onions, and cucumbers. Just before serving toss with vinaigrette, orégano, and salt and pepper to taste. Serves 12.

HOT HERB BREAD

2 loaves French bread
½ pound butter, softened
2 large cloves garlic, crushed

1 cup finely chopped parsley
1 cup finely chopped onion
Salt, freshly ground pepper

Preheat oven to 375 degrees.
  Slice bread almost through, leaving it joined at bottom, at 2-inch intervals. Cream butter with garlic, parsley, onion, and salt and pepper to taste and generously spread between each slice. Wrap in foil and bake in 375-degree oven until hot, about 10 to 15 minutes. Serves 12.

OLYMPIAN CAKE

4 1-ounce squares unsweetened chocolate
3 tablespoons sugar
6 tablespoons water

8 eggs, separated
3 packages of ladyfingers,
   split (36 ladyfingers)
1 cup heavy cream

Combine chocolate, sugar, and water in a small, heavy saucepan and melt over low heat. Beat until smooth. Cool. Beat egg yolks until thick and lemon-colored and add to chocolate mixture. Beat the egg whites until stiff and fold into the chocolate mixture.

Line bottom of an 8 by 12-inch serving dish with 1⅓ of the lady-fingers. Pour half the filling over them. Spread with half the remaining ladyfingers, and pour in the remaining filling. Top with remaining lady-fingers. Cover with foil or plastic wrap and refrigerate overnight. Whip the cream until stiff. Just before serving, unmold cake and spread with whipped cream. Serves 12.

Puerto Rican

Fiesta for Eight

*Escabeche
*Candied Plantains
*Asopao
*Orange Custard

"Bienvenida a Nueva York." "Welcome to New York." Spanish is New York's second language, so numerous are our Puerto Rican residents. You can watch Spanish programs on television, read a Spanish newspaper, even be wooed to buy products on Spanish billboards. Puerto Rico is honored on a special day with a parade up Fifth Avenue.

This menu represents Puerto Rican cuisine at its finest. It begins with *escabeche*, a variation of *seviche*—marinated raw fish or scallops. Here the fish is cooked for just a moment and then marinated. A different serving idea would be an avocado half filled with *escabeche*. Then try *asopao*, a hearty chicken and rice dish, and candied plantains. Dessert is a light orange custard.

Capture Spanish gaiety and drama in your table settings. Dramatic red and black would be effective, perhaps inexpensive black lace over red tablecloths for theatrical contrast. Castanets (wired together) would be clever holders for place cards and favors for your guests.

"Muchas gracias, Puerto Rico, para ésta comida. Salud!"

ESCABECHE

1 Spanish onion or 2 medium
   white onions, thinly sliced
2 cloves garlic, peeled
2 bay leaves
1 cup red wine vinegar
Salt
10 black peppercorns

1 cup small stuffed Spanish
   olives
1 cup olive oil
3 pounds halibut or sole fillets
Boston lettuce leaves or
   avocado halves

Prepare the marinade: combine onions, garlic, bay leaves, vinegar, 1 ta-blespoon salt, and peppercorns in a saucepan, cover, and simmer until the onions are tender, about 20 minutes. Cool the marinade and add the olives and ¾ cup olive oil. Meanwhile, cut the fillets into 1½- to 2-inch wide pieces, and sprinkle lightly with salt. Heat the remaining olive oil in a large skillet, and sauté the fish for about 1 minute on each side, or until barely done. If all the fish does not fit in one layer, sauté in stages, adding more olive oil as needed. Transfer the fish to a glass or ceramic bowl or dish. Pour the marinade over the fish, cover the bowl or dish, and chill for at least 24 hours. Remove the bay leaves and garlic. Serve the escabeche on Boston lettuce leaves or in avocado halves with a gener-ous portion of olives, onions, and marinade. Serves 8 as a first course.

CANDIED PLANTAINS

4 very ripe plantains
¼ pound butter
1½ to 2 cups sugar
1 cup water

2 cinnamon sticks
¼ cup dry sherry or ver-
   mouth (optional)

Peel plantains and slice diagonally. Melt butter in a large heavy skillet and sauté plantains until lightly browned. Add sugar, water, cinnamon, and sherry or vermouth if desired and blend. Cover and cook over low heat about 45 minutes, until syrup is thick and coats plantain slices. Serves 8.

ASOPAO

2 3- to 3½-pound chickens,
  each cut into 8 serving
  pieces and skinned
4 cloves garlic, peeled
1 teaspoon salt
1 teaspoon dried orégano
4 or 5 black peppercorns
Olive oil
1 large onion, finely chopped
2 ounces cooked ham,
  chopped
1 green pepper, seeded and
  chopped
2 tablespoons *sofrito* (a pungent flavoring paste, optional but available in
  many large supermarkets
  and Spanish groceries)

1½ pounds fresh or canned
  tomatoes, peeled and
  chopped (drain canned tomatoes)
6 cups chicken stock
2 cups long-grain rice
Salt, freshly ground pepper
1 cup cooked baby peas
½ cup freshly grated Parmesan cheese
¼ cup small stuffed olives
1 tablespoon drained capers
2 pimientos, cut into thin
  strips
8 to 10 white asparagus tips
  (optional)

Rinse the chicken pieces and dry thoroughly.

Prepare the marinade: mash the garlic, salt, orégano, and peppercorns in a mortar and pestle and moisten generously with olive oil. Rub the marinade well into the chicken pieces and marinate several hours or overnight.

Heat ¼ cup olive oil in a large skillet and sauté the chicken over medium to high heat until lightly browned. Remove the chicken to a heavy 4-quart flameproof casserole. Add the chopped onion, ham, green pepper, and sofrito to the skillet in which the chicken was cooked, add-ing more olive oil as necessary, and cook over medium heat until the onion is soft. Add the tomatoes and cook for 3 minutes. Pour the mix-ture over the chicken, cover the casserole, and cook over low heat at a gentle simmer until the chicken is tender, about 30 minutes. Remove the chicken from the casserole and set aside. If desired, you may re-move the casserole from the heat and cool until the chicken can be handled. The dish may be prepared ahead to this point.

Reheat the tomato mixture if the dish has been prepared ahead to this point. Add chicken stock, rice, and salt and pepper to taste to the casserole. Cover and cook over moderate heat for 20 to 25 minutes, or until the rice is tender.

Stir the peas, Parmesan cheese, olives, and capers into the rice, and add the chicken pieces. Garnish with pimiento strips. Cover and simmer 10 to 15 minutes or until the chicken is heated through. The rice will not absorb all the liquid. Heat asparagus tips, and garnish the asopao. Serves 8.

ORANGE CUSTARD

3 cups fresh orange juice
¾ cup sugar
12 eggs, well beaten
¾ cup dark rum

1½ cups heavy cream, whipped
2 tablespoons grated orange zest

Preheat oven to 350 degrees.

Mix the orange juice and sugar and stir until the sugar is dissolved. Blend in the eggs and dark rum. Pour into a 6-cup soufflé dish or 8 oven-proof custard molds and put in a shallow pan of hot water. Bake the custard in a 350-degree oven for 20 minutes. Test by inserting a knife in center. If the knife comes out clean, the custard is cooked. Chill several hours. Serve with whipped cream and grated orange zest. Serves 8.

A Farewell to Summer

Cocktail Party

*Country Pâté
  Cornichons
*Cheese Tray
*Hot Roasted Nuts (see Index)
*Fresh Pear Cubes in Prosciutto
*Hard-cooked Eggs with Crab and Chives
*Mushrooms Stuffed with Mussels
  A variety of Unsalted Crackers, Water Biscuits, and
    Thin-sliced French and Dark Breads

As summer draws to a close there is a feeling of nostalgia. Everyone would like a last chance to sit on the grass and enjoy a balmy evening with friends. That feeling inspired this idea for an outdoor cocktail party set at the obelisk in Central Park. But anywhere you plan it, first check out the physical aspects, and if it is to be held on public grounds, also check with the proper authorities to see if permission is required.

For invitations, line tiny wicker baskets with a small square cut from an orange and yellow print fabric and fill them with a scroll announcing the time, date, and a map of the site of the party, then deliver them. On the evening of the party, prior to guests' arrival, decorate the site with baskets filled with Queen Anne's Lace, Black-eyed Susans, and timothy hay. Tablecloths and napkins could be of marigold colors, as could be the paper plates and plastic glasses. And, to provide soft, flickering light, fill the bottom of small colorful paper bags with sand and stand a candle in them.

The menu offers a potpourri of canapés—both hot and cold, from country pâté served with cornichons to mushrooms stuffed with mussels. Most of the organizing can be done at home in advance. Ideally, you should be able to arrive and set everything up in minutes. Hors d'oeuvres can be arranged on a platter and covered with plastic wrap at home with its accompanying utensils and condiments. Reserve food should be stashed in plastic containers, ready to replenish trays later on. Keep the hot food hot by wrapping it in foil and nestling it in metal containers with hot bricks. Cold food can be kept on ice in a large Styrofoam hamper. And don't forget ice—you'll need plenty of it—so be sure to have a second hamper. Everything can be transported to the site in wagons, shopping carts, or baby carriages.

Just imagine for a moment the setting for this fabulous farewell to summer: little groups of guests gathered on the green, faces illuminated by flickering light. The backdrop is shimmering with thousands of tiny lighted windows—the most glamorous panorama in the world.

COUNTRY PÂTÉ

1 ½ pounds fresh pork fat
1 pound boneless veal
1 pound boneless pork shoul-
    der
1 pound lightly smoked ham
½ pound pork liver
4 cloves garlic
6 shallots
¼ cup heavy cream

3 eggs
¼ cup scotch or bourbon
4 teaspoons salt
2 teaspoons freshly ground
    pepper
½ teaspoon allspice
½ teaspoon cinnamon
½ cup flour

Preheat oven to 400 degrees.

Slice ½ pound of the pork fat thinly, then finely grind half of the remaining pork fat with the veal and pork shoulder. Line a 3-quart mold, or 2 1½-quart molds (or loaf pans) with the sliced pork fat, letting the long ends hang over the edge of the pan. Dice the ham and mince or grind coarsely remainder of the pork fat. Purée the liver in a blender with the garlic, shallots, cream, eggs, and scotch or bourbon. Gradually add about a third of the veal-pork mixture.

Combine all the ground and puréed meats in a large bowl and add the remaining seasonings and flour, mixing all thoroughly. Fill the mold or molds with the pâté mixture and fold the overlapping strips of fat over the top. Cover tightly with a double thickness of aluminum foil. Put the mold in boiling water (in a bain-marie) and bake on the middle rack of a 400-degree oven for 3 hours. Replenish water if necessary. Remove the foil and continue baking until the top of the pâté is browned, approximately 20 minutes longer. Weight the pâté and cool. Yields 3 quarts, enough to serve 12. Serve with cornichons.

CHEESE TRAY

Try a selection of cheeses based on whatever your budget permits and whatever is available at your market: Chèvre, St. Marcellin, La Grappe, Coulommiers, Belle-Étoile, Boursin, King Christian, Brie, Roquefort, and perhaps a large Edam or Gouda, hollowed out, arranged in the traditional French style on a wicker tray with a border of fresh grape or lemon leaves.

Serve with a variety of unsalted crackers, water biscuits, and thin-sliced French and dark bread.

FRESH PEAR CUBES IN PROSCIUTTO

6 ripe pears, peeled and cored
Lime juice

¼ pound best-quality domestic or imported prosciutto

Cut pears into 1-inch cubes and prosciutto into 1-inch wide strips. Brush pear cubes lightly with lime juice. Wrap each pear cube with a thin strip of prosciutto and secure it with a toothpick. Serves 12.

HARD-COOKED EGGS WITH CRAB AND CHIVES

½ cup frozen or canned king crabmeat, defrosted and/or drained
1 large or 2 small tomatoes, peeled, seeded, juiced, and chopped
8 hard-cooked eggs
¼ to ½ cup Mayonnaise (see Basic Recipes)

Fresh chives (never dried; substitute fresh parsley, add ¼ teaspoon of dried tarragon if chives are not available)
Salt, freshly ground pepper
Minced fresh parsley or chives
Tabasco sauce

Chop the crabmeat finely and reserve. Put chopped tomatoes in a sieve to drain off juices. Halve the eggs lengthwise, put the yolks in a small bowl and mash well with a fork. Mix in the crabmeat, tomatoes, the chives or tarragon, salt and pepper to taste, a dash of Tabasco, and enough mayonnaise to moisten. Stuff the egg halves and garnish with extra chives or parsley and chill before serving.

Extra filling makes a delicious tea-sandwich filling.

MUSHROOMS STUFFED WITH MUSSELS

36 mussels
½ cup dry white wine
36 large mushrooms
2 tablespoons butter
1 tablespoon minced parsley
2 tablespoons minced shallots
1 small clove garlic, minced
Salt, freshly ground pepper

Olive oil
½ to ¾ cup fresh bread
   crumbs (see Basic Rec-
   ipes)
Butter
Minced parsley
Lemon wedges

Scrub the mussels and cut off attached beard with a sharp short knife. Steam the mussels in white wine until shells open, about 5 minutes, shell them, and set aside. Remove the stems of the mushrooms and chop them finely. Melt the butter in a large skillet, add the chopped stems, parsley, shallots, garlic, and salt and pepper to taste. Sauté briefly. Brush the mushroom caps with olive oil and broil them, bottom side up, well below the flame, for about 5 minutes, or until tender. Fill each cap with the seasoned, cooked stems and place a mussel atop each cap, then sprinkle with bread crumbs, and dot with butter. Brown quickly under the broiler, sprinkle with parsley, and serve on a heated dish with lemon wedges. Serves 12.

Early September Supper

for Eight

*Cannelloni with Spinach and Ricotta
*Chicken Piccata
*Broccoli with Lemon Butter
  Arugula Salad with *Lemon Vinaigrette (see Basic Recipes)
  Fresh Pears
*Gorgonzola Mousse

Although for most of us Labor Day marks the beginning of autumn—the flavor of summer still lingers in many inviting ways. One of those ways is homegrown tomatoes—plump, ripe, sun-kissed—really at their peak in the final month of summer. An unusually delicious way to take advantage of the crop is by creating the cream sauce served with the cannelloni which is suggested as a first course on this menu. The sauce beautifully blends the essence of tomato with rich fresh cream—a perfect complement to the spinach-and-ricotta-stuffed pasta.

The chicken piccata, served as a main course, is a preparation ordinarily reserved for veal. In this recipe, ultra-thin scallops of chicken are sautéed in butter and served simply with broccoli and lemon butter. After a salad of tart, crisp arugula, you can present a dessert that's out of the ordinary. It's a smooth Gorgonzola cheese mousse served with succulent ripe pears.

To enhance your September supper, the table setting combines the warm yellow of summer with the cool blue of a September sky. A blue and white paisley sheet covers the table and is brightened by crisp yellow napkins of heavy linen. A yellow wicker basket containing bachelor buttons, yellow marigolds, and baby's breath would serve enchantingly as a centerpiece. And since many think September is the loveliest month of the year for sailing, for place cards you might want to cut sailboats out of yellow construction paper and write the names in with royal blue ink.

CANNELLONI WITH SPINACH
AND RICOTTA

Salt

3 pounds fresh spinach, thoroughly washed

4 scallions, finely chopped

⅔ to ¾ cup freshly grated imported Parmesan cheese

½ pound mozzarella cheese, cut into very small dice

1 pound ricotta cheese

2 eggs, lightly beaten

Freshly ground pepper

Freshly grated nutmeg

24 4 by 6-inch squares fresh pasta, either green or white (or packaged manicotti tubes)

Olive oil

Tomato Cream Sauce (see recipe below)

1 to 1½ cups mixed fresh bread crumbs and freshly grated Parmesan cheese

3 tablespoons butter, melted

Preheat oven to 375 degrees.

Bring a large pot of salted water to a boil and plunge in the spinach. Cook the spinach 3 to 4 minutes, until just wilted. Drain well, and when cool enough to handle, extract all liquid by squeezing between the palms of the hands in small handfuls, or use a potato ricer. Chop finely. Combine the scallions, Parmesan, mozzarella, ricotta, and eggs, blending well. Mix in the chopped spinach. Season to taste with salt, pepper, and a generous amount of nutmeg.

Bring a large pot of water to a boil; add salt and 1 tablespoon of olive oil, and cook the pasta squares until just tender, about 5 minutes, or follow package directions for manicotti tubes. Drain on a cloth dish towel (they will stick to paper towels). Butter 2 ovenproof dishes about 12 by 15 inches. Trim the squares so that they are the same length. Spread 2 to 3 tablespoons of the spinach mixture along a long side of each pasta square and roll up. Arrange 9 cannelloni in each baking dish.

Pour sauce over cannelloni and sprinkle with Parmesan-bread crumb mixture. Dribble melted butter over top. Bake in a 375-degree oven for 15 to 20 minutes, until bubbling and top has colored. Serves 8.

Tomato Cream Sauce

6 tablespoons butter
12 scallions, finely chopped
9 large or 12 medium ripe
    tomatoes, peeled, seeded,
    and diced
2 to 3 tablespoons chopped
    fresh basil, or 1 ½ tea-
    spoons dried

3 cups heavy cream
Salt, freshly ground pepper
Freshly grated nutmeg

Melt butter and sauté scallions gently until tender. Add tomatoes, raise heat, and cook rapidly, watching carefully, until liquid has evaporated. Stir in basil and heavy cream and simmer 5 to 10 minutes, until thickened. Season to taste with salt, pepper, and nutmeg.

Note: To seed tomatoes: cut in half and squeeze seeds out, cut side down.

Note: Cannelloni may be prepared in advance and refrigerated or frozen, then sauced and baked just before serving. This dish is also excellent as the main course for lunch or a light supper.

CHICKEN PICCATA

8 whole chicken breasts,
    boned, skinned, and halved
Salt, freshly ground white
    pepper

Thyme
½ pound unsalted butter,
    clarified (see Basic Rec-
    ipes)

Put the chicken breasts between sheets of wax paper and pound them to a ¼ to ½-inch or less thickness. Season with salt, pepper, and thyme to taste. Sauté in clarified butter until delicately browned and tender, about 5 to 10 minutes. Serves 8.

BROCCOLI WITH LEMON BUTTER

2 bunches fresh broccoli   ¼ pound unsalted butter
Salt   Juice of 1 large lemon

Break the broccoli into flowerets and peel the stems with a sharp knife.
Cut a small cross into the bases of the stems so that the stems will cook
as quickly as the flowerets. Drop into a large pot of salted boiling
water. Return to the boil and cook about 8 minutes, until just tender,
then drain.

Melt the butter, add the lemon juice, and pour over the drained
broccoli before serving. Serves 8.

GORGONZOLA MOUSSE

Oil   ⅓ cup cold water
1 cup Gorgonzola cheese   ¼ cup boiling water
¼ pound unsalted butter,   3 egg yolks
    softened   1 ½ cups heavy cream,
2 envelopes unflavored   whipped
    gelatin   Salt

Oil a 4-cup ring or other shape mold. Mash Gorgonzola until smooth,
then blend well with butter.

Soften gelatin in cold water, then add ¼ cup boiling water and stir
until dissolved. Combine egg yolks with gelatin and mix well. Combine
egg yolk mixture and cheese mixture. Fold in whipped cream. Season
with salt to taste. Put into mold and refrigerate until set.

When ready to serve, unmold the mousse by dipping the bottom of
mold into hot water until it loosens. Serves 8.

Autumn

A Packable Dinner Party

for Moving Day for Six

*Duckling and Wild Rice à l'Orange en Casserole

Salad of Endives and *Marinated Mushrooms (see Index) with
   *Watercress Vinaigrette (see Basic Recipes)

Salt Sticks

*Phoebe's Chocolate Mousse

Here's a welcome surprise—a three-course meal that can make the day bearable for good friends who are moving, be it across town or across the street. This is a dinner that you prepare in your kitchen and move to their new one with minimum hassle. It includes a casserole that's worthy of a house-warming or a formal dinner and a dessert that's cause for celebration.

The movers may not have completely unpacked kitchen and dining essentials, so you'll want to be prepared. Details are important. In addition to the food itself, tuck all the dining necessities—knives, forks, spoons, plates, napkins, glasses, even salt and pepper—in a basket, along with a pretty tablecloth or place mats, for a completely packaged party. If you're really feeling expansive, you might tote an ice-filled bucket and a bottle or two of champagne. This menu definitely merits it.

The meal begins with a main course—the sumptuous casserole of boned duckling and nutted wild rice in a delicious fruit-flavored wine sauce. All the assembly and preparation can be done by you in advance, and it need only be heated through at your friends' new home. Serve it with a special wiltproof salad that can travel and wait well: endive and sliced marinated mushrooms dressed with a watercress vinaigrette. Then for dessert—what a dessert—a melt-in-your-mouth mousse: super-rich chocolate with just a hint of orange. It's the perfect ending to a great meal—and a very warm welcome.

DUCKLING AND WILD RICE
À L'ORANGE EN CASSEROLE

DUCKS AND STOCK

2 5- to 6-pound ducks
Salt
1 onion stuck with 4 cloves
1 teaspoon peppercorns
1 bay leaf

3 sprigs parsley
2 sprigs fresh thyme (or ¼
   teaspoon dried)
2 celery stalks with leaves

Prick ducks all over with the tines of a fork. Remove innards and liver, and reserve. Put ducks in a large pot and add cold water to cover. Add salt to taste, the onion with cloves, peppercorns, bay leaf, parsley, thyme, and celery. Bring to a boil and simmer, uncovered, for about 1 hour and 15 minutes or until the ducks are tender.

    Remove ducks from stock and set aside until cool enough to handle. Remove skin and fat and discard. Remove meat from bones and set aside. Return scraps and carcass to stock pot and continue to simmer until it is reduced by half. When the stock is reduced, add the innards and simmer for 10 minutes or until tender, then add the liver and simmer for 5 minutes more. Strain the stock through a piece of damp cheesecloth or flannel. Pour strained stock into refrigerator containers, cool, then refrigerate overnight. Skim off the fat before using stock.

SAUCE À L'ORANGE

3 tablespoons butter
3 tablespoons flour
1 cup reserved duck stock
½ cup currant jelly
½ cup dry white wine
1 garlic clove, put through
   a press
⅓ cup orange liqueur (Curaçao, Triple Sec, or Grand
   Marnier)

Zest of 1 orange, slivered,
   blanched, and drained
Juice of 1 orange
Salt, freshly ground pepper

Melt butter over low heat. Stir in flour to make a roux and cook gently for 2 minutes. Add the duck stock gradually, stirring constantly until sauce has thickened. Add currant jelly and stir until melted. Blend in white wine, garlic, liqueur, zest, and juice of orange. Stir and simmer together for a few minutes. Season with salt and pepper to taste.

RICE

1 cup wild rice	2 tablespoons butter
4 cups reserved duck stock (if enough is left—if not, add chicken broth)	½ cup chopped almonds Salt, freshly ground pepper

To wash rice, put it in a pan of warm water, stir thoroughly, drain. Repeat this step twice. Then rinse thoroughly in a strainer with cold running water. Return rice to pan, cover with warm water. Bring to a boil and boil for 5 minutes. Drain. Add stock to the rice. Bring to a boil, cover, and simmer for about 45 minutes—or until grain has opened up but the rice is still a bit chewy. Drain. Add butter, almonds, and salt and pepper to taste.

FINAL PREPARATION

Butter	Duck or chicken stock or
Salt, freshly ground pepper	fresh orange juice, if necessary

Preheat oven to 350 degrees.

Butter a shallow, heavy, ovenproof 3-quart casserole. Spread ½ of the rice in the bottom, arrange ½ of the duck meat over the rice, and pour ½ the sauce over it. Make sure all layers are well salted and peppered. Add the remaining rice, then the duck, and pour the remaining sauce over all. Cover. Bake in a 350-degree oven for ½ hour or until heated through. If the casserole seems to be drying out, add more hot stock or orange juice. Serves 6.

Note: This rather elaborate recipe must be started at least a day in advance—and can be started as much as five days in advance if the cooked duck is frozen, then defrosted, before the final preparation. It can be doubled and would make a nice main course for a holiday buffet.

SALAD OF ENDIVES AND
MARINATED MUSHROOMS

6 Belgian endives
1 cup sliced marinated mushrooms, drained (see Index)

Watercress Vinaigrette (see
   Basic Recipes)
1 tablespoon chopped parsley

Belgian endive is the only green that can be tossed with its dressing up
to 3 or 4 hours in advance and remain unwilted. Cut the endives lengthwise into thin strips, or crosswise into ½-inch slices and combine with
the marinated mushrooms. Toss with just enough vinaigrette to coat the
endives lightly, about ½ cup. Refrigerate until ready to serve. Mix in
parsley just before serving. Serves 8.

PHOEBE'S CHOCOLATE MOUSSE

8 ounces imported Swiss
   extra bittersweet chocolate
Grated zest and juice of 1
   orange

4 eggs, separated

Slowly melt the chocolate with 1 tablespoon water in the top of a
double boiler over simmering water. Beat in the orange zest and juice,
and add the egg yolks. Beat the egg whites until stiff and carefully
fold into chocolate mixture. Pour into champagne glasses, or perhaps
something more easily portable, and chill. Serves 4.

A Committee

Lunch for Twelve

*Vitello Tonnato
*Rice Salad (see Index)
*Leeks Vinaigrette
*Sesame Seed Toasts
*Apricot Ice
*Chocolate Chiffon Cookies

When the time comes to start things clicking with your favorite charity, one of the pleasantest and most persuasive ways of ensuring the desired result is to invite the committee to your house for lunch. Not only will it give the newcomers a chance to get acquainted, but a lunch party provides just the right atmosphere to help create camaraderie—so necessary to the teamwork upon which a successful fund-raising event relies.

A good way to warm up this informal meeting would be with a selection of apéritif wines such as Lillet or Dubonnet Blond, served with salted pecans. Of course, you'll want to have your table attractively set before the committee arrives. If the dining table isn't large enough for everyone, why not set up several smaller tables and devise a seating arrangement that strategically teams the most enthusiastic committee members with those who need a little more convincing?

The menu suggested here, however, is more than just palatable persuasion. It's light—but lovely enough to serve as a bridesmaids' luncheon. And the cold main course can keep you out of the kitchen—even at serving time. Vitello tonnato, a classic Italian dish, is a cold roast of veal that's swathed in a rich, tuna-fish-flavored sauce that's spiked with anchovies and capers. Here it's served with sesame toasts and an unusual accompaniment—leeks vinaigrette—and followed by a refreshing apricot ice and chocolate chiffon cookies.

Although there's no certain guarantee of the success of your committee, you can be sure that a luncheon as thoughtfully prepared as this one is bound to be richly rewarded.

VITELLO TONNATO

4 pounds boneless veal shoul-
    der, rolled and tied
2 bottles dry white wine
2 cups water
2 teaspoons salt
8 or 9 onions, peeled and
    halved

4 carrots, scraped and quar-
    tered
2 tablespoons lemon juice
Tonnato Sauce (see recipe
    below)
Lemon slices
Minced parsley

Put veal in large casserole with lid, cover with dry white wine and add 2 cups water, salt, onions, carrots, and lemon juice. Cover and slowly bring to a boil, skimming off scum that rises. Cook until tender, 2 to $2\frac{1}{2}$ hours. Remove scum that may have formed during the cooking and let veal cool in its broth. When cold, cut in thin slices and cover with the tonnato sauce. Garnish with lemon slices and minced parsley. Serves 12.

Tonnato Sauce

2 7-ounce cans tuna fish in
    olive oil (preferably im-
    ported)
4 anchovy fillets in olive oil
3 tablespoons capers, rinsed
    in cold water

4 cup Mayonnaise, prefer-
    ably homemade (see Basic
    Recipes)
Juice of 2 lemons
Veal stock, if necessary

Crush tuna fish, anchovies, and capers in mortar and pestle and combine with mayonnaise and lemon juice. If sauce is too thick to spread easily on veal slices, add some of the veal broth, first straining it through damp cheesecloth or a linen towel twice.

LEEKS VINAIGRETTE

30 leeks, with most of green
  cut off, washed well under
  cold running water
Salt

Vinaigrette Sauce (see Basic
  Recipes)
Chopped parsley

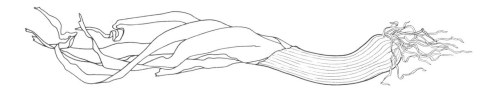

Put leeks into boiling salted water and cook until tender, about 15
minutes. Cool to room temperature. Dress with vinaigrette right before
serving, and sprinkle with chopped parsley. Serves 12.

SESAME SEED TOASTS

18 slices good-quality white
  bread
¼ pound unsalted butter,
  melted

Sesame seeds

Preheat oven to 350 degrees.

Cut bread into rounds with a 2- or 2½-inch cookie cutter, 2 rounds
to a slice. Brush with melted butter on 1 side, or quickly dip round into
butter. Put on a baking sheet and sprinkle liberally with sesame seeds.
Bake in a 350-degree oven for 10 to 12 minutes, until crisp and lightly
browned. Serve hot. Serves 12.

VARIATION: Split open 3 pita breads and cut each disc into 6 wedges.
Brush with melted butter, sprinkle with sesame seeds, and bake in a
350-degree oven for 8 to 10 minutes, until crisp and lightly browned.

APRICOT ICE

3 30-ounce cans peeled apricots (or 5 ½ pounds fresh
   apricots)
1 ½ cups sugar
1 tablespoon unflavored gelatin, softened in ¼ cup cold
   water

Salt
1 pint heavy cream, whipped
   and flavored with rum and
   crushed almonds

Drain syrup from canned apricots and cook with sugar in heavy saucepan over moderate heat for 5 minutes. If using fresh apricots, peel and stew in heavy saucepan with 1 ½ cups sugar and just enough water to cover bottom of pan until tender, about 15 to 20 minutes. Add gelatin for last few minutes of cooking and stir to dissolve thoroughly. Mash fruit with syrup and put through a coarse strainer. Add 3 pinches salt and chill for 1 hour. Beat in a bowl and freeze. Serve with the flavored whipped cream. Serves 12.

CHOCOLATE CHIFFON COOKIES

½ pound butter
1 ¼ cups confectioners' sugar
6 ounces imported sweet
   chocolate, finely grated
1 ½ cups flour, sifted

1 teaspoon vanilla
Salt
1 cup pecans or walnuts,
   finely chopped

Preheat oven to 250 degrees.

Cream the butter and sugar thoroughly. Add the grated chocolate, flour, vanilla, a pinch of salt, and chopped nuts. Form into ¾ inch balls and flatten on ungreased cookie sheets. Bake in a 250-degree oven for 35 to 45 minutes. Makes 5 dozen.

A Tail-gate
Picnic for Four

*Shrimp Pâté (see Index)
*Melba Toast (see Index)
  Crudités
*Cream of Scallop Soup
*Beef and Potato Salad in Bread Rounds
  Pickles, Olives
  Apples
*Brownies
*Ginger Almond Cakes

Tail-gating has gotten to be quite the craze these days—but this picnic menu will do equally well at outdoor concerts, in a box at a baseball game, or on a leafy college campus lawn. The soup is delicious served hot or cold, and the crusty bread round stuffed with hearty beef and potato salad and garnished with cherry tomatoes is a meal in itself—both dramatic and attractive. Somehow the idea that it comes in an edible container seems just right for a picnic.

The soup, after a vigorous stir to bring up the scallops sunk to the bottom, can be served hot in special all-temperature paper beverage cups. The salad is easy to eat from paper plates, and the rest of the menu is finger food, so you need carry along only forks and serving utensils.

If you have yet to invest in a handsome, roomy picnic hamper, you could carry the edibles in a simple tote bag. Each guest could be supplied with his own brightly colored mini-shopping bag containing the cups, plates, vegetables, utensils, and napkins that he will need, and perhaps a half bottle of wine—depending upon how expansive you feel. If it is to be a college football game, a good way to be supportive of your team is to choose paper supplies in the team's colors. Even if they lose—your picnic's bound to be a winner.

CREAM OF SCALLOP SOUP

2 cups dry white wine	2 cups water
1 onion, sliced	1 pound fresh or frozen sea
1 carrot, peeled and sliced	scallops
1 or 2 stalks fennel (when	3 tablespoons butter
available), sliced	4 tablespoons flour
Thyme	1 ½ cups milk, hot
1 bay leaf	2 egg yolks
1 clove garlic, mashed	1 cup heavy cream
6 peppercorns	Salt, freshly ground pepper
4 sprigs parsley	Cumin

Prepare a court bouillon: Combine wine, onion, carrot, fennel, a generous pinch of thyme, bay leaf, garlic, peppercorns, and parsley with water in a large saucepan; bring to a boil, and simmer 10 minutes, then strain. Cut raw scallops into small dice. Return liquid to a boil, add scallops, and simmer 2 to 3 minutes, until barely done. Drain scallops immediately, reserving the liquid.

Prepare a velouté: Melt butter in a large saucepan, stir in flour, and cook the roux gently for 2 minutes. Add court bouillon to roux, stirring constantly. Blend in milk and cook a few minutes, stirring. Mix yolks and cream in a small bowl. Blend in a bit of the hot soup to warm yolks, then pour mixture into saucepan, add scallops, and season to taste with salt and pepper and a pinch of cumin. Cook, stirring, for 1 to 2 minutes, but do not let soup boil. Chill if desired, or pour immediately into Thermoses, and shake before serving. Serves 4.

BEEF AND POTATO SALAD
IN BREAD ROUNDS

1 pound boiling potatoes
Salt
1 cup Mayonnaise, gener-
ously seasoned with Dijon
mustard and 1 tablespoon
vinegar (see Basic Recipes)
1½ pounds rare roast beef,
thinly sliced
½ pound mushrooms, thinly
sliced and marinated in ½
cup vinaigrette sauce
(see Basic Recipes),
flavored with salt, freshly

ground pepper, minced
onion, garlic, and parsley
2 shallots, chopped
2 tablespoons chopped
parsley
Freshly ground pepper
1 10-inch round of sour-
dough or French bread, or
2 smaller rounds, or 4 large
sourdough rolls
Butter
1 cup cherry tomatoes

Peel potatoes and cook in boiling salted water until tender. Slice potatoes and dress with some of the mayonnaise while still hot. Cut roast
beef into finger lengths; drain marinade from mushrooms, reserving the
marinade.

Toss potatoes, beef, and mushrooms together gently to keep potatoes
from breaking up, and carefully mix in reserved marinade, shallots,
parsley, more mayonnaise as needed, and salt and pepper to taste.

Slice off top of bread round and scoop out center, leaving a shell
about ¾ to 1 inch thick. Butter generously, then fill with salad. Put top
on and refrigerate until ready to pack picnic basket or serve. Accompany
with cherry tomatoes. Serves 4.

Note: Potato preparation and marinating of mushrooms may be done
a day ahead, as well as roasting of beef. Salad may be packed into bread
shell several hours before serving.

BROWNIES

4 tablespoons butter
5 ounces German's sweet
  chocolate
2 eggs
1 cup sugar
½ cup flour

1 teaspoon vanilla
2 tablespoons rum
½ cup chopped walnuts
Butter
Walnut halves (optional)

Preheat oven to 350 degrees.

Melt butter and chocolate over hot water. Cool. Beat eggs until thick; add sugar and blend well. Add chocolate mixture, flour, vanilla, rum, and walnuts. Butter an 8-inch square cake pan and pour in mixture. Top with walnut halves if desired. Bake in a 350-degree oven for 35 minutes. Cool before cutting into squares. Makes 16 2-inch squares.

GINGER ALMOND CAKES

1 ¾ cups flour, sifted
1 cup sugar
1 egg
½ pound unsalted butter,
  soft
½ cup preserved ginger,
  finely chopped (drain
  syrup)

1 tablespoon grated orange
  zest
½ cup very finely chopped
  almonds or pecans
2 tablespoons dark rum
Salt

Preheat oven to 350 degrees.

Combine flour, sugar, egg, butter, ginger, orange zest, almonds, rum, and a generous pinch of salt. Knead until well blended. Put into a 9-inch square pan and smooth top. Bake in a 350-degree oven for 20 minutes, then lower heat to 325 degrees and bake 25 to 30 minutes longer, until lightly browned and a toothpick inserted in center comes out clean. Cool a few minutes, then cut into 25 small squares.

Note: For pretty little cakes, bake in individual brioche molds. Makes 10.

A Salute to the Game Season

for Eight

*Chicken and Ham Rolls

*Cheese Wine Soup

*Roast Pheasant with Madeira

*Purée of Celery Root and Potatoes

*Spiced Apple Rings

  Salad of Endives with *Watercress Vinaigrette (see Basic
    Recipes)

*Cassis and Champagne Sherbet

*Macaroons (see Index)

This is a dinner to be served in autumn to honor the first of the season's game birds—be they bought at one's butcher or the gift of a friendly hunter. A simple, elegant, and classic French menu, it is difficult neither in preparation nor presentation for an experienced cook and hostess. The entree specified is roast pheasant, but partridge of any type could be substituted.

The table setting is imaginative, colorful, and in keeping with the game season theme. A dark green felt tablecloth provides the background for brass candlesticks, flickering dark green candles, and a rich, dark antique box filled with pheasant plumage. At each setting, one could carry out the feather motif with little place cards adorned with feathers and feather-patterned napkins.

The menu contrasts the simple soup and roasted bird—larded before roasting with sheets of fat—with such elegant touches of haute cuisine as the delicious purée of celery root and potato, and the cassis and champagne sherbet. It also allows for much of the cooking to be done in advance. The cheese-wine soup, for instance, may be partially prepared the day before, the sherbet easily done the morning of the dinner party.

As well as being a tribute to the game of the season, this festive dinner also provides a pleasing occasion to sample a selection of wines. It progresses from the white wine in the cheese soup which introduces the meal to a majestic burgundy or Bordeaux served with the entree to the flourish of champagne!

CHICKEN AND HAM ROLLS

2 chicken breasts, boned and
   skinned
3 thin slices of smoked ham
Dried basil, crushed
Salt, freshly ground pepper
Butter

1 small clove garlic, put
   through a press
2 teaspoons lemon juice
Paprika
Bread or toast rounds
   (optional)

Preheat oven to 350 degrees.

Put chicken breasts, skinned side down, on board and pound to ¼-inch thickness. Sprinkle with a pinch of basil and salt and pepper to taste. Put 1½ slices of ham on each breast, to cover. Roll lengthwise with ham inside, and secure with wooden toothpicks. Butter a rectangular baking dish and put both rolls, seam side down, in it. Combine the garlic with lemon juice, and dribble over chicken rolls. Sprinkle lightly with paprika. Bake in a 350-degree oven for 35 to 40 minutes, until tender. Chill. Cut into ¼-inch slices. These may be served on small bread or toast rounds but are equally good alone. Makes about 24.

CHEESE WINE SOUP

3 tablespoons butter
3 tablespoons flour
4½ cups milk, hot
2 cloves garlic, peeled
2 cups firmly packed finely
   grated extra sharp natural
   Cheddar cheese

1½ cups of dry white wine
   or vermouth
Salt, freshly ground pepper
3 egg yolks
¼ cup heavy cream
½ cup grated sharp natural
   Cheddar cheese
Freshly grated nutmeg

Melt the butter in a heavy 3-quart saucepan. Stir in the flour and cook the roux gently for 2 minutes. Beat the milk in gradually with a wire whisk, add the garlic, and cook over low heat for 25 minutes, stirring frequently. Do not let the milk boil. Remove the garlic cloves and discard. Soup may be prepared in advance to this point. Stir in the cheese and wine or vermouth, ½ cup at a time, to taste, and season with salt and pepper to taste. Continue stirring until the cheese is melted. Beat the egg yolks with the heavy cream. Stir the mixture gradually into the soup, and simmer for 5 minutes, but do not let soup boil. Serve immediately, garnished with grated Cheddar and a little grated nutmeg. Serves 8.

ROAST PHEASANT WITH MADEIRA

4 2½- to 3-pound pheasants
2 or 3 lemons, cut in half
Fresh pork fat, very thinly
  sliced, or ¾ pound
  unsalted butter (do not
  use salt pork)

Salt, freshly ground black
  pepper
Pinch of thyme
3 cups madeira

Preheat oven to 500 degrees.

Wash pheasants inside and out, pat dry with paper towels, and rub with lemon, inside and out. Lard the breast of each pheasant with thin slices of fresh pork fat. If pork fat is unavailable, rub each bird well all over with 7 tablespoons of the butter, putting extra butter on the breast.

Roast the birds for 15 to 20 minutes. Open the oven door, leaving it ajar slightly to help reduce the oven heat, and reduce heat to about 250 degrees. Remove the pork larding at this time to brown the pheasant. Continue to roast the pheasant for 20 to 25 minutes (no more), basting occasionally with the pan juices and 1½ cups madeira. Remove the pheasant from the pan to a warm platter. Add remaining madeira, salt and freshly ground pepper to taste, a pinch of thyme, the remaining butter, and swirl, scraping up all brown bits to make a simple *jus*. This method should ensure tender, moist birds. Carve and serve the breast meat first, then the legs and thighs. Wings are not generally served. Serves 8.

PURÉE OF CELERY ROOT AND POTATOES

2½ pounds celery root
Lemon juice
Butter
3 cups chicken stock
   (approximately)

2 pounds baking potatoes
Salt, freshly ground pepper
Freshly grated nutmeg
Heavy cream

Peel celery root and cut into ½-inch slices. Drop into lemon juice mixed with water to keep celery root white. Remove from water, put in a heavy saucepan with 1 tablespoon butter and enough chicken stock to barely cover celery root. Cover and simmer—braise—until tender, about 20 minutes.

Peel potatoes, quarter or cut in ½-inch slices, and cook in salted water until tender, or braise with celery root in stock; just add to stock 5 minutes after celery root has begun to cook. Put vegetables through ricer or food mill to make a purée. Add a little braising liquid and additional butter. Season to taste with salt, pepper, and nutmeg. Just before serving, add 2 to 3 tablespoons heavy cream and blend well. Serves 8.

Note: This recipe may be prepared substituting parsnips for celery root. Cook parsnips with potatoes in water, drain and purée, and season with salt, pepper, madeira, and a few drops of lemon juice. Put into a baking dish, cover with buttered bread crumbs (see Basic Recipes), and bake in a 350 degree oven for 30 minutes.

SPICED APPLE RINGS

4 tart apples, cored but not
   peeled
1 cup Calvados or apple
   brandy, or more, to cover
   apples
6 whole cloves

2 2-inch cinnamon sticks
3 bay leaves
1 cup sugar
½ cup wine vinegar
1 cup water

Cut the apples into slices about ½ inch thick. Combine Calvados, cloves, cinnamon, and bay leaves and marinate the apples for 30 to 45 minutes. Drain the apples, remove bay leaves, but reserve the marinade.

Combine the sugar, vinegar, and water, and cook over low heat until thickened slightly, about 15 minutes. Add the apple rings, and cook another 10 minutes or until tender. Mix the marinade into syrup and serve with game, or drain, if desired, before serving. Serves 8.

CASSIS AND CHAMPAGNE SHERBET

1 cup sugar	¼ to ⅓ cup cassis, prefera-
2½ cups water	bly imported
Grated zest and juice of 2	2 egg whites
lemons (strain juice)	Additional cassis
1 cup brut champagne	Champagne (optional)

Combine the sugar and water in a saucepan. Bring to a boil over medium heat and boil 5 minutes. Add the lemon zest. Refrigerate until cool, then add the lemon juice.

Pour into refrigerator trays or a rectangular Pyrex baking dish, and freeze until the mixture is mushy around the edges. Pour into a chilled bowl and beat hard for 1 minute. Stir in the champagne and cassis and return to the baking dish. Freeze again until mushy.

Beat the egg whites until stiff peaks form. Pour the wine-cassis mixture over the whites and mix thoroughly. Return to the freezer tray and continue freezing, stirring every hour to prevent cassis from settling on the bottom.

Serve in chilled coupe champagne glasses. Pass a sauceboat of cassis at the table for guests to spoon a bit over each serving. Champagne may also be poured over the sherbet. This is especially good served with champagne. Serves 8.

Hearty Fare After Touch Football
in Central Park for Eight

*Chili con Queso

*Tostadas

*Rabbit or Chicken in Salsa Verde

  Rice (see Index)

  Salad of Curly Endive, Sliced Red Onions, and Tomatoes with
    *Vinaigrette (see Basic Recipes)

*Pumpkin Soufflé

New York's Central Park is unique. While it appears to be entirely natural, even wild, it was designed by Frederick Law Olmstead and entirely man-made in the early part of the nineteenth century. Central Park was ingeniously devised to provide recreation and relaxation for every New Yorker. At its southern end lies a gem of a children's zoo; both ends have an ice skating rink. The Metropolitan Museum of Art dominates the east side; The Museum of Natural History stands across from its western edge. There is the Ramble—an overgrown wild area, a model boat pond that's the scene of many a mini-America's Cup, numerous bridle paths, a bandshell, fountains, and sculptured walks. Formally landscaped gardens lie behind a grilled door on upper Fifth Avenue. Shakespeare comes to the park in the summer and the Sheep Meadow is the scene of summer concerts, attended by thousands of music lovers who picnic under the star-filled summer skies. There is even a hill near the Metropolitan Museum that is the informal meeting place of dogs and dog fanciers, with every breed of dog and every size and shape of fancier. And a game of some kind is always being played, but baseball, touch football, and romance seem the perennial favorites.

After a game of touch football in the park, the hearty fare on this menu might be just the thing. Featured are a chili-cheese dip that can be as spicy as you like, followed by an unusual chicken or rabbit in salsa verde, a pale delicate sauce with a delayed piquancy. The pumpkin soufflé is chilled and pungent with ginger, cinnamon, and rum.

If you want to reflect the football theme in your table setting, cover the table with green felt and mark yard lines with strips of white ribbon or chalk. Cut white felt numbers for the lines. Attach autumn leaves to a football for a centerpiece. Pin ivy leaves to plain white place cards, and either use white candles or echo the fall colors with yellow, rust, gold, and dark green. Arrange the table early in the day. The dinner can be prepared ahead and kept on warming trays since the dishes wait well. Serve either chilled beer or a hearty jug of red wine to complement the spicy supper. Your guests will thank you for an imaginative autumn afternoon of sports and good food.

CHILI CON QUESO WITH TOSTADAS

1 medium onion, diced
6 tablespoons butter
1 clove of garlic, put through a press
3 medium tomatoes, peeled, seeded, and chopped
2 4-ounce cans green chili peppers, drained, seeded, and chopped (for a less spicy dip)
3½ tablespoons flour
1 cup heavy cream

½ pound Monterey Jack cheese, grated coarsely (available in special cheese stores), or another mild cheese, such as Münster
Tabasco sauce
Salt, freshly ground pepper
Homemade tostadas (see below) or corn chips (preferably from a health food store)

Sauté onion in 4 tablespoons butter until wilted. Add garlic, tomatoes, and chili peppers, and simmer together until thick and all juice evaporates.

Stir in remaining butter, add flour, and cook, stirring 1 to 2 minutes. Add the heavy cream, blend well, then stir in the cheese and cook over low heat, stirring, until thickened to a good dipping consistency. Season to taste with Tabasco, salt and pepper. Serve in a chafing dish, preferably with tostadas, made by cutting fresh or frozen (defrosted) tortillas into 6 wedges and deep-frying in hot lard until crisp.

Note: If there are leftovers, pour over toasted English muffins as a quick supper dish, a south-of-the-border sort of rarebit.

RABBIT OR CHICKEN IN SALSA VERDE

2 frozen rabbits, thawed, dried, and cut into serving pieces, or 8 legs and thighs, or 8 chicken breasts, split
Olive oil
6 stalks celery, chopped
1 large onion, chopped
1 fresh hot green chili (or 2 or 3 canned jalapeño chilies), chopped

40 cloves garlic, about 2 heads, peeled (see Lapniappe)
Salt, freshly ground pepper
½ cup dry white wine
1 can tomatillos (Mexican green tomatoes, available in specialty stores), drained
1 cup plain yogurt
Fresh coriander or Italian parsley, finely chopped

Preheat oven to 350 degrees.

Dip the rabbit or chicken pieces in oil, coating all sides. Make a bed of the chopped celery, onion, and chili(es) in the bottom of a deep earthenware or enameled cast-iron casserole with a lid. Arrange rabbit or chicken pieces on top, tucking the garlic cloves in among them, and sprinkling with salt and pepper to taste.

Pour the wine over, bring to a simmer on top of the stove, then cover with aluminum foil and the lid to prevent steam from escaping and cook in a 350-degree oven for 1 hour. Test to see if meat is tender (it should not be falling from bones). Add green tomatoes and heat through. Remove rabbit or chicken pieces to a serving platter and keep warm.

Put remaining contents of casserole in blender container and whirl until it is a smooth purée. Add yogurt, and blend until incorporated.

Skim off fat if necessary. Return sauce to casserole and heat through, but do not allow to boil. Correct seasoning, if necessary.

Pour sauce over rabbit or chicken and sprinkle with coriander or parsley. Serve with rice. Serves 8.

COLD PUMPKIN SOUFFLÉ

Oil	½ teaspoon ginger
1 ½ envelopes unflavored gel-	½ teaspoon mace
atin	¼ teaspoon ground cloves
6 tablespoons dark rum	¼ cup chopped preserved
6 eggs	ginger
½ cup granulated sugar	1 ½ cups heavy cream,
1 ½ cups cooked pumpkin	whipped
purée	Rum
¾ teaspoon cinnamon	

Prepare soufflé dish: oil a 6-inch band of wax paper and tie it around a 1 ½-quart soufflé dish, oiled side in, to form a collar.

Sprinkle the gelatin over the rum to soften it. Stand this mixture in its bowl in a pan of simmering water and heat until gelatin dissolves. Beat the eggs thoroughly. Gradually add the sugar and beat the mixture until very smooth and thick.

Mix gelatin and egg mixture with pumpkin, cinnamon, ginger, mace, and cloves, being sure the gelatin is thoroughly mixed in. Fold in ⅔ of the whipped cream, pour mixture into prepared soufflé dish and chill. Flavor remaining whipped cream with rum and serve with soufflé. Serves 8.

A Theater or Benefit

Supper for Twelve

*Smoked Salmon and Asparagus Quiche
*Zucchini Quiche
*Sausage and Mushroom Quiche
*Quiche Louisiane
*Spinach Quiche
*Quiche Lorraine
  A Make-Your-Own Salad
*Green Goddess Dressing
*South Carolina "Low Country" Dressing
*Vinaigrette Sauce (see Basic Recipes)
*Baked Stuffed Pears

If you are entertaining before or after the theater, the opera, or a bene-fit, this might be the answer to your menu planning. The meal can be entirely prepared ahead and served at room temperature, or, schedule permitting, put in the oven for the final cooking just before serving. The menu offers a variety of quiches, all basically the same classic quiche formula but differing in taste from zesty sausage quiche to delicate zucchini quiche to classic quiche Lorraine. Quiches are easy to eat, hearty enough for men, and not so heavy that your guests feel uncomfortable or sleepy at the theater.

There is great visual appeal in the salad service. Crisp greens—ro-maine, Bibb, curly endive, watercress—in a bowl as big as the Waldorf are surrounded by smaller bowls containing marvelous make-your-own garnishes: chopped onion, green pepper, sliver-thin sliced mushrooms, olives, diced avocado, crumbled bacon, grated Parmesan cheese, crumbled blue and feta cheeses, anchovies, cherry tomatoes, croutons, and any-thing else you choose. Offer a choice of salad dressings. The dessert is sweet but light—baked pear halves stuffed with honey and nutmeats, followed by coffee and brandies.

The meal works, whether you're trying to make a deadline curtain time or celebrating after the opera. And just to make things easier, many New York hostesses today hire buses to transport guests to the theater. The guests may carry their coffee, laced with brandy or not, aboard to launch a gala theater evening.

SMOKED SALMON AND
ASPARAGUS QUICHE

12 to 18 asparagus, trimmed
  and cooked until just tender
9-inch Pastry shell, partially
  baked in 400-degree oven
  for 10 to 12 minutes (see
  Basic Recipes)

¼ to ⅓ pound smoked
  salmon
3 egg yolks
1 ½ cups heavy cream
Salt, freshly ground pepper
Freshly grated nutmeg
¼ cup grated Swiss cheese

Preheat oven to 350 degrees.

Arrange asparagus in bottom of pastry, then cover with smoked salmon. Combine egg yolks and cream and season with salt, pepper, and nutmeg. Pour custard mixture over asparagus and salmon and sprinkle grated cheese on top. Bake in a 350-degree oven about 30 minutes, until custard is just set and top is lightly browned. Serves 4 to 6.

ZUCCHINI QUICHE

3 zucchini, grated
Salt
1 ½ cups heavy cream
3 egg yolks
¼ teaspoon freshly ground
  white pepper
1 teaspoon chopped chives
1 tablespoon chopped parsley

1 small onion, chopped
9-inch Pastry shell, partially
  baked in 400-degree oven
  for 10 to 12 minutes (see
  Basic Recipes)
½ cup grated Swiss or
  Gruyère cheese

Preheat oven to 375 degrees.

Toss grated zucchini with salt and put in colander or spread on dish towels. Let zucchini sit for at least ½ hour to extract moisture, and squeeze thoroughly dry in potato ricer or dish towel. Mix cream with egg yolks, pepper, chives, parsley, and onion. Put zucchini in pastry shell and pour custard over. Sprinkle with cheese. Bake in a 375-degree oven for 30 to 35 minutes or until custard is just set and top is golden brown. Serves 4 to 6.

Note: Filling may be used to make a zucchini custard, a delicious vegetable accompaniment for meats, poultry, or fish. Use 6 zucchini. Butter a shallow baking dish, pour in zucchini custard mixture, and sprinkle cheese on top. Bake in a 375-degree oven for 25 to 30 minutes, until custard is just set and top is golden brown. Serves 4 to 6.

SAUSAGE AND MUSHROOM QUICHE

1 pound hot and/or sweet Italian sausages
¾ pound mushrooms, thinly sliced
4 tablespoons butter
1 cup heavy cream
2 egg yolks, lightly beaten
1 tablespoon flour
1 tablespoon melted butter

1 tablespoon lemon juice
½ teaspoon salt
Freshly ground pepper
9-inch Pastry shell, partially baked in 400-degree oven for 10 to 12 minutes (see Basic Recipes)
½ cup freshly grated imported Parmesan cheese

Preheat oven to 350 degrees.

Squeeze sausage meat out of casing and cook in frying pan until lightly browned, breaking up meat with a fork. Remove from pan with slotted spoon and drain on paper towels. Sauté mushrooms in butter. Mix cream, egg yolks, flour, butter, lemon juice, and salt and pepper to taste. Put sausage and mushrooms into pastry shell, pour custard over, sprinkle with cheese and bake in a 350-degree oven for 35 minutes or until puffy and lightly browned. Serves 4 to 6.

QUICHE LOUISIANE

3 tablespoons chopped scallions
½ green pepper, chopped
4 tablespoons butter
2 tablespoons tomato paste
1 cup shrimp, shelled and deveined
Tabasco sauce
2 tablespoons chili sauce

9-inch Pastry shell (see Basic Recipes)
¼ pound Swiss cheese, grated
3 eggs
1 cup heavy cream
Salt
Cayenne pepper

Preheat oven to 425 degrees.

Sauté scallions and pepper in 2 tablespoons butter; add tomato paste, shrimp, Tabasco to taste, and chili sauce. Rub remaining butter over sides and bottom of pastry shell and fill with shrimp mixture. Sprinkle cheese over shrimp. Combine eggs, cream, salt to taste, and a dash of cayenne. Pour into pastry shell.

Bake for 15 minutes at 425 degrees, then reduce heat to 325 and bake about 30 to 40 minutes, until a knife inserted in center comes out clean. Serves 4 to 6.

SPINACH QUICHE

2 tablespoons butter
2 tablespoons minced onion
3 egg yolks
1 ½ cups heavy cream
Salt, freshly ground pepper
1 ½ pounds fresh spinach,
    finely chopped or 10-ounce
    box frozen chopped spin-
    ach, cooked, and squeezed
    in potato ricer or paper
    towel to extract all liquid

9-inch Pastry shell, partially
    baked in 400-degree oven
    for 10 to 12 minutes (see
    Basic Recipes)
¼ cup grated Swiss cheese

Preheat oven to 375 degrees.

Heat butter in a small skillet and sauté onion until soft.

Beat together egg yolks, cream, and salt and pepper to taste. Blend in spinach, then add onion. Pour into pastry shell. Sprinkle with cheese and bake in a 375-degree oven for 25 to 30 minutes, until custard has just set and a knife inserted in center comes out clean. Serves 4 to 6.

QUICHE LORRAINE

12 slices bacon (¾ pound)
9-inch Pastry shell, partially
   baked in 400-degree oven
   for 10 to 12 minutes (see
   Basic Recipes)
1½ cups grated Swiss cheese
3 egg yolks
1 cup heavy cream

½ cup milk
½ teaspoon salt
¼ teaspoon freshly ground
   pepper
1½ teaspoons chopped chives
½ teaspoon dry mustard
Freshly grated nutmeg
Cayenne

Preheat oven to 375 degrees.

Sauté bacon until cooked but not crisp. Arrange in pastry shell and sprinkle cheese on top. Beat egg yolks, cream, milk, salt, pepper, chives, mustard, and a dash each of nutmeg and cayenne together and pour into pastry shell. Bake in a 375-degree oven for 45 minutes, or until custard has set and top is brown. Serves 4 to 6.

GREEN GODDESS SALAD DRESSING

¼ cup coarsely chopped
   onion
1 clove garlic, quartered
1 shallot, quartered
6 tablespoons wine vinegar
1 generous teaspoon an-
   chovy paste

1 cup Mayonnaise, prefer-
   ably homemade (see
   Basic Recipes)
½ cup heavy cream
1 tablespoon lemon juice
½ cup fresh parsley, coarsely
   chopped

Combine onion, garlic, shallot, and vinegar in blender container and whirl at medium speed until well blended. Add anchovy paste and mayonnaise and blend until smooth.

Whip cream lightly just until beaters leave traces on the cream. Add lemon juice and mix well. Add the cream to the mayonnaise mixture and blend until well mixed. Add parsley and blend no more than 10 to 15 seconds.

Chill in refrigerator overnight: the dressing will keep in the refrigerator for 2 to 3 weeks. Makes about 2 cups.

SOUTH CAROLINA
"LOW COUNTRY" DRESSING

1 pint Mayonnaise, preferably homemade (see Basic
   Recipes)
12-ounce bottle chili sauce
2 tablespoons India relish
2 tablespoons Worcestershire
   sauce

Tabasco sauce
1 teaspoon steak sauce
2 tablespoons grated onion
1 teaspoon lemon juice
Salt, freshly ground pepper

Combine mayonnaise, chili sauce, relish, Worcestershire, a few dashes of Tabasco, steak sauce, onion, and lemon juice. Blend well and season to taste with salt and pepper. Makes about 4 cups.

Note: This sauce is excellent for a seafood cocktail, on grapefruit salad, or as a dip for raw vegetables.

BAKED STUFFED PEARS

8 firm, ripe pears (preferably
   Comice or Bartlett)
5 tablespoons lemon juice
4 cups water or red wine
1 cup sugar
1½ cinnamon sticks
5 to 6 cloves
Large strip lemon zest
Butter

2 cups honey
½ cup raisins
½ cup chopped pecans
2 tablespoons finely chopped
   preserved ginger (drain
   syrup)
Freshly grated nutmeg
Salt

Preheat oven to 325 degrees.

Peel pears carefully, halve, and remove cores and seeds, leaving a neat small hollow for stuffing. Put in a bowl of water with 2 tablespoons lemon juice to prevent their discoloring.

Combine water or wine, sugar, cinnamon sticks, cloves, lemon zest, and remaining lemon juice in a saucepan large enough to hold all pear halves. Bring to a boil, partially cover, and cook 5 to 8 minutes. Drop in the pear halves, and lower heat so that syrup barely simmers. Poach for about 7 to 8 minutes, until just tender.

Butter an attractive 12 by 16-inch baking dish. Drain the pear halves and arrange in 1 layer in baking dish, hollowed side up. Combine honey, raisins, pecans, ginger, nutmeg to taste, and a pinch of salt. Put about ⅓ cup of the mixture in and over each pear and bake in a 325-degree oven for 15 to 20 minutes. Serves 16.

A Comforting Autumn
Dinner for Four

*Mrs. Pilkington's Eggs
*Flank Steak in Teriyaki Marinade
*Purée of Butternut Squash
*Snow Pea and Shallot Salad
*Strawberries Marsala

Warn your guests to work up an appetite—this dinner is designed to satisfy hunger pangs and comfort the weary. It's a flavorful menu that will appeal to meat-and-potato people as well as those with less definite tastes.

The first course, an ultra-rich dish originally devised by the British Mrs. Pilkington (bless her whoever she may be!) blends cream, butter, and sliced hard-cooked eggs with an abundance of onions. This dish is easy to prepare, and can stand by itself at lunch.

The flank steak acquires new dimension with the help of a teriyaki marinade, quietly spiced with ginger. It is served with an unusual purée of squash—a more imaginative accompaniment than plain mashed potatoes, you'll agree.

The snow pea salad is a delicious surprise. These Chinese vegetables are crisp and wiltless. The snow peas are combined with shallots and a zesty dressing—pretty to look at and sensational to eat.

Strawberries with an Italian touch are the finale to this meal. Served as they are with a light marsala sauce, they provide a wonderful finish to this richly satisfying menu.

MRS. PILKINGTON'S EGGS

12 to 16 medium to large
   onions (3 to 4 per person),
   thinly sliced
¼ to ½ pound butter
¾ cup chopped parsley
Dry bread crumbs, made
   from 12 thin slices of
   white bread (see Basic
   Recipes)

8 hard-cooked eggs (2 per
   person)
Salt, freshly ground pepper
2 to 4 cups heavy cream
   (varying amount explained
   in procedure)

Preheat oven to 350 degrees.

Sauté onions in ¼ pound butter in a large, heavy skillet over very low heat, adding more butter if necessary, until soft and lightly browned. This takes up to 1 hour. Mix parsley and bread crumbs. Slice hard-cooked eggs (this can be done while layering). Layer in a 2-quart soufflé dish in the following order: bread crumbs, sliced eggs, and sautéed onions—ending with a bread-crumb layer. Season layers with salt and pepper. Fill dish with cream until it reaches the top and bake in 350-degree oven until bubbly (check after 25 minutes). Serves 4.

A large number of onions are necessary because they reduce greatly when sautéed.

Note: As an easy light dinner; the bread crumb, egg, onion layers can be fortified with layers of salmon. Accompanied only by a green salad, it's an easy and satisfying dinner.

FLANK STEAK IN TERIYAKI MARINADE

2 tablespoons ground ginger
   or 3 tablespoons finely
   minced fresh or canned
   ginger root
1 medium onion, grated, or 2
   cloves garlic, put through
   a press

2 tablespoons granulated
   sugar
½ to 1 cup imported soy
   sauce, according to taste
½ cup sherry or dry ver-
   mouth
2-pound flank steak, or other
   type steak

Mix ginger, onion or garlic, sugar, soy sauce, and sherry together. Marinate steak in the marinade for no longer than 3 hours. Broil the flank steak for 2 minutes on each side for rare, and carve diagonally across the grain into thin slices to serve. Serves 4.

Note: This marinade is also good with chicken pieces, which are marinated, then oven-roasted for 1 to 1½ hours in a moderate oven (350 degrees) basting occasionally with the marinade and juices. Serves 4.

PURÉE OF BUTTERNUT SQUASH

1 medium butternut squash
Salt
1 beef bouillon cube
⅓ cup milk
¼ teaspoon nutmeg

1 small white onion, finely
    chopped
3 tablespoons butter
Salt, freshly ground pepper

Peel the squash with vegetable peeler. Slice into discs about ¾ inch thick. Remove any seeds. Drop into boiling salted water, return to a boil, and cook for 15 minutes, until tender. Mash with a fork, or purée in a blender or food mill until smooth. Grate the bouillon cube and sprinkle over milk. Blend the milk, nutmeg, onion, butter, and salt and pepper to taste into the squash. Turn into an ovenproof serving dish and keep warm in a low oven until ready to serve. Serves 4.

SNOW PEA AND SHALLOT SALAD

1 pound fresh snow peas or
    2 6-ounce boxes frozen
    snow peas
Salt
4 shallots, finely chopped

½ cup Lemon Vinaigrette,
    approximately (see Basic
    Recipes)
Boston lettuce

If using fresh snow peas, wash and string them. Defrost frozen snow peas. Cook snow peas in boiling salted water for 1 to 2 minutes. Cool. Mix shallots and peas, toss with vinaigrette, and serve on individual beds of lettuce. Serves 4.

STRAWBERRIES MARSALA

2 boxes strawberries, washed and hulled
1 ½ cups granulated sugar
2 cups water

1 cinnamon stick
½ cup sweet marsala
Lemon juice

Put strawberries in a serving bowl. Put sugar, water, and cinnamon stick in a heavy saucepan and cook 10 to 15 minutes to make a syrup. Stir in marsala and add a few drops lemon juice to sharpen the flavor. It should not, however, be lemony. Remove cinnamon stick. Cool. Pour over strawberries and chill well. Serves 4 to 6.

A Canapé Dinner
for Twenty-four

*Tiropites p. 241-2 huh!!
*Shrimp Spread
  Rye Bread Rounds + turkey?
*Toasted Sardine Rolls (see Index)
*Pâté Mold 242-3
*Chicken Liver Pâté 243
*Melba Toast Rounds (see Basic Recipes)
*Cheese Puffs
*Marinated Chicken Wings
*Croques Monsieurs 245
*Hot Anchovy-Cheese and Meat Turnovers 245-6
  Oysters and Clams on the Half Shell
*Horseradish Sauce
*Shallot Sauce
Cold Shrimp
*"Low Country" Dressing (see Index) or *Rémoulade Sauce
*Steak Tartare 247
  Dark Bread
*Endive or Cooked Artichoke Leaves with Sour Cream and
    Caviar 248
*Duxelles Strudels 248-9

If you're tired of the "little dinner" . . . bored by cocktail binges . . . in the mood for something really unusual in the way of entertaining —invite your guests for this abundance of riches: an offering of hors d'oeuvres that should stagger even the most sophisticated palate. It's a "dinner" where guests dine on more than thirteen different canapés— possibly the fulfillment of many a wild food fantasy.

For this kind of feasting you'll want to think on a grand and glamorous scale when it comes to table decor. So get out chafing dishes, sterling silver bowls and trays, and provide plenty of small plates and forks for the non-finger foods. The oysters and cherrystone clams are best presented on beds of crushed ice next to their two very special sauces. Other fish offerings include cold shrimp, cream cheese and anchovy turnovers, shrimp spread, sardine rolls, artichoke and endive leaves with caviar and sour cream. In the meat category are cold chicken wings marinated in a gingery soy sauce, steak tartare balls, and tiny croques monsieurs— little hot fried sandwiches filled with ham and melted cheese. There are also two pâtés—one creamy, the other mousselike, cheese puffs, and strudels filled with savory duxelles. Of course, you may not want to serve all of these at one time. If it seems a surfeit of riches, simply pick and choose what you will.

Since this is a dinner rather than a cocktail party—a festive way to serve it might be with a selection of wines. To suit everyone's taste, you might offer at least three: a chilled dry white, a rosé, and a light young red Bordeaux or California Cabernet Sauvignon.

This unusual way to dine is sure to tempt even the most confirmed anti-cocktail crowd.

TIROPITES

¾ pound feta cheese
¾ pound creamed cottage
   cheese
2 large eggs, lightly beaten
2 tablespoons finely minced
   parsley

1 pound phyllo or strudel
   pastry
¾ pound unsalted butter,
   melted

FILLING

Crumble or chop feta rather finely and blend with cottage cheese, eggs, and parsley. (This can be done the night before.)

PREPARATION OF PASTRY

These pastries are spectacular and practical to have in the freezer, so don't be put off by the lengthy directions. Phyllo pastry is fun to work with but has a few eccentricities. It dries out quickly and becomes unworkable, so take the following precautions. If pastry has been frozen, either keep it in the refrigerator overnight, or allow it ample time to defrost—about 1 to 2 hours on the kitchen counter, sealed in its plastic bag. If it is unrolled before it has been thoroughly defrosted, it will crack into pieces and be completely useless. Remove phyllo pastry from plastic bag and put on a cutting board. Square the edges as well as possible, then cut the pile of pastry sheets in half lengthwise. Cut once again lengthwise into quarters. (You should have four piles of strips about 1½ to 2 inches wide.) Keep one pile of strips out to work with, and put the other three on a sheet of wax paper over a well-wrung out damp dish towel. Cover with a second sheet of wax paper, another damp towel, and refrigerate. Working steadily, brush top strip with melted butter. Put a scant teaspoon of filling in center at one end, and fold corner of pastry diagonally over spoon in a triangle, using pastry to push filling off spoon. Keep folding triangle flag style until pastry is used up.

    Freeze the first batch while working on the second. They freeze rather quickly and, once they are frozen, are easier to store with economy of space. Tiropites may be closely packed, the layers separated with wax paper. Folding "flag style" takes a bit of practice. (You might want to try it first with strips of paper.)

COOKING

    Preheat oven to 425 degrees.

Put frozen tiropites on a cookie sheet and cook until the triangle corners begin to brown lightly, about 7 to 8 minutes.

This makes a cocktail size, but you can cut the sheets in halves or thirds to make a first course size. Also fat-free cottage cheese and sweet corn-oil margarine are acceptable substitutes for the cottage cheese and butter and hardly affect the taste. Makes about 120.

Note: Filling for Spanakopita (see Index) may also be used. Fill and assemble as directed above.

SHRIMP SPREAD

2 3-ounce packages cream cheese, softened
1 ½ tablespoons blue cheese
1 ½ cups Mayonnaise, preferably homemade (see Basic Recipes)
1 tablespoon horseradish
1 medium sour pickle, finely chopped
1 garlic clove, put through a press

3 pounds shrimp, cooked, cleaned, and chopped
¼ cup minced scallions
½ small white onion, grated
2 pimientos, chopped
6 dashes Tabasco sauce
1 tablespoon salt
1 tablespoon paprika

Cream the cheeses and mayonnaise together. Blend in remaining ingredients. Chill for 2 hours to allow the flavors to blend before serving. This will hold a day, but no longer. Serve in crocks with rye bread rounds or on the rounds as canapés. Makes about 4 cups.

PÂTÉ MOLD

1 tablespoon unflavored gelatin
2 ½ cups green turtle soup or beef consommé
2 3-ounce packages cream cheese

2 tablespoons heavy cream
¼ teaspoon minced garlic
½ teaspoon Beau Monde seasoning
½ cup mashed foie gras or cooked chicken livers

Soften gelatin in ¼ cup green turtle soup or consommé. Heat remaining soup to boiling and add gelatin mixture, stirring until dissolved. Soften cream cheese with cream and blend in garlic and Beau Monde.

Pour ½ soup into a 4-cup ring mold and chill until it starts to jell.

Drop pâté by teaspoon into soup and refrigerate. When set, spread softened cream cheese over all and pour rest of soup into mold and refrigerate.

Unmold and serve with toast or crackers. Serves 15.

CHICKEN LIVER PÂTÉ

1 pound fresh chicken livers	Thyme
½ pound unsalted butter	Basil
4 to 5 shallots, coarsely chopped	Salt, freshly ground pepper
	Freshly grated nutmeg
3 to 4 tablespoons cognac	

Remove fat and membranes from chicken livers. Melt half the butter in a heavy skillet and lightly sauté shallots for 5 minutes, until soft. Add chicken livers and sauté about 5 minutes, until just firm and lightly browned but still quite pink inside. Add remaining butter, 3 tablespoons cognac, a pinch of thyme, about ½ teaspoon dried basil, about 1 teaspoon salt, and a generous amount of pepper and nutmeg. Cook gently about 2 minutes, until butter is almost melted and cognac slightly evaporated.

Pour into blender container and whirl until smooth. Taste carefully: add cognac, thyme, basil, salt, pepper, and nutmeg if necessary; the flavor should be quite intense as it will not be so strong when chilled. Pour into ramekins and cover tightly with plastic wrap. It is best to refrigerate until the following day to permit the flavor to develop. Makes about 2 cups. Serve with fresh Melba toast (see Basic Recipes).

CHEESE PUFFS

8-ounce package cream
   cheese, softened
1 egg yolk
1 tablespoon onion juice
Salt, freshly ground pepper

10 to 12 slices white bread,
   medium-thick slice, firm
   "country-loaf" type
Paprika

Preheat oven to 400 degrees.

Mix cream cheese with egg yolk, onion juice, and salt and pepper to taste. Cut circles from slices of bread with 1½-inch round cookie cutter (about 4 to each slice).

Heat bread on cookie sheet in 400-degree oven until toasted lightly. Cool. Spread each circle with the cheese mixture, peaking it at the center. Sprinkle with paprika. Reduce temperature to 375 degrees and cook about 10 minutes, then run under broiler quickly to brown tops. Makes about 40.

MARINATED CHICKEN WINGS

1 cup soy sauce
1 tablespoon sugar or ¼ cup
   pineapple juice
¼ cup white wine
2 cloves garlic, put through a
   press
¼ cup corn oil

⅛ teaspoon monosodium
   glutamate
1 teaspoon ground ginger
2 to 3 pounds chicken wings,
   tips cut off and discarded
   (or frozen to use in stock)

Preheat oven to 325 degrees.

Combine the soy sauce, sugar or pineapple juice, wine, garlic, corn oil, monosodium glutamate, and ginger. Pour this mixture over the chicken wings and marinate 16 to 20 hours, turning occasionally. Arrange in one layer in a shallow baking pan and bake in a 325-degree oven for 1½ to 2 hours, until crisp and brown. Serves 12 to 16.

CROQUES MONSIEURS

12 slices good-quality bread
Dijon mustard
24 slices Swiss cheese, cut to
    fit the bread
12 slices boiled ham, cut to
    fit the bread

1½ cups milk
2 eggs, beaten
½ pound butter, clarified
    (see Basic Recipes)

Make 6 ham and cheese sandwiches: spread each slice of bread with mustard, and use 2 slices of cheese with 1 slice of ham sandwiched in the center. Combine milk and eggs. Cut crusts off sandwiches and dip into the egg and milk batter. Heat butter in a heavy skillet and sauté sandwiches until well browned on each side. Drain on a paper towel. Cut into quarters and serve hot. These may be cooked ahead on the day of the party and reheated, although they are best when served immediately. Makes about 2 dozen.

HOT ANCHOVY-CHEESE or ~~AND~~ MEAT TURNOVERS

Pastry

¼ teaspoon salt
4½ cups flour
2 cups vegetable shortening
¾ cup water
½ cup vinegar

1 egg
Anchovy-Cheese or Meat
    Filling (see recipes below)
3 tablespoons melted butter

Mix salt with flour. Cut in shortening. Add ¾ cup water and vinegar gradually, and mix in with a fork. Beat the egg lightly and stir into the dough. Turn out onto wax paper and press into a ball. Chill overnight. Makes enough pastry for about 200 turnovers.

Cut the dough into 4 sections. Roll out 1 at a time to ⅛-inch thickness. Cut into 2½-inch circles with a cookie cutter or a glass.

Preheat oven to 425 degrees.

Put 1 teaspoon of the filling on half of each piece. Fold over pastry to make a semicircle. Moisten the edges with water and press together with the tines of a fork. Freeze the turnovers, if desired, on a flat tray and wrap in plastic freezer wrap. When ready to bake, brush with melted butter and bake in a 425-degree oven for 20 minutes.

Anchovy-Cheese Filling

4 8-ounce packages cream
  cheese
¼ cup chopped chives

2-ounce tube of anchovy
  paste
5 tablespoons heavy cream

Soften cheese. Combine all ingredients and mix thoroughly. Makes about 4½ cups, enough for about 100 turnovers.

Meat Filling

1 pound lean ground beef
6 tablespoons butter
2 medium onions, chopped
2 scallions, chopped
2 tablespoons flour
1 cup canned tomatoes,
  drained and crushed

¼ cup dry marsala
¼ cup chopped parsley
¼ cup chopped fresh dill or
  1 tablespoon dried dill
1 ½ teaspoons salt
¼ teaspoon cayenne
½ teaspoon paprika

Sauté beef in 4 tablespoons of the butter until brown. Remove meat and chop it very fine. Heat the remaining 2 tablespoons of butter in skillet, and cook onions and scallions until lightly browned. Stir in flour and add tomatoes and wine. Cook until thickened. Stir in parsley, dill, salt, cayenne, paprika, and meat. Cool before making turnovers. Makes about 4 cups, enough for about 100 turnovers.

HORSERADISH SAUCE

1 cup olive oil
⅓ cup lemon juice
1 to 2 tablespoons prepared
    horseradish

Salt, freshly ground pepper

Mix olive oil, lemon juice, and horseradish, and salt and pepper to taste. Serve in a bowl by oysters and clams. Makes 1⅓ cups.

SHALLOT SAUCE

3 shallots, chopped
½ cup hearty red wine

10½-ounce can beef bouillon
¼ cup chopped parsley

Cook the shallots in the red wine until the wine is reduced to about ¼ cup. Add bouillon and cook for a few minutes more. Cool and add parsley before serving. Makes about 1½ cups.

STEAK TARTARE

1 pound top round or bone-
    less sirloin, twice ground
1 tablespoon Dijon mustard
2 tablespoons prepared
    horseradish
¼ teaspoon Tabasco sauce
2 tablespoons capers
1 tablespoon Worcestershire
    sauce

1 medium onion, finely
    chopped
1 tablespoon steak sauce
2 tablespoons cognac
Salt, freshly ground pepper
Parsley

Mix beef, mustard, horseradish, Tabasco, capers, Worcestershire, onion, steak sauce, cognac, and salt and pepper to taste together. Hand mixing is best to blend fully. Serve either in a flat-bottomed ball shape, garnished with sprigs of parsley and surrounded by pumpernickel bread or, for easy passing and handling, on toothpicks in individual bite-size balls rolled in chopped parsley. Serves 6 to 8.

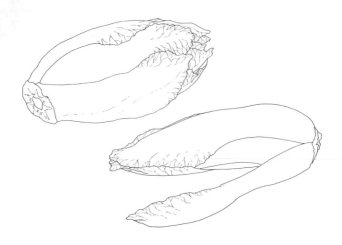

ENDIVE OR COOKED ARTICHOKE LEAVES WITH SOUR CREAM AND CAVIAR

3 or 4 endives or the leaves of   1 cup sour cream
2 or 3 cooked artichokes   6 ounces red or black caviar

Separate the leaves of the endives (or cooked artichoke) and coat the
end with sour cream. Put a small dab of caviar on the sour cream
(be careful not to overwhelm the vegetable taste with that of the sour
cream or caviar—a little goes a long way). Serves about 10, with other
hors d'oeuvres.

DUXELLES STRUDELS

p.355

1½ cups Duxelles (see Basic   ¼ pound unsalted butter,
  Recipes)   melted
1 tablespoon finely chopped
  parsley
2-ounce package strudel pastry, or 4 sheets phyllo pastry (the sheets are about
  16 by 22 inches)

Combine duxelles and parsley, and set aside. Dampen a dish towel, wring out well, and spread out. Put 1 sheet of pastry on towel; set the others aside covered with wax paper and another damp towel. Brush pastry lightly with melted butter. Spread 4 to 6 tablespoons duxelles along a long edge of pastry. Carefully roll up: this is easily done by lifting the towel to guide the roll. Put long roll on a baking sheet and brush with butter. Repeat with remaining pastry and duxelles. Refrigerate.

When long rolls are chilled, trim ends and cut into 1¼-inch pieces. These may be frozen until ready to serve. Bake in a 375-degree oven until pastry is well browned, about 20 minutes, if cooked thawed; 25 to 30 minutes if baked when frozen. Makes about 70.

A V.I.P.

Dinner for Eight

*Cucumber Boats Filled with Shrimp
*Chicken Breasts in Phyllo Pastry
*Braised Watercress
Salad of Boston Lettuce, Sliced Beets, Radishes, and Green
Onions with *White Wine Vinaigrette (see Basic Recipes)
*Poire Hélène

This is the night you'll want to use your best things—the frills, the flowers, the finest china, crystal, and silver. And when that very important person is coming to dinner—be it a boss or a best friend—the occasion calls for an important menu. This one begins and ends with cold dishes—and has a main course that can be totally prepared in the afternoon or a day earlier and needs only to be baked before serving. Therefore, it allows you to spend the evening out of the kitchen, entertaining your guest. Yet each course is distinctive enough to require a separate wine—a flourish that is always impressive.

The first course is a festive presentation of cold shrimp swathed in a piquant capered mayonnaise and served in individual hollowed-out cucumber boats. It is accompanied by a dry white wine. As a main course chicken breasts and cognac-spiked duxelles are wrapped in leaves of phyllo pastry. Braised watercress complements them. Served with a light, red wine and followed by a fresh, crisp salad—who would believe that the best is yet to come?

The *pièce de résistance* is the meltingly rich dessert—poire Hélène—served with champagne. It's an elaborate dish of whole poached pears nestled on a bed of frangipane and doused in chocolate sauce. The rather elaborate preparation required for this creation is more than justified by the results.

CUCUMBER BOATS FILLED WITH SHRIMP

4 6-inch cucumbers, peeled, halved lengthwise, and seeded
2 cups chicken broth
½ cup dry vermouth
Bay leaf
Thyme
Salt, freshly ground pepper
1 cup mayonnaise
2 tablespoons chopped parsley
2 tablespoons olive oil
2 tablespoons chopped chives
1 tablespoon capers
1 tablespoon very finely minced scallion

1 teaspoon anchovy paste (optional)
1 pound shrimp, cooked and coarsely chopped
4 large or 6 small artichoke bottoms cut into large dice, or thin strips
Additional capers
Mixed chopped parsley, basil, and scallions
1 hard-cooked egg, the yolk sieved, white cut into strips
1 or 2 pimientos, cut into thin strips

Put cucumbers into a skillet, placing them quite close together. (They tend to spread out and become rafts rather than boats, and so need each other's support while cooking and cooling.) Pour over broth and vermouth and add bay leaf, thyme, salt and pepper to taste. Simmer gently until tender but still firm, about 10 minutes. Cool in broth and refrigerate until well chilled.

Meanwhile prepare shrimp filling. Combine mayonnaise, parsley, olive oil, chives, capers, scallion, and anchovy paste if desired to make sauce. Gently toss shrimp and artichoke bottoms in sauce. Before serving, spoon filling into cucumber halves. Serve on individual plates, and garnish prettily: sprinkle with a few capers, a mixture of chopped parsley, basil, and scallions, the hard-cooked egg, and 1 or 2 thin strips of pimiento. Serves 8.

CHICKEN BREASTS IN PHYLLO PASTRY

6 whole chicken breasts, split, boned, and skinned
½ pound unsalted butter
4 tablespoons olive oil
⅓ cup cognac
12 sheets phyllo pastry (strudel pastry may be substituted)

Duxelles (made from 1 ½ pounds mushrooms, 6 shallots, ¼ pound unsalted butter, cognac or Madeira to taste, and 2 tablespoons minced parsley)

Sauté chicken breasts in ¼ pound butter and the oil in a heavy skillet until lightly browned on each side, about 1 to 2 minutes. Remove to a plate (reserve butter and juices). Heat and ignite cognac and pour over chicken breasts. When flames are extinguished, pour liquid into skillet and set aside. Melt remaining butter in a clean saucepan. Spread a sheet of pastry on a damp cloth, brush with butter, fold in half, and brush again with butter. Put a chicken breast at narrow end, spread with Duxelles, and fold to make a rectangular package.

Butter a jelly-roll pan and put chicken packages on it; brush tops with butter. (The recipe may be prepared in advance up to this point, wrapped, and refrigerated.) When ready to serve, bake in a 400-degree oven 25 to 30 minutes, until puffed and brown. Serve with either of the following sauces:

Sauce

½ to ¾ cup white wine
2 cups chicken stock
1 carrot, peeled and sliced
2 or 3 shallots, coarsely chopped
2 sprigs parsley
1 bay leaf
Thyme
Chervil

2 or 3 truffles, chopped, with juice (optional)
1 teaspoon meat glaze available in specialty stores (optional)
Salt, freshly ground pepper
1 tablespoon arrowroot
1 tablespoon unsalted butter

To make sauce, add wine to cognac and juices in pan in which chicken was browned and cook to reduce slightly, scraping up brown bits. Add chicken stock, carrot, shallots, parsley, bay leaf, and a good pinch of thyme and simmer 30 minutes. Strain. It is best to put it now in freezer for a while, or in the refrigerator overnight, so that fat rises to the top and solidifies. Remove fat. Heat and add a good pinch of chervil, truffles, and juice, if desired. Stir in meat glaze if desired and season to taste with salt and pepper. Make a paste of the arrowroot and a little hot sauce or water and add to sauce. Stir until thickened. Just before serving, beat in the butter.

For a simpler sauce, heat reserved butter and juices. Blend in ½ to ¾ cup chicken stock. Season to taste with salt and pepper. Serves 8.

BRAISED WATERCRESS

4 pounds watercress (8 to 10 bunches, depending on size)	2 to 3 tablespoons flour
	⅓ cup chicken stock
	⅓ cup heavy cream
Salt	Freshly ground pepper
¼ pound unsalted butter	

Wash the watercress and cut off the very thick stems only. Bring a large pot of water to a boil, add 2 tablespoons salt, then the watercress. Boil until wilted and just tender, about 4 to 5 minutes. Drain, run under cold water, then press with the back of a wooden spoon to extract as much liquid as possible. This may be done in advance.

Melt butter in a large skillet. Add watercress and cook over high heat, tossing it with the butter, for 1 to 2 minutes, to evaporate excess moisture. Sprinkle with flour, stir to blend well, then blend in chicken stock. Cook for 1 minute, stir in cream, season to taste with salt and pepper, and serve immediately. Serves 8.

POIRE HÉLÈNE

Pears

2⅔ cups water	8 ripe, small whole pears
2 cups sugar	(such as Comice), peeled
3-inch piece of vanilla bean	

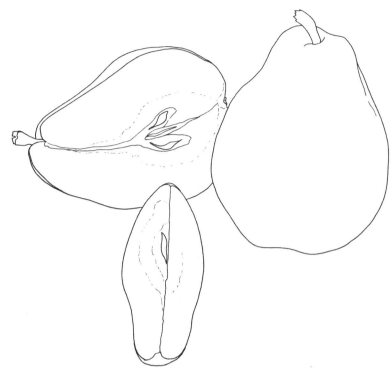

Combine water, sugar, and vanilla bean in a large saucepan and boil for several minutes. Then add the pears, and simmer, covered, for 10 to 15 minutes, or until tender. Drain and cool.

Frangipane

1⅓ cups sugar, sifted (if superfine is used it need not be sifted)
7 egg yolks
1 cup sifted flour
2⅔ cups boiling milk

1⅓ tablespoons butter
1 tablespoon vanilla
3 tablespoons cognac or rum
1 cup coarsely chopped walnuts

Gradually beat the sugar into the yolks with an electric mixer or whisk and beat until pale yellow and thickened. Then add the flour and beat briefly until well mixed. While still beating, gradually add the boiling milk in a slow, thin stream, then pour into a saucepan and set over medium heat. Stir with a whisk until the sauce comes to a boil; it will become lumpy, but it will smooth out as it cooks. When it boils, reduce the heat and beat for several minutes until it smooths out, but do not let it scorch bottom of the pan. Remove from heat and beat in the butter, then the vanilla and cognac or rum. When completely cooled, add the walnuts. Chill.

Chocolate sauce

1⅓ pounds grated semi-
    sweet Swiss chocolate
2⅔ cups water

Vanilla
Rum or cognac to taste

Combine chocolate with water and bring to a boil. Flavor with home-made vanilla (see Lagniappe) or commercial vanilla and rum or cognac, to taste.

Note: Sauce may be frozen.

To serve the pears, make a bed of frangipane in an attractive serving dish or platter and arrange the pears upright on it. At the last minute, warm the chocolate sauce and pour it over the pears in small, dribbling amounts. Reserve remaining sauce to pass separately. Some of the chopped nuts should be visible in the frangipane. Frangipane is usually flavored with almonds or macaroons; the walnuts in this dish are rather special. Serves 8.

An Election Night

Celebration for Twelve

*Whole-wheat Cheese Biscuits (see Index)
  Cherry Tomatoes
*Billi Bi
*Beef with Beer
*Potato Pudding
*Salad of Hearts of Palm and Zucchini
*Hazelnut Torte
*Walnut Torte

The ballots are cast, the results are coming in. Will your candidate win? Why not plot an exciting evening watching election returns with your friends and offer a hearty yet simple buffet set against a color scheme of red, white, and blue.

For lively discussion, gather friends of varying political persuasion. Take advantage of candidates' headquarters for posters, hats, and buttons. In advance, prepare scorecards to chart the candidates' progress as the returns from various states or precincts begin to come in. And if possible, arrange to have more than one television set so that you can tune into different channels and avoid congestion.

The buffet is more easily charted than today's politics. There'll be no unexpected upsets. The menu is made up of dishes that hold well over a long period of time and are ready to accommodate deliciously those guests who pop in late—even the most straggling poll watchers.

The Billi Bi may be served in a large, colorful tureen surrounded by mugs. The hot dishes can be prepared well in advance and kept warm for several hours with no flavor loss. The salad is also designed to stand up to time wiltlessly. You'll want to have plenty of bottled beer set out in an enormous ice-filled tub to complement the beer-flavored beef and onions. And perhaps you'll also want a large supply of a hearty country red wine for non-beer drinkers. After the returns are in serve the rich dessert tortes with a big urn of coffee. You'll find that even the most avid political foes agree that this is an enjoyable way to spend election night.

BILLI BI

9 pounds mussels
9 shallots, chopped
6 small onions, quartered
6 sprigs parsley
4½ cups dry white wine
6 tablespoons butter

1½ bay leaves
1½ teaspoons thyme
Salt, freshly ground pepper
Cayenne
6 cups heavy cream
3 egg yolks, lightly beaten

Scrub mussels and pull out beards. Put in kettle with shallots, onions, parsley, wine, butter, bay leaves, thyme, salt and pepper to taste, and a pinch of cayenne. Bring to a boil, then lower heat and steam for 5 to 10 minutes, until shells open. Strain liquid through cheesecloth into large, heavy sauce pot. (Reserve the mussels to be used in another dish.) Just before serving, blend cream and egg yolks. Stir a little of the hot mussel liquid into the egg/cream mixture, then pour this mixture into mussel broth. Stir over low heat until slightly thickened and heated through. Serve immediately. Serves 12.

Note: The mussel broth may be prepared in advance and frozen.

BEEF WITH BEER

6 pounds top round of beef,
   cut into 2-inch cubes
½ cup bacon drippings or
   peanut oil
6 cups thinly sliced onions
4 tablespoons flour
4½ cups each light and dark
   beer
Tied in a cheesecloth: 2 teaspoons whole allspice, 2
   bay leaves, ½ teaspoon
   thyme, 6 peppercorns

4 pounds whole mushroom
   caps
Salt, freshly ground pepper
12 to 16 slices French bread
Seeded French mustard
Butter

Preheat oven to 375 degrees.

Dry meat with paper towels and brown in hot drippings in a heavy pot. Remove meat and set aside. Add the onions to oil in the pot, and cook until browned, then sprinkle with flour and stir in beer. Return the meat to the pot and simmer gently, uncovered, for 25 minutes. Add the cheesecloth bag of spices, and simmer, covered, for 1 hour. Uncover, and continue cooking for 30 minutes. Add mushroom caps 20 minutes before end of cooking time. Season to taste with salt and pepper. Spread one side of the bread with mustard, and butter other side lightly. Pour beef into a deep, heavy, ovenproof casserole, put bread on top buttered side up, and put in a 375-degree oven for 20 minutes to toast lightly. Serves 12 to 14.

POTATO PUDDING

6 egg yolks, beaten
2 cups grated Gruyère cheese
2 cloves garlic, finely minced or put through a press
12 medium baking potatoes, baked, scooped out, and mashed (approximately 8 cups)

1 cup heavy cream
½ teaspoon freshly ground white pepper
Freshly grated nutmeg
Salt
Butter
Bread crumbs

Preheat oven to 350 degrees.

Add egg yolks, grated cheese, and garlic, to mashed potatoes and blend well. Gradually add cream, pepper, a pinch of nutmeg, and salt to taste.

Liberally butter sides and bottom of 10 to 12-cup round baking dish, then shake in bread crumbs to coat bottom and sides, discarding excess crumbs. Fill dish with potato mixture and bake 1 hour at 350 degrees. Turn out onto serving platter. If you wish, sprinkle with more cheese and brown under broiler. Serves 12.

SALAD OF HEARTS OF PALM
AND ZUCCHINI

½ cup olive oil
3 tablespoons lemon juice
1 clove garlic, minced
2 to 3 shallots, minced
Marjoram
Orégano
Salt, freshly ground pepper
10 small or 8 medium zuc-
chini

2 14-ounce cans hearts of
palm
1 to 2 heads romaine, depending on size, the leaves separated, washed, and dried
3 to 4 tablespoons chopped
parsley

Combine olive oil, lemon juice, garlic, shallots, a generous pinch each
of marjoram and orégano, and salt and pepper to taste. Scrub zucchini,
cut off ends, trim to the same length as hearts of palm, and cut into thin
strips. Drain the hearts of palm and cut into similar-size thin strips.
Combine the palm and the zucchini, and pour the dressing over. Let
stand several hours to allow the flavors to blend. Taste, and correct
seasoning if necessary.

Before serving, line a salad bowl with romaine leaves. Put the hearts
of palm and zucchini mixture in the center and sprinkle the parsley on
top. Serves 12.

HAZELNUT TORTE

2 cups (1 pound) peeled and
finely ground hazelnuts
(see note)
½ teaspoon powdered instant
coffee or 1 tablespoon unsweetened cocoa, or both
6 eggs, separated
1 cup sugar
1 teaspoon grated lemon zest

1 teaspoon vanilla, preferably
homemade (see Lagni-
appe)
½ cup sifted flour
Butter for cake pans
2 cups Orange Butter Cream
(see recipe below), or 2
cups heavy cream,
whipped and flavored with
vanilla
Ground hazelnuts for garnish

Preheat oven to 350 degrees.
Combine ground nuts with instant coffee and/or cocoa. Beat the egg

yolks with ½ cup sugar until it forms a "ribbon" when a spoonful is dribbled onto the surface, then add the lemon zest and vanilla. Blend in ground nut mixture.

Beat the egg whites until very stiff but not dry, adding the remaining sugar gradually. Mix ¼ of the whites into nut mixture to lighten it, then fold in the remaining whites alternately with the flour. Generously butter 2 8-inch cake pans, pour in the batter, smoothing the surface, and bake in a 350-degree oven for 30 minutes. Remove pans from oven and cool layers on rack. Assemble torte with orange butter cream or flavored whipped cream. Dust top with ground hazelnuts. Refrigerate until 30 minutes before serving. Serves 6 to 8.

Note: To peel hazelnuts more easily, put them in a 250-degree oven for 20 minutes to loosen the skins. Cool and peel by rubbing in a towel.

Orange Butter Cream

3 egg yolks
4 tablespoons sugar
2 tablespoons fresh orange juice
Finely grated zest of 1 orange
1 tablespoon of orange liqueur (Grand Marnier, Cointreau)

¾ to 1 cup unsalted butter (half should be soft, the rest cold and firm)

Put egg yolks, sugar, orange juice, grated zest, and liqueur in blender and blend at low speed for 2 to 3 minutes. Add the softened butter, blending gradually until it is absorbed by this mixture, then add the firm butter in small chunks until the cream is well thickened. Taste, and, if desired, add an additional tablespoon of liqueur.

WALNUT TORTE

4 eggs, separated
1 cup sugar
1 cup graham cracker crumbs, finely ground in blender
1 teaspoon baking powder

1 teaspoon vanilla
1 cup finely ground walnuts
1 cup heavy cream, whipped and flavored with vanilla and cognac

Preheat oven to 375 degrees.

Beat the egg yolks with ½ cup sugar until pale yellow and thick; then add the crumbs, baking powder, and vanilla.

Beat the egg whites until stiff, gradually adding the remaining sugar. Stir ½ of the whites into the yolk mixture to lighten it, add the ground walnuts gently, then fold in the remaining egg whites.

Generously butter a 9-inch square or round pan and pour in batter, smoothing the surface. Bake on middle rack in a 375-degree oven for 25 minutes. Test for doneness by inserting a toothpick—it should come out clean. If not, continue cooking 5 to 10 minutes and retest. Serve with the flavored whipped cream. Serves 6 to 8.

Black Tie Buffet

for Twenty

Crudités with *Taramasalata
*Curried Chicken Liver Turnovers
*Parsleyed Ham in Aspic
*Paupiettes de Boeuf
Rice
*Fish Mousse with Shrimp Sauce
Salad of Mixed Greens with *Vinaigrette Sauce (see Basic
Recipes)
*Fruit Compote
*Chocolate-Chestnut Soufflé

One marvelous way to make an evening memorable is to invite your guests to come in formal dinner dress. However, the meal you offer should be as dressed up as your company. This menu will do elegantly for a black tie buffet—and it can be prepared entirely in advance.

The curried chicken liver turnovers can be frozen and then baked just before serving. The main course, paupiettes de boeuf, is a good choice for any sort of buffet. It has all the good qualities of a stew: it freezes well, it makes meat go further, and it can sit in a chafing dish for a long period of time without losing flavor or spoiling. Yet, it makes prettier servings and is far more elegant than stew. The parsleyed ham in aspic takes a long time to make, but it is not difficult and can be done a week ahead. The fish mousse is a nice balance to the other two dishes, and it can be done the day before your party. And, the rice will stay fluffy all evening long if you toss it with beaten egg yolk and melted butter.

A note on the chocolate-chestnut soufflé: the recipe can be assembled an hour in advance of cooking if the beaten egg whites are added to the soufflé base while it is warm and the soufflé is covered by a large bowl to protect it from drafts while it waits to go into the oven. Everyone is sure to agree that it is a coup for any hostess to be able to serve soufflés to a crowd.

Since few people have a room large enough to seat twenty people comfortably, why not set tables for four all over the house? The children's bedrooms can even be used successfully if a kind friend will invite *them* out to dinner.

If you do use the small tables, salad can be served in a separate bowl at each table, along with a variety of cheeses. One of the guests will be glad to oblige by serving it for her table. That will allow time for you to arrange the buffet table with the compote and soufflés. And if you have room, dancing would be a gala way to end the evening.

TARAMASALATA

4 regular slices white bread,
  or 6 diet-thin slices
4-ounce jar *tarama* (carp roe,
  available in Greek and
  other specialty stores)

Juice of 1 to 1½ lemons
1 cup olive oil
Freshly ground white pepper

Cut the bread into small cubes and sprinkle with 2½ tablespoons water. Combine with the tarama and juice of 1 lemon and beat with an electric mixer on low speed until well blended. Begin adding olive oil in a very thin, slow stream, increasing speed of beater to medium. Continue beating until all the oil has been added and mixture is smooth. Taste and season with pepper and more lemon juice if desired. Makes about 2 cups.

Suggested crudités: zucchini sliced diagonally, cauliflower flowerets, celery sticks, raw mushrooms, and endive leaves.

CURRIED CHICKEN LIVER TURNOVERS

Filling

½ to ¾ pound chicken
  livers
4 tablespoons butter
3 hard-cooked eggs, minced
1 tablespoon good-quality
  imported curry powder
2 teaspoons grated onion

Salt, freshly ground pepper
Cream Cheese Pastry (see
  recipe below)
Egg glaze: 2 egg yolks beaten
  with 2 tablespoons cold
  water

Sauté chicken livers in butter until firm but still pink inside, about 5 minutes. Cool and mince finely. Combine with eggs, curry powder, onion, and salt and pepper to taste. This may be done a day in advance.

Preheat oven to 400 degrees.

Dough should be firm but malleable. Roll out until it is ⅛ inch thick, and cut into 2-inch circles. Put about 1 teaspoon of filling in center and fold pastry over to form a crescent. Seal edges with a fork. Refrigerate any scraps of dough before rolling out again, as dough becomes difficult to work with when it is too warm. Prepared turnovers may be frozen at this point in a large refrigerator box with wax paper between layers. When ready to serve, paint tops with egg glaze and bake in a 400-degree oven about 10 to 15 minutes, until browned and pastry is cooked. Makes 6 to 7 dozen turnovers.

Cream Cheese Pastry

2 3-ounce packages cream cheese

½ pound butter
2 cups flour

Cream the cheese and butter together until blended. Cut in flour and work until dough can be gathered into a ball. Chill or freeze.

PARSLEYED HAM IN ASPIC

7-pound mild cured ham or picnic shoulder
2 cups dry white wine
2 small onions, each studded with a clove
1 carrot, sliced
2 leeks
A cheesecloth bag containing 4 or 5 whole allspice, 5 peppercorns, 2 large whole peeled garlic cloves, 1 bay leaf, large pinch of thyme, 6 sprigs of parsley
Calf's foot
A few veal bones

½ cup egg whites (4 or 5 egg whites)
2 envelopes unflavored gelatin (use if unable to obtain calf's foot and veal bones)
2 cups coarsely chopped parsley
1 clove garlic, put through a press
1 tablespoon tarragon
Freshly grated nutmeg
1 tablespoon minced shallot
1 ½ teaspoons wine vinegar

Simmer ham with wine, onions, carrot, leeks, cheesecloth bag, calf's foot, veal bones, and water to cover for about 2 hours, until tender, occasionally skimming surface of stock. Allow ham to cool in the stock until it can be easily handled. Remove and cut away rind and as much fat as possible. Tear ham apart, discarding fat, and cut into 2-inch cubes. Arrange in a 3-quart serving dish with a few spoonfuls of the stock.

Strain remaining stock and boil to reduce to about 5 cups. Cool. Clarify stock: Skim fat from cooled stock. Beat egg whites slightly, add to stock, and bring to a simmer. Simmer 10 minutes, then pour through a sieve lined with dampened cheesecloth or a linen dish towel into a clean bowl. If calf's foot or veal bones are unobtainable, soften gelatin in ½ cup water, then add to hot stock and stir until completely dissolved. Test for jelling by pouring a bit of stock into a cold saucer and refrigerating until set.

Sprinkle about 1 cup parsley into crevices between ham pieces and liberally over each layer of ham. Combine remaining parsley with garlic, tarragon, a pinch of nutmeg, shallot, and vinegar, mix with aspic, and pour over ham. Chill until set. Any leftover aspic can be chilled in a large baking dish and chopped or cut into decorative shapes to decorate the top of the ham dish. If aspic is quite stiff, unmold before serving; otherwise, serve it from the bowl. Serves 20.

PAUPIETTES DE BOEUF

20 ½-inch-thick slices of top round, about 6 to 7 inches long	2 eggs
	¼ cup chopped parsley
3 cups minced onions	1 teaspoon each orégano and basil
6 tablespoons butter	Salt, freshly ground pepper
¾ pound pork, ground with some fat	Peanut oil
3 slices light rye bread, torn into small pieces	½ cup dry vermouth
	Beef stock
8 tablespoons Dijon or seeded mustard	1 bay leaf
	½ teaspoon thyme
5 large cloves garlic, put through a press	Arrowroot (optional)

Preheat oven to 325 degrees.

Pound meat slices between pieces of wax paper until very thin. Sauté onions in butter until soft but not brown, then combine with pork, bread, mustard, garlic, eggs, parsley, orégano, and basil, and salt and pepper to taste. Put 2 to 3 spoonfuls of this stuffing on each piece of meat and roll up. Do not try to overstuff. Tie at each end with string.

Brown the beef rolls lightly in a skillet on all sides in peanut oil. Put into a flameproof casserole. Pour off excess fat, deglaze the skillet with vermouth, and add to casserole. Add enough stock barely to cover beef rolls; put bay leaf on top, and sprinkle with thyme. Bring to a simmer on top of stove. Cover, and bake in a 325-degree oven, regulating the heat so that stock simmers gently, about 30 to 45 minutes, until tender. Do not overcook, as rolls will continue to cook while cooling, and will be reheated. Remove the strings when cool enough to handle. Refrigerate until ready to serve. This may be done 2 or 3 days in advance. Remove fat that accumulates on surface, then reheat and serve in a chafing dish. Pour broth over, thickened with a little arrowroot if desired. Serves 20.

FISH MOUSSE WITH SHRIMP SAUCE

4 pounds white fish fillets (such as sole, flounder, or halibut)
8 egg whites (defrosted frozen ones may be used)
5 cups heavy cream
Salt, freshly ground white pepper
Cayenne
Butter
Shrimp Sauce (see recipe below)
Parsley

Preheat oven to 375 degrees.

Put fish through food grinder, then slowly work in the egg whites. Purée in a blender a little bit at a time; work in cream, and purée in blender again until fish flesh is completely smooth. Season to taste with salt, pepper, and a pinch of cayenne.

Butter 2 8-cup charlotte or ring molds. Pour in mousse and put molds in a pan or pans of simmering water reaching halfway up side of dish. Put a buttered piece of wax paper over mold, buttered side down, to prevent top from becoming crusty, and bake in a 375-degree oven for about 25 minutes, until a knife inserted in center comes out clean. Unmold before serving. Serve with shrimp sauce, garnished with parsley. May be served hot or cold with the hot sauce. Serves 16 to 20 in buffet.

Shrimp Sauce

3 to 4 cups Béchamel Sauce
   (see Basic Recipes)
Tomato juice
Dry sherry
Salt, freshly ground pepper

1 pound shrimp, cooked,
   peeled, and deveined
2 tablespoons chopped fresh
   dill or 2 teaspoons dried

Color béchamel sauce with tomato juice to taste, but use no more than ¼ cup, and flavor to taste with sherry, salt, and pepper. Stir in the shrimp and dill.

FRUIT COMPOTE

1 cup sugar
1 cup water
6 whole cloves
2 cinnamon sticks
6 whole allspice
(*Or* ¼ teaspoon anise instead of other spices)
Salt
3 large apples, unpeeled and
   cut into large, uniform, attractive pieces

3 large pears, peeled and cut
   into large, uniform, attractive pieces
6 Italian prune plums, halved
   and pitted
1 ½ cups melon balls from
   cantaloupe, Cranshaw, or
   casaba melons
Mint leaves

Simmer sugar, water, cloves, cinnamon sticks, and allspice, or the anise, and a dash of salt together very slowly for about 10 minutes. Poach apples and pears in syrup until tender, about 15 to 20 minutes. Cool and refrigerate, removing spices. Before serving add plums and melon balls, and garnish with mint leaves. Serves 10 to 12.

CHOCOLATE-CHESTNUT SOUFFLÉ

Butter and sugar for preparing soufflé dishes
4 1-ounce squares unsweetened chocolate
2 cups unsweetened chestnut
  purée, fresh or canned
2 cups milk

1 cup sugar
4 tablespoons butter
4 tablespoons flour
2 teaspoons vanilla
8 eggs, separated
Whipped cream (optional)

Preheat oven to 375 degrees.

Butter 2 6-cup soufflé dishes well and sprinkle with sugar. Melt
chocolate in a Pyrex measuring cup put in a pan of simmering water.
Beat chestnut purée, milk, and sugar with a rotary beater until smooth.
Melt butter in a large saucepan. Remove from heat and blend in flour.
Add chestnut mixture and stir over low heat until it reaches the boiling
point. Remove from heat and stir in melted chocolate and vanilla. Beat
yolks in a large bowl, then add chestnut mixture and beat until blended.
Cool. Beat the whites, preferably in a copper bowl, with large whisk or
electric beater until stiff peaks form. Gently fold into soufflé base. Pour
soufflé mixture into prepared soufflé dishes. Put in a pan (or pans) of
boiling water and bake in a 375-degree oven for about 40 minutes, until
well puffed. Serve immediately, with whipped cream if desired. Serves
12 to 16.

Note: If preparing in advance for an hour's wait, fold whites into
chocolate-chestnut base while it is still warm.

A Delicious

Dessert Party

*Chef Oliver Brown's Snow Pudding with Custard Sauce
*Southern Trifle
*Devil's Food Cake
*South Carolina Pound Cake
  Bowl of Sherbet Balls
*Brown Sugar Cookies
*Butter Cookies
*Chocolate Chiffon Cookies (see Index)
  Fresh Fruit

Drinks
A Chilled Sparkling Wine such as Vouvray
Mulled Red Wine
Coffee

After an evening meeting, after a benefit performance, after a Knicks game, after almost anything—invite the crowd back to your home for a dessert party, which can be accomplished even if both time and budget are limited. Most of the desserts suggested here can be prepared days—or even weeks—in advance if carefully wrapped, covered, and refrigerated or frozen.

Plan to be home a few minutes ahead of your guests to light candles and put out those desserts that needed refrigeration. Everything else can be set up before you leave for the evening. The table should be as tempting as the desserts. Bedeck it with a bright cloth and napkins. Use the most glittering plates, bowls, and cake stands that you have or can borrow and intersperse them with candles of differing heights.

The menu offers a selection of eight richly caloric enticements that will be hard to resist. But for any friends who are dieting, you might also offer some fresh fruit and cheese. The less prudent can choose from luscious cookies, truly sinful chocolate devil's food cake, a shamefully rich southern trifle, a light and meltingly lovely orange snow pudding served with custard sauce, and a crunchy butterscotch mold as well as sherbet balls of different flavors and colors and plain but perfect pound cake. The sherbet balls can be scooped, arranged in a pretty bowl, and put in the freezer in advance.

Accompany the sweets with a selection of dessert wines—and offer coffee demitasses. This festive party is an easy way to entertain—and it's bound to tickle anyone with a sweet tooth.

CHEF OLIVER BROWN'S SNOW PUDDING
WITH CUSTARD SAUCE

1 cup sugar
2 cups water
Juice of 2 lemons
Juice of 3 oranges
1 envelope unflavored gelatin

2 tablespoons cold water
Grated zest of 2 oranges
1 cup egg whites (8 to 10)
Custard Sauce (see recipe below)

Combine sugar, water, and juices in a saucepan and bring to a boil. Meanwhile, soften gelatin in cold water. Pour boiling mixture over softened gelatin and stir until dissolved. Add grated zest, cool, and refrigerate until slightly thickened.

Beat egg whites until stiff. Fold into gelatin mixture. Chill and serve with custard sauce. Serves 8.

Custard Sauce

1 whole egg plus 2 egg yolks
½ cup sugar

2 cups milk
1 teaspoon vanilla

Beat egg, yolks, and sugar together in top of double boiler until thick and lemon-colored. Blend in milk, and cook, stirring, over simmering water until thickened, and mixture lightly coats the back of spoon. Blend in vanilla. Chill to serve with Snow Pudding or serve warm over cakes, jellies, or fruits. Makes about 2½ cups.

SOUTHERN TRIFLE

4½ cups milk
1¼ cups sugar
5 tablespoons cornstarch
6 eggs, lightly beaten
1 tablespoon vanilla
3 packages ladyfingers, halved (36 ladyfingers)

10- to 12-ounce jar currant jelly
10-ounce package toasted slivered almonds
1½ cups sherry
Whipped cream (optional)

Make custard: combine milk, sugar, and cornstarch, and heat until luke-warm. Whisk in eggs, return to heat and cook, stirring constantly, until mixture thickens; do not boil. Strain, and cool in refrigerator for at least 4 hours, then add vanilla.

Line a silver or crystal bowl with ladyfinger halves, and spread with currant jelly. Cover with half of the custard and half of the almonds. Pour half of the sherry over. Repeat layers, covering top with almonds. Put in refrigerator overnight. Decorate with whipped cream, if desired. Serves 8 to 10.

DEVIL'S FOOD CAKE

3 1-ounce squares unsweet-ened chocolate
2 ¼ cups cake flour (not self-rising)
2 teaspoons baking soda
½ teaspoon salt
¼ pound butter, at room temperature
2 ½ cups light brown sugar, firmly packed

3 eggs, at room temperature
½ cup buttermilk, at room temperature
2 teaspoons vanilla
1 cup boiling water
Butter and flour for prepar-ing cake pans, if needed
Whipped Cream Chocolate Frosting (see recipe below)

Preheat oven to 375 degrees.

Melt chocolate in a glass measuring cup in a pan of boiling water. Sift cake flour, measure 2 ¼ cups, and sift it again with baking soda and salt.

Cream the butter, preferably with an electric mixer. Add brown sugar, a little at a time, beating until light and fluffy. Beat in eggs, one at a time, beating hard after each addition. Add the chocolate and mix thoroughly. Sift about ⅓ of the flour mixture over the batter and stir in. Stir in half of the buttermilk. Repeat, ending with the flour. Add vanilla and water. Stir until blended. The batter will be thin. Line 3 8-inch cake pans with silicone parchment, or butter and flour them. Pour in batter. Bake in a 375 degree oven for about 25 minutes, until a toothpick inserted in center comes out clean. Remove from the oven, cool for 15 minutes, then turn out on racks to cool. When cool, frost with whipped cream chocolate frosting. Serves 8.

Whipped Cream Chocolate Frosting

2 cups heavy cream
6 tablespoons sugar

3 tablespoons unsweetened
  cocoa
¾ teaspoon vanilla

Mix well all of the ingredients with an electric mixer but do not beat. Chill in the refrigerator for at least 2 hours or longer. Beat until thick and mixture stands in peaks. Frost between layers and on top, and the sides if you wish.

Note: The cake layers may be prepared and frozen in advance, then defrosted and iced several hours before serving.

SOUTH CAROLINA POUND CAKE

1-pound box confectioners'
  sugar
1 tablespoon granulated
  sugar
¾ pound butter
7 eggs
3 cups cake flour (not self-
  rising)

½ teaspoon salt
½ teaspoon baking powder
1 teaspoon vanilla extract
½ teaspoon almond extract
Butter and flour for cake pan
Icing (see recipe below)
Confectioners' sugar
  (optional)

Preheat oven to 300 degrees.

Cream together the sugar and butter until smooth and fluffy. Beat in eggs one at a time. Sift the flour, salt, and baking powder together. Blend a little at a time into the creamed ingredients, then add the vanilla and almond extracts.

Butter and flour a 9-inch tube pan and pour in batter. Bake in a 300-degree oven for 30 minutes, then lower heat to 275 degrees and bake about 45 minutes longer, until a toothpick inserted in center comes out clean.

Let cool a few minutes, then invert onto a rack. Ice when completely cooled or sprinkle with confectioners' sugar. Serves 8.

Icing

3 ½ cups sugar   3 egg whites, stiffly beaten
1 cup water

Combine sugar with the water in a heavy saucepan, and cook until syrup reaches 238 degrees on a candy thermometer or the soft-ball stage. Beat in a slow, steady stream into egg whites.

Note: The cake may be prepared and frozen in advance, then defrosted and iced the day it is to be served.

BROWN SUGAR COOKIES

¼ pound butter   ¼ pound finely chopped
½ cup dark brown sugar   pecans (approximately 1
½ cup granulated sugar   cup)
1 egg   Butter for cookie sheets
½ cup flour, sifted

Preheat oven to 350 degrees.

Cream butter and sugar well. Blend in the egg, flour, and finally the nuts. Butter cookie sheets and drop by ½ teaspoonfuls onto cookie sheets about 2 inches apart. Bake in a 350-degree oven for about 8 minutes, until lightly browned. The cookies should be quite thin and lacy. Remove quickly from the cookie sheet with a spatula. If they stick, warm for several seconds in oven. Makes about 4 dozen cookies.

Note: Do not prepare these cookies on a humid day—humidity affects their crispness. Store cookies in an air-tight tin.

BUTTER COOKIES

1 pound butter   2 teaspoons baking powder
2 cups sugar   1 tablespoon flavoring such
2 eggs   as vanilla, rum, or brandy
2 egg yolks   Butter for baking sheet
6 cups flour

Preheat oven to 350 degrees.

Cream butter, add sugar, and mix well. Blend in eggs and yolks thoroughly. Sift flour and baking powder together, then add to butter mixture. Add flavoring and mix well. Chill dough until firm.

Butter cookie sheets. Roll out dough ¼ inch thick and cut into desired shapes with fancy cookie cutters, or put through cookie press. Arrange cookies on buttered sheets. Bake in a 350-degree oven for 10 minutes or until lightly browned. Makes about 10 dozen.

Note: These make excellent refrigerator cookies. Form dough into a roll about 1½ inches in diameter and refrigerate or freeze. Slice ¼ inch thick and bake as directed.

The Liberated Cook's Small Apartment

Thanksgiving Dinner for Six

*Cold Purée of Pumpkin Soup
*Almond Ducklings à l'Orange
*Potatoes au Gratin
*Celery Root Salad
  Brie
  French Bread
*Cinnamon–Brown-Sugar Crêpes with Coffee Ice Cream

This meal proves that even with limited time and space it's possible to feast at Thanksgiving (or any time) with an unusual, untraditional menu. This fancy dinner for six puts the emphasis on festive flavors—pumpkin, nutmeg, orange, almonds, cinnamon, brown sugar—yet requires few pots and pans or elaborate equipment. And it liberates you to enjoy your family and company because almost all of the preparation can be accomplished in advance. Final preparation only requires the ducks be roasted and basted, the potatoes baked, the crêpes warmed—all at the same oven temperature: 375 degrees.

Rather than ending with sweet, conventional pumpkin pie, our unconventional menu begins with a smooth, subtle, cold pumpkin soup. It can come to the table in a whimsical tureen and centerpiece fashioned from a hollowed-out real pumpkin. The celebration then continues with the most defatted ducklings this side of a Chinese restaurant with a crispy outer texture made crispier with the addition of chopped almonds. They're the perfect foil for the satiny gratin potatoes—seemingly bland but with a whisper of garlic. The tart, refreshing salad has a real crunch to it and is served as a separate course with Brie and warmed French bread. The finale—a gala note—dessert of cinnamon-brown-sugar crêpes and rich coffee ice cream. Espresso and brandy anyone?

COLD PURÉE OF PUMPKIN SOUP

1 onion, chopped
2 tablespoons chopped leeks
2 tablespoons butter
2 cups Chicken Stock, home-
    made or canned (see Basic
    Recipes)
2 cups unsweetened canned
    pumpkin or puréed,
    cooked, fresh pumpkin

½ teaspoon sugar
½ teaspoon mace
¼ teaspoon nutmeg
½ teaspoon salt
Freshly ground white pepper
Light cream
½ cup heavy cream,
    whipped and salted

Sauté onion and leeks in butter until transparent. Mix in stock and pump-kin and heat thoroughly. Purée the mixture in a blender, then push through a strainer or food mill. Add sugar, mace, nutmeg, salt and pepper to taste, and chill. Before serving, adjust seasonings if necessary and thin to desired consistency with light cream. Serve garnished with salted whipped cream. Serves 6.

ALMOND DUCKLING
À L'ORANGE

2 5-pound ducks, fresh or
  frozen, thawed
4 quarts fresh or frozen
  orange juice, plus 2 cups
  fresh

6 tablespoons coarsely
  chopped almonds
4 tablespoons flour
Salt, freshly ground pepper
Watercress

In advance, bring the 4 quarts of orange juice to a boil. With a sharp fork, puncture the skin of each duck in many places so that the fat will run out. Submerge each duck in the boiling orange juice. (You may do this one at a time if the pot will not accommodate both—using the same orange juice over again. If necessary add a little water or more orange juice so that the duck is completely covered. Boil briskly for ½ hour.)

Meanwhile, combine the 2 cups fresh orange juice with the almonds, flour, and salt and pepper to taste. Set aside.

Remove the ducks from orange juice and drain. When cool enough to handle, rub the inside of the duck with the almond-orange juice mixture, truss the duck, and rub the outside skin with the juice mixture. If they are completely cooled, the ducks may be stored for several hours in the refrigerator at this point. Reserve the remaining almond-orange juice mixture.

Final preparation: Preheat oven to 350 degrees. Put ducks on a rack in roasting pan. Roast for 1 hour, basting every 20 minutes with reserved juice mixture. Raise oven heat to 375 degrees and continue roasting for ½ hour, basting often. To serve, remove trussing string and present on a platter surrounded by watercress. Serves 6.

POTATOES AU GRATIN

1 ½ pounds baking potatoes
Milk as needed
1 clove garlic, peeled and
   halved
Salt, freshly ground pepper,
   and nutmeg

1 ½ tablespoons butter,
   softened
1 cup heavy cream

In advance, scrub and peel potatoes. Cut them into slices less than ¼ inch thick. Drop slices as they are sliced into a bowl of cold water. Before proceeding, pat dry on paper towels. Put the slices in a large pan and add just enough milk to cover. Sprinkle with salt, pepper, and nutmeg. Add garlic halves. Bring to a boil, cover, and simmer for 10 minutes. Drain off any excess milk. Discard the garlic.

Preheat oven to 375 degrees.

Butter a shallow flameproof baking dish with half the butter. Make one layer of overlapping potato slices. Sprinkle with salt and pepper and nutmeg. Add half the cream. Make another layer of potatoes, salt, pepper, nutmeg, and remaining cream. Dot with remaining butter.

Bring to a simmer, uncovered, on top of the stove. Put in oven and bake ½ hour, or until the potatoes have absorbed the cream, are tender and delicately browned on top. For a browner top, run the dish under the broiler for a moment. Serves 6.

CELERY ROOT SALAD

1 cup julienne strips of
   celery root
2 endives, washed and sliced
   lengthwise into match-
   stick strips
Grated zest of ½ orange
Grated zest of ½ lemon
½ cup pitted black olives
½ cup chopped parsley

2 bunches watercress,
   washed, dried, and tough
   stems removed
½ cup olive oil
⅓ cup freshly squeezed
   lemon juice
1 clove garlic, peeled and
   halved
Salt, freshly ground pepper

Put celery root, endive, orange and lemon zest, olives, and parsley in a salad bowl, with watercress covering all. Cover the salad with plastic wrap, and chill in refrigerator.

Meanwhile, mix oil, lemon juice, garlic, and salt and pepper to taste. Let stand at room temperature for 1 to 2 hours.

To serve, remove garlic and toss dressing with salad. Serves 6.

CINNAMON–BROWN-SUGAR CRÊPES

18 basic Dessert Crêpes, using ½ teaspoon cinnamon
   in the batter (see Index)
10 tablespoons brown sugar
5 tablespoons unsalted butter

1 teaspoon cinnamon
Coffee ice cream
½ cup cognac
½ cup Kahlúa

In advance, make basic dessert crêpes. Spread 1 teaspoon brown sugar and ½ teaspoon butter on each crêpe.

Fold the crêpes in half and arrange them, in a slightly overlapping fashion, in a buttered flameproof baking pan. Sprinkle with the remaining 4 tablespoons of sugar, the cinnamon, and dot with the 2 tablespoons butter.

Preheat the oven to 375 degrees. Warm crêpes in oven for 15 minutes to melt butter. Just before serving, combine cognac and kahlúa and heat. Ignite and pour over crêpes. Serve immediately with coffee ice cream. Serves 6.

Winter

A Warming Winter
Dinner for Eight

*Iced Curry Soup with *Apricot Port Cream
*Pork Roasted with Cassis and Coarse Salt
*Purée of Turnips
*Salad of Cabbage, Endive, and Mushrooms
*Crème Brûlée

This menu offers a contrast of fire and ice, of interesting textures and non-cliché taste combinations. It also offers a wonderful, wintry way to add a glow to old friendships and take the chill from the new. You set the mood for this somewhat hearty meal by stressing seasonal contrasts in a grouped table centerpiece of vases of dried flowers and lush, potted wintertime greens interspersed with candles. The candlelight flickering on crystal and silver will cast subtle shadows and a spell all its own.

Warm up slowly with a delicate cold curried soup. It's an unusual but not unwelcome way to start a winter's meal. Pass the apricot port cream garnish in a sauceboat and let everyone stir in his own. This soup's very special combination of flavors offers just the right icy prelude to the very unique hot loin of pork roast to follow. The handsome roast, cooked with an outer crust of coarse salt and cassis can be easily and dramatically carved at the table. It's served with a hearty purée of turnips and followed by an absolutely sensational salad of cabbage, mushrooms, and endive.

The utterly lavish dessert—crème brûlée—with its cracked caramel crust, would be dramatic served at fireside. And for the final fuel to kindle lasting friendships—coffee, cordials, and lots of good conversation.

ICED CURRY SOUP

2 medium onions, chopped
3 ribs celery, chopped
¼ pound butter
2 tablespoons flour
1 tablespoon good quality
  imported curry powder

2 apples, peeled, cored, and
  chopped
2 quarts chicken stock
1 bay leaf
Apricot Port Cream (see
  recipe below)

Sauté onions and celery gently in butter in a medium skillet until soft. Add flour and curry powder, stir well, and cook for several minutes. Transfer the mixture to blender container. Add apples and 1 cup of the stock. Blend until smooth. Combine puréed mixture with remaining stock in a 3-quart saucepan, heat until well blended, add bay leaf, and chill. Stir in apricot port cream when serving, or pass it separately. Serves 8.

Apricot Port Cream

1 cup port
½ cup apricot purée (made
  from fresh or canned apricots)

2 teaspoons curry powder
½ cup heavy cream, slightly
  whipped

Reduce port by half over high heat. Add the purée and curry and cook for 5 minutes over gentle heat. Cool and stir in the cream.

Note: The apricot port cream serves as a lovely sauce for cold meats.

PORK ROASTED WITH CASSIS AND COARSE SALT

6- to 7-pound loin roast of
  pork
10 bay leaves, or more if necessary
Coarse salt, such as sea salt or
  kosher salt

Peppercorns
1 cup ice water
1 cup cassis

Preheat oven to 500 degrees.

Cut slits the length of the roast, at even intervals (a little under an inch) on the fat side of the pork loin. Fill slits with pieces of bay leaf and about 3 peppercorns per slit. Pour coarse salt heavily over roast, and put it on a rack in a roasting pan. Put in oven and after 5 minutes pour ice water over the roast. Lower heat to 350 degrees and roast for 30 minutes per pound. Thirty minutes before roast is cooked, pour the cassis over the roast and baste 2 to 3 times during final cooking period. Serves 6 to 8.

PURÉE OF TURNIPS

3 pounds small white turnips   Cayenne
½ pound piece of salt pork   Salt
    or 8 thick slices bacon   2 tablespoons butter
Freshly ground black pepper

Wash and peel turnips and cut into thin slices. Combine the turnips with salt pork or bacon and water to cover in a saucepan, and cook uncovered, about ½ hour, until tender. Drain if necessary, reserving cooking liquid.

Purée the turnips with half the salt pork or bacon and season to taste with pepper, salt (if necessary), and the butter. Add cooking liquid if too thick. Serves 8.

SALAD OF CABBAGE, ENDIVE, AND MUSHROOMS

1 egg yolk
1 teaspoon dry mustard
4 tablespoons vinegar
2 cloves garlic, put through a press
Salt, freshly ground pepper
1 cup plus 9 tablespoons olive oil
¼ to ½ cup commercial mayonnaise

2 tablespoons Dijon mustard
1 pound raw mushrooms, sliced to retain the mushroom outline
½ head green cabbage, cut into julienne strips
6 endives, sliced crosswise
1 to 2 heads Boston lettuce, separated into leaves

Mix egg yolk, dry mustard, 1 tablespoon vinegar, garlic, salt, and pepper to taste with whisk until thick and creamy. Add 1 cup olive oil drop by drop, whisking constantly. Then add enough commercial mayonnaise to thicken and whisk lightly until well blended.

Mix the remaining oil and vinegar, and mustard. Then blend with the tangy mayonnaise until it is thinned to a light-cream consistency. Pour this dressing over the mushrooms, cabbage, and endive and toss together. (Any remaining dressing may be kept in sealed jar in refrigerator.) Line salad bowl with Boston lettuce leaves and spoon dressed mushroom, cabbage, and endive mixture on top. Serves 8.

CRÈME BRÛLÉE

3 cups heavy cream
1 tablespoon sugar
2-inch piece of vanilla bean

6 egg yolks
Salt
1¼ cups light brown sugar

Preheat oven to 350 degrees.

Scald cream with sugar and vanilla bean. Beat egg yolks until light and mix slowly into cream with a pinch of salt. Blend well. Strain into a shallow 10-inch ovenproof dish (such as a porcelain flan dish or a Pyrex pie plate). Set in a pan of hot water and bake in a 350-degree oven for 50 to 60 minutes, until a knife inserted in center comes out clean. Chill overnight.

Preheat broiler.

Sieve brown sugar. Spread very evenly on top of custard. Put under broiler, turning dish so it broils evenly, until sugar has caramelized. Refrigerate until chilled. To serve, crack crust with back of spoon. Serves 8.

Note: The custard may also be baked in 8 individual ½-cup ramekins. Reduce cooking time to 20 to 30 minutes.

A Pasta Party

Antipasti: *Garbanzo Salad
                *Marinated Mushrooms (see Index)
                 Sliced Prosciutto and Genoa Salami
                 Provolone Cheese
                *Carrot Salad with Lemon Vinaigrette
                 Roasted Sweet Red Peppers and Anchovies
                *Fennel, Cucumber, and Radish Salad
                *Caponata

*Lasagna Milanese
*Pimiento-Walnut Sauce with Pasta
*Chicken Liver Sauce (see Index) with Pasta
*Shells San Marino
  Grissini, Italian Bread, Rolls
*Apple and Plum Tart

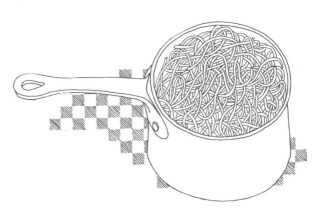

The Italian section of New York, known as Little Italy, has made an indelible impression on our cuisine. It has served as the inspiration for countless Italian regional restaurants throughout the city and offers New Yorkers the easy availability of fresh pasta of every description. Also to be had: wonderful fresh bread, tiny fresh amaretti, festive Christmas panettone and even tiny cookies decorated in the colors of the Italian flag.

Inspired by this Italian culinary exposure, the menu suggested here is not a dinner requiring lots of last-minute preparation, and as such is ideal for an informal gathering of close friends after a long walk in the cold or a game of boccie in Central Park. It features unusual antipasti (all of which may be prepared in advance) followed by pots of different pasta such as linguine and tagliatelle and a selection of sauces from which to choose. Also suggested is a light northern Italian lasagna, bound with a Béchamel sauce instead of ricotta and mozzarella cheeses.

For decor you might cover the table and sideboard with red-checkered cloths, and use red bandanna napkins. As a centerpiece, line a straw basket with a bandanna napkin and heap it with Italian breads, rolls, and breadsticks. Write the menu with a red felt tip pen on a wide lasagna noodle. And instead of conventional place cards, inscribe the guests' names on smaller noodles.

The sideboard is the setting for the pots of pasta and their accompanying sauces to be selected and tossed by the guests themselves. All you need to do in the kitchen before dinner is boil the pasta, heat the sauces, bake the assembled lasagna, and ask a guest to help set out the antipasti. *Grazie*, Little Italy, for this delicious idea.

GARBANZO SALAD

2 2-pound 4-ounce cans gar-
    banzos or chickpeas
5 scallions, minced
2 4-ounce jars pimientos,
    chopped
½ cup chopped parsley
    (preferably the flat-leaf
    Italian parsley)

½ cup wine vinegar
½ cup olive oil
1 teaspoon salt, or more to
    taste
Freshly ground pepper

Drain and rinse the garbanzos. Combine the garbanzos in a large mixing bowl with the scallions, pimientos, parsley, vinegar, oil, salt, and freshly ground pepper, and stir gently to mix well. Refrigerate, covered, for several hours before serving to allow flavors to blend. Serves 8.

CARROT SALAD
WITH LEMON VINAIGRETTE

6 to 8 medium carrots
½ to ¾ cup Lemon Vinai-
    grette (see Basic Recipes)
Salt, freshly ground pepper

2 to 3 tablespoons chopped
    parsley (preferably the
    flat-leaf Italian parsley)

Scrub and peel carrots. Shred or grate coarsely, then dress lightly with lemon vinaigrette. Season to taste with salt and pepper. Just before serving, toss with parsley. Serves 8 as part of antipasti.

FENNEL, CUCUMBER,
AND RADISH SALAD

1 large cucumber
1 bulb fennel
5 to 6 radishes
1 tablespoon finely chopped
    fresh mint, or ½ to 1 tea-
    spoon dried

1 small clove garlic, minced
    (optional)
½ cup olive oil
3 tablespoons lemon juice
Salt, freshly ground pepper

Peel cucumber, halve it, and scoop out seeds. Cut into ¼-inch slices. Cut the fennel into ¼-inch slices and chop the feathery top. Slice the radishes thinly. Combine cucumber, fennel, radishes, mint, and garlic if desired. Mix olive oil and lemon juice, season to taste with salt and pepper, and dress the salad. Serves 8 as part of antipasti.

CAPONATA

1 medium eggplant, about 1 pound
Salt
½ cup olive oil
½ cup finely chopped onion
1 cup finely chopped celery
2 to 3 tablespoons finely chopped carrot
1 to 2 cloves garlic, minced
1 pound ripe tomatoes, peeled and chopped, or 1½ cups canned Italian plum tomatoes, drained and chopped

1 tablespoon tomato paste
4 oil-cured black olives, or large green olives, pitted and slivered
3 tablespoons red wine vinegar
1 tablespoon capers
2 anchovy fillets, minced
Salt, freshly ground pepper
Sugar (optional)
2 to 3 tablespoons chopped parsley, preferably the flat-leaf Italian parsley

Cut eggplant into ½-inch cubes. Sprinkle generously with salt and spread on paper towels. Cover with more towels, and weight with plates. Leave ½ hour, then pat dry.

Heat 3 tablespoons olive oil in a large, heavy skillet and sauté onion, celery, carrot, and garlic over medium-low heat 8 to 10 minutes, until soft but not brown. Remove from skillet and set aside. Heat remaining oil, add eggplant cubes, and sauté over high heat, stirring and tossing constantly, until lightly browned. Stir in sautéed vegetables, tomatoes, tomato paste, olives, vinegar, capers, anchovies, and salt and pepper to taste. Bring to a boil, then lower heat and simmer, uncovered, about 10 to 15 minutes, until eggplant is tender but still holds its shape. Taste, and if desired, add 1 to 2 teaspoons sugar. Put in a serving dish and refrigerate. Remove from refrigerator 20 to 30 minutes before serving; it should not be served ice cold. Stir in parsley just before serving. Serves 8 as part of antipasti.

LASAGNA MILANESE

1 medium onion, finely
  chopped
½ carrot, finely chopped
1 stalk celery, finely
  chopped
4 tablespoons butter
¼ cup finely diced ham or
  lean bacon
½ cup dry white wine
1 pound ground lean beef,
  such as round
Salt, freshly ground black
  pepper
⅛ teaspoon freshly grated
  nutmeg

2 tablespoons tomato paste
1½ cups stock, water, or tomato juice
½ pound mushrooms, sliced
2 tablespoons heavy cream
2 cups Béchamel Sauce (see
  Basic Recipes)
12 2-inch wide lasagna noodles
Butter or oil for preparing
  the baking dish
2 cups freshly grated im-
  ported Parmesan cheese
3 tablespoons butter

Prepare the sauce: sauté the onion, carrot, and celery in 2 tablespoons butter in a medium saucepan until soft but not browned. Add the diced ham or bacon and cook for 3 to 4 minutes. Add the wine, and cook until almost evaporated. Add the ground beef, salt and pepper to taste, and nutmeg, and continue cooking, stirring, about 5 minutes. Dissolve the tomato paste in the stock, water, or tomato juice and add to the meat mixture. Taste and correct seasoning. Cover and simmer 45 minutes. Sauté the mushrooms in the remaining 2 tablespoons of butter, and add to the meat mixture with the heavy cream. (While the sauce is simmering, prepare the béchamel sauce.)

Bring about 6 quarts water to a boil in a large saucepan. Add 3 table-spoons salt. Add the noodles and cook for about 12 to 14 minutes, until tender. If using fresh pasta, reduce the cooking time to 5 to 6 minutes. Drain the noodles and remove to a linen towel (they will stick to paper towels).

Preheat oven to 350 degrees.

Butter an attractive 9 by 13 by 2-inch baking dish, and put 4 lasagna noodles on the bottom, overlapping slightly. Cover with ½ of the meat sauce, ⅔ cup béchamel sauce, and ⅔ cup grated Parmesan. Repeat with the noodles, sauce, béchamel, and cheese, twice, finishing with the cheese. Dot with butter. Bake uncovered at 350 degrees until heated through and lightly browned. The dish may be prepared ahead and refrigerated before baking. Serves 8. For 16, prepare 2 casseroles, doubling all ingredients.

PIMIENTO-WALNUT SAUCE

1 cup chopped scallions (or
   1 large onion, chopped)
3 tablespoons best-quality
   olive oil
2 medium cloves garlic, put
   through a press (or more
   to taste)
8-ounce can walnuts,
   chopped medium-fine
3 4-ounce cans pimientos,
   chopped medium-fine

1 cup chopped parsley
1 teaspoon dried basil, or 1
   tablespoon chopped fresh
   basil
1 cup sliced, pitted ripe
   olives (optional)
½ pound butter, melted
2 pounds linguine, cooked al
   dente
Bowl of freshly grated imported Parmesan cheese

Sauté scallions or onion in oil with garlic until wilted. Combine with walnuts, pimientos, parsley, basil, olives, and butter, heat through, and pour over a platter of hot linguine. Serve with Parmesan cheese. Makes enough sauce for 2 pounds of pasta. Will serve 8 to 10 generously.

SHELLS SAN MARINO

3 chicken breasts, boned and
   skinned
2 tablespoons flour
2 tablespoons olive oil
2 tablespoons butter
½ cup dry white wine or
   dry vermouth
¾ to 1 cup milk
Salt, freshly ground white
   pepper

2 egg yolks
1 pound pasta shells
1 ½ cups grated imported
   Parmesan cheese, or a mixture of grated Parmesan,
   Romano, and Sardo
¾ cup heavy cream, heated

Place the chicken breasts between sheets of wax paper, and pound to about ½-inch thickness with a heavy mallet or meat cleaver. Dust the breasts lightly with 1 tablespoon flour. Heat the olive oil and butter in a heavy sauté pan or frying pan and sauté the breasts until golden. Remove from the skillet, and cut into very thin julienne strips. Return to the skillet and toss with the rest of the flour. Stir in the white wine or vermouth, and cook over medium high heat until the wine is reduced by half. Boil the milk in a separate saucepan; add the milk to the chicken. Add salt and pepper to taste, and stir to blend thoroughly.

Remove the pan from the heat and stir in the egg yolks carefully. Return to the heat and simmer very gently, covered, for 25 minutes. Meanwhile, cook the shells in 8 quarts of boiling salted water for 15 minutes. They should be just al dente or firm to the bite. Drain and put the shells in a preheated 4-quart serving bowl. Add all the sauce and ¾ cup grated cheese. Toss until thoroughly mixed. Add the heavy cream and toss again to mix. Cover with the remaining ¾ cup grated cheese, and correct seasoning, if necessary. Serves 8.

APPLE AND PLUM TART

2 cups sugar
1 cup water
3 tart cooking apples, peeled and cored
1 dozen prune plums, halved and pitted
10-ounce jar red currant jelly

10-inch Pastry shell (see Basic Recipes), prebaked
¾ to 1 cup applesauce flavored with 2 tablespoons Kirsch
Crème Fraîche (see recipe below)

Combine sugar and water and cook until syrup reaches 220 degrees on candy thermometer. Slice apples into attractive, uniform slices, about ⅛ to ¼ inch thick. Poach apple slices in barely simmering sugar syrup for 3 to 5 minutes, or until tender. Be careful not to overcook. Drain. The plums are not cooked.

Melt the currant jelly, and boil 1 to 2 minutes. Paint the bottom of the pastry shell with some of the melted jelly to seal it. Spread a generous layer of applesauce over the bottom, and then arrange the fruit attractively, perhaps in overlapping rings alternating apples in one ring and plums in the next. Put a plum half in the center. Paint the top with the remaining jelly glaze. Serve with crème fraîche. Serves 8.

Crème Fraîche

1 cup heavy cream   1 teaspoon buttermilk

Combine cream and buttermilk and leave in a warm spot, covered, until thickened, 1 to 3 days. Refrigerate. This is wonderful and zingy on many fruit desserts. Makes 1 cup.

The Last-minute Christmas Shopper's

Soup Supper for Four

Hot Buttered Rum
Hot Apple Cider Spiced with Cinnamon
*Dutch Erwtensuppe
Whole-grain Bread
Sweet Butter
Gouda and Edam Cheeses
*Dutch Apple Flensjes

You're feeling festive but tired . . . hungry but hurried. So on your way home after tracking down that last Christmas gift, pick up a loaf of dark, crusty, whole-grain bread. Then relax . . . if you've planned this menu. It's a no-nonsense, economical evening supper that makes an occasion of that splurging-shopping day. The main course is a Dutch recipe that can be completely concocted days in advance: Erwtensuppe —or split pea soup. And, anytime you plan to serve it you can simply double the proportions and reserve half in the freezer for a later date.

This appetite- and soul-satisfying supper might provide the inspiration for a family Christmas present wrap-in or the prelude to trimming the tree. So be sure to have all the wrapping and trimming essentials on hand and Christmas music in the background. To evoke the Christmas spirit you might serve around the fireplace—starting with soothing hot buttered rums for you and hot apple cider for the children. Then pass the non-cliché pea soup—thick, hearty, and herb-scented—cooked with a pig's knuckle, ham, and sausage (or ham bone) for subtle flavor and texture. The soup could be served from a tureen or simply ladled into oversized ironstone mugs accompanied by the bread you bought, sweet butter, and beer. For dessert, a basket of fresh fruit will suffice, and in keeping with the Dutch motif, Gouda and aged Edam cheeses. Or, if the time permits, Dutch apple pancakes would make a delicious and Christmasy dessert alternative.

ERWTENSUPPE
(DUTCH SPLIT PEA SOUP)

1 pound dried split peas
1 ½- to 2-pound shank or
   butt end of smoked ham
1 pig's knuckle, smoked if
   possible
3 quarts water
3 large onions, coarsely
   chopped
1 leek, sliced
2 celery ribs, coarsely
   chopped

2 carrots, coarsely chopped
1 potato, coarsely chopped
2 teaspoons thyme
Salt, freshly ground pepper
4 knockwurst, sliced
1 tablespoon hickory smoked
   salt (optional)
¼ cup chopped parsley

If the peas require soaking, soak overnight in water to cover. Drain before starting the soup.

Combine the ham and knuckle with the peas and 3 quarts of water in a 6-quart Dutch oven or heavy pot. Bring to a boil, reduce the heat, and cook 30 to 40 minutes, skimming frequently. Add the onions, leek, celery, carrots, and potato. Add thyme, season well with salt and pepper, and simmer slowly, uncovered, about 5 hours or until very thick, stirring occasionally. Remove the pig's knuckle and discard. Remove the ham, cut into pieces, and return to the soup with the sliced knockwurst 30 minutes before serving. Add the optional smoked salt and stir in parsley. Serve with whole-grain bread and sweet butter. Serves 8.

APPLE FLENSJES
(DUTCH APPLE PANCAKES)

1 cup all-purpose flour
1 cup dark beer
2 eggs, separated
4 to 6 tablespoons sugar, depending on desired sweetness
1 teaspoon cinnamon
¼ pound unsalted butter

4 tart apples (McIntosh are
   good), cored and sliced in
   4 or 5 rings
Dark brown or confec-
   tioners' sugar, sweetened
   whipped cream, or vanilla
   ice cream

Mix the flour and beer in a large bowl, and beat in the egg yolks and
sugar thoroughly. Beat the egg whites until stiff, and add to the flour-
and-beer mixture spoonful by spoonful, stirring well after each addition.
Add the cinnamon.

Melt 4 tablespoons butter in a large, heavy skillet and sauté the apple
slices for about 2 to 3 minutes on each side, until they are tender
but not too soft. Remove to a plate. This may be done in advance. Butter
the skillet, arrange a few apple slices in it about 2 inches apart, and ladle
some batter over each apple slice to make a pancake. Cook about 2 to 3
minutes, turn, and cook another 2 to 3 minutes, until pancake is done.
Sprinkle generously with brown or confectioners' sugar, or serve with
sweetened whipped cream or vanilla ice cream. If brown sugar is used,
the pancakes may be put under the broiler quickly, about 2 minutes, to
melt the sugar. Serve immediately. Serves 6 to 8.

An Extended

Christmas Eve Buffet

*Chef Oliver Brown's Avocado Mousse
*Pâté en Croûte
*Poached Salmon with *Cucumber and Dill Mayonnaise and
   *Caviar Mayonnaise
*Glazed Ham
*Eggplant Mozzarella
*Bourbon Balls
*Sugared Pecans
*Mincemeat Turnovers
*English Fruitcake
*Devil's Food Cake (see Index)
*Southern Eggnog

The invitation reads: "Drop in anytime after six on Christmas Eve for drinks and dinner. And please do bring the children." Since Christmas Eve presents certain logistics problems for most families, your invitation offers the flexibility of a welcome buffet dinner or a simple cup of holiday cheer to those who might also have to cope with family, last-minute chores, church, and children who must be home in bed. It's a bounteous buffet designed to fit any family's schedule—since the hour of arrival and departure is completely optional.

Before your guests are expected, throw the windows open to bring down the temperature and allow for the heat of a fire and the crowd. To absorb the odor of smoke, you might put little bowls of ammonia behind curtains and in safe corners of the room. You'll want to check the room regularly throughout the evening for dirty glasses, ashtrays, and dishes. A party that has people coming and going over an extended period requires that extra effort to assure that rooms look inviting at all times.

Extend your dining room table to its fullest point for a look of festive generosity. The main dishes, set with forks and plates by each, occupy its four corners. They are a lovely pâté en croûte, elegant whole poached salmon served with a selection of herbed and seasoned mayonnaises, glazed ham, and luscious eggplant mozzarella. As a centerpiece, a beautiful wreath or a silver bowl heaped with shiny Christmas balls, and plenty of candles both on the table and throughout your party rooms will add to the decor. Placed around the main dishes on cake stands and compotes, offer candies: bourbon balls and sugared pecans, cakes, and mincemeat turnovers. At a strategic location set up a bar: wines, whiskeys, and a very special eggnog.

During the height of the festivities you might keep the young guests busy in another room stringing popcorn or making Christmas-tree-patterned place mats of felt-backed contact paper with ornaments cut out for each child to arrange on his mat himself. For this most festive time of the year, entertaining is an extension of the generosity of the season. And this buffet is a beautiful way of giving.

CHEF OLIVER BROWN'S
AVOCADO MOUSSE

3 cups mashed ripe avocado
6 tablespoons lemon juice
1 ½ tablespoons finely grated
   onion
2 ½ teaspoons salt
Tabasco sauce

¾ cup mayonnaise
2 tablespoons unflavored gelatin
¼ cup cold water
1 ¼ cups hot water
2 to 3 pints cherry tomatoes

Mix the mashed avocado with the lemon juice, onion, salt, a dash of
Tabasco, and mayonnaise. Soften the gelatin in the cold water. Add
hot water to the gelatin and stir well to dissolve. Add the gelatin to the
avocado mixture and blend thoroughly. Oil a 6-cup mold and rinse out
with cold water. Pour in avocado mixture and chill for at least 3 hours.
Unmold and serve surrounded by cherry tomatoes. Serves 8.

PÂTÉ EN CROÛTE

½ pound boiled ham, cut in
   ¼-inch thick slices (about
   2 slices)
1 pound veal scaloppine
Salt, freshly ground pepper
Thyme
Allspice
½ cup cognac
¼ cup dry white wine
¼ cup minced shallots
1 pound pork ground with
   ¼ pound fresh pork fat
1 egg
2 teaspoons cornstarch,
   mixed to a paste with a little cold water

¼ cup shelled pistachios
   (optional)
Butter
Pastry (see recipe below)
3 to 4 chicken livers, quickly
   seared in butter, or 3 to 4
   diced truffles, marinated in
   cognac (optional)
1 bay leaf (optional)
Egg glaze: 2 egg yolks
   beaten with 2 tablespoons
   cold water

Cut the ham and veal into ¼-inch strips and arrange in a flat dish.

Sprinkle with big pinches of salt, pepper, thyme, and allspice, and pour the cognac and white wine over. Marinate 12 to 24 hours.

Mix the shallots, ground pork and fat, egg, cornstarch mixture, and marinade. Season to taste with salt and pepper. Add ¼ teaspoon allspice and ½ teaspoon thyme. Mix well, then sauté a small spoonful in butter and taste for seasoning. Since the terrine will be served cold, it should be a little salty when hot. Season if necessary.

Butter a baking sheet or jelly-roll pan. Divide pastry in thirds and roll out one third ¼-inch thick into a rectangle about 9 by 12 inches. Put on a baking sheet. Spread ⅓ of the ground pork mixture in a neat rectangle in center, leaving a 2-inch border. Sprinkle with half the pistachios (do not use if using truffles). Arrange half the veal and ham strips on top, and spread this layer with half the remaining pork mixture. Sprinkle with remaining pistachios, and if desired, arrange chicken livers or truffles in a line down the center. Cover with remaining veal and ham strips, then spread with remaining pork mixture. If desired, put bay leaf on top.

Roll out remaining pastry ¼-inch thick. Brush egg glaze on edge of bottom sheet of pastry around meat and lay second sheet over pâté, enveloping it. Trim away excess pastry with a sharp knife, leaving a ½- to 1-inch border, and press edges together. Roll out pastry scraps and cut into decorative shapes. Brush entire surface of pastry with egg glaze, arrange pastry decorations, and brush them with egg glaze. Cut 2 small holes in top of pastry and insert little foil funnels. Bake in a 350-degree oven about 1½ hours, until juices (which can be seen in funnels) are clear or yellow and pastry is golden brown. If pastry browns too much, cover lightly with foil. Cool before serving. May be prepared 1 day in advance and refrigerated. Serves 12 to 16.

Pastry for Pâté en Croûte

5 cups cake flour (not self-rising)	Salt
	1 egg
12 to 14 tablespoons unsalted butter, cold and firm	¼ cup cold water
	Flour

Put the flour on a board or in a bowl and make a well in the center. Cut the butter into tiny pieces and put into the well. Put in a large pinch of salt and the egg. Mix quickly with fingertips, gradually drawing in flour, until mixture resembles oatmeal. Sprinkle on 2 to 3 tablespoons water and mix. If dough does not adhere and gather into a ball, sprinkle on remaining water, or enough so dough forms a ball.

Flour board. Put dough on it, and with heel of hand push down and break away a 1- to 2-inch piece of dough, smearing it across board. Repeat until all dough has been handled in this way. Gather into a smooth ball and refrigerate until firm, about 1 to 2 hours.

CHRISTMAS SALMON

Poach an 8-pound salmon according to basic poaching directions (see Index). Drain, and chill. Remove the skin from the top half of the salmon. Serve with bowls of seasoned mayonnaises.

Cucumber and Dill Mayonnaise

1 large cucumber, peeled
2 cups homemade Mayonnaise (see Basic Recipes)
1 tablespoon finely snipped fresh dill, or 1 teaspoon dried

3 to 4 tablespoons, cooked, drained, and puréed spinach
Salt, freshly ground pepper

Cut the cucumber in half, lengthwise and remove seeds. Chop the cucumber as finely as possible. It should almost be a purée. Mix cucumber into the mayonnaise with the dill. Add the spinach, 1 tablespoon at a time, to color it delicately. The mayonnaise should be a pretty pale green. Season to taste with salt and freshly ground pepper. Makes 2 ½ cups.

Caviar Mayonnaise

1 tablespoon tomato sauce
2 cups homemade Mayonnaise (see Basic Recipes)

4 ounces good-quality red caviar

Stir the tomato sauce into the mayonnaise. The mayonnaise should be a pale pink. Fold the caviar into the mayonnaise and chill. Makes 2¼ cups.

GLAZED HAM

10- to 12-pound country ham, or a good-quality canned ham

¾ cup Dijon mustard
¾ cup dark brown sugar

Preheat oven to 350 degrees.

Follow directions for preparing country ham (see Index). If using a good-quality canned ham, no preliminary cooking is required. Combine mustard and sugar. Score the fat of the ham, and spread the glaze generously over the surface of the ham. Bake in a 350-degree oven 30 to 45 minutes, until the glaze is brown and crusty. Serves 12.

EGGPLANT MOZZARELLA

4 large or 8 small eggplants, peeled and cut into *thin* slices crosswise
Salt
4 to 6 eggs
1 cup flour, or more, if necessary

Butter and peanut oil
Spaghetti Sauce (see recipe below)
3 pounds mozzarella cheese, grated

Set eggplant slices in flat pan in layers, sprinkling generous amount of salt over each layer. Separate layers with paper towels. Weight with heavy objects to squeeze out the juice. Allow to sit for 1 to 2 hours, so that juices run out of eggplants and they are limp. Drain and wipe dry. Put eggs in a bowl, and flour in another. Dip each piece of eggplant in egg, coat with flour, then sauté in hot oil and butter, in a large heavy skillet. (Change the oil and butter when it begins to get dark and full of sediment.) Drain browned eggplant on paper towels. Do not be discouraged by the length of this process.

Preheat oven to 375 degrees.

Layer eggplant, sauce, and cheese twice in two 12 by 15-inch baking dishes. Eggplant can be frozen at this point. Bake in a 375-degree oven until browned on top and bubbly, about 45 minutes. If frozen, be sure to bring it to room temperature before baking. Also, note that recipe does not call for salt. The soaking with salt seems sufficient. Serves 12.

Spaghetti Sauce

4 pounds ground round steak
8 to 10 tablespoons good
 olive oil
6 cloves garlic (more if desired), put through a press
2 35-ounce cans Italian tomatoes with tomato paste and
 basil leaf

12 carrots, washed (not
 peeled) and cut into pieces
 to fit into saucepan
8 medium onions, peeled
Salt, freshly ground pepper

Sauté ground meat in the olive oil until browned, then add garlic, tomatoes, carrots, and onions, and cook on low simmer uncovered until carrots are soft (about 1 hour). Season to taste with salt and pepper. Remove the onions and carrots and discard (children usually take care of discarding the carrots). Serve over spaghetti or in Eggplant Mozzarella. Makes about 8 cups.

Note: To make a chicken liver sauce, sauté ¾ pound chicken livers in butter until they are just firm but still pink inside. Add to sauce and cook 10 to 15 minutes.

BOURBON BALLS

2 cups fine, dry cake or
 cookie crumbs
1 cup confectioners' sugar
1 cup chopped toasted
 pecans

2 tablespoons light or dark
 corn syrup
¼ cup bourbon whiskey
Additional confectioners'
 sugar

Combine crumbs, sugar, pecans, corn syrup, and bourbon, mixing well. Form into 1-inch balls and roll in additional confectioners' sugar. Store in a covered jar in refrigerator. They are best made a day or two before serving. Makes about 40 to 50.

Note: White or yellow cake are the traditional choices, but chocolate or spice cake crumbs would be equally delicious.

SUGARED PECANS

1 cup sugar
¼ teaspoon salt
6 tablespoons milk
1 to 2 teaspoons grated
    orange zest

½ teaspoon vanilla
2 to 3 cups pecan halves

Combine sugar, salt, milk, and orange zest in a large, heavy saucepan. Cook until mixture reaches the soft-ball stage (238 degrees on candy thermometer), stirring often.

Remove from heat and blend in vanilla, then nuts. Stir until grainy and nuts are coated. Turn out onto wax paper, separating each nut. Cool and pack as gifts, or serve in candy dishes. They are best if aged several days in an air-tight jar before serving.

MINCEMEAT TURNOVERS

Cream Cheese Pastry for
    turnovers (see Index)
Mincemeat (see recipe be-
    low)

Egg glaze: 2 egg yolks com-
    bined with 2 tablespoons
    cold water

Preheat oven to 400 degrees.

Prepare cream cheese pastry. Roll to ⅛-inch thickness, and cut into 2½-inch rounds. Spoon about 1 teaspoon mincemeat onto the pastry, fold to form a crescent, and pinch the edges together with the tines of a fork. Brush with egg glaze, and bake in a 400-degree oven for 10 to 12 minutes, until golden brown. Makes 6 to 7 dozen.

Mincemeat for Turnovers or Pie

2 pounds boneless chuck, cut
    into 1-inch cubes
Boiling water
1 ½ pounds beef suet
3 pounds cooking apples,
    peeled, cored, and coarsely
    chopped
1 quart apple cider
1 tablespoon cinnamon
1 tablespoon allspice
1 ½ teaspoons powdered
    cloves

1 ½ teaspoons powdered
    mace
3 cups sugar
3 cups seedless raisins
5 cups currants
½ cup finely minced Can-
    died Orange Peel (see
    Index)
2 teaspoons salt
1 cup brandy

Put meat in a deep, heavy-bottomed saucepan. Add boiling water to cover. Cover the saucepan and simmer for 2 hours. Remove the meat, and continue to boil the stock until reduced to 1 ½ cups. Put the beef and beef suet through the coarse blade of a food chopper. Mix the meat mixture with the stock, apples, cider, cinnamon, allspice, cloves, mace, sugar, raisins, currants, candied orange peel, and 2 teaspoons salt. Cover the mixture and bring to a boil. Simmer 1 hour, stirring occasionally. Add brandy, spoon immediately into sterilized jars, and seal. Store in a cool place. This makes about 4½ quarts, keeps indefinitely, and makes nice gifts.

ENGLISH FRUITCAKE

Butter for cake pan
½ pound butter
1 ¼ cups sugar
4 eggs
2 ¼ cups flour
Salt
2 cups currants
2 cups seedless raisins
2 ounces glacéed citron,
    coarsely chopped

2 ounces glacéed pineapple,
    coarsely chopped
2 ounces glacéed cherries,
    halved
1 scant teaspoon baking pow-
    der
2 tablespoons Cointreau
1 tablespoon cognac or dark
    rum

Preheat oven to 300 degrees.

Butter two 8 by 5-inch loaf pans. Cream the butter and sugar together thoroughly, and add the eggs, one at a time, stirring well after
each addition. Add the flour, about ⅔ cup at a time, alternately with the
fruit. Stir in the Cointreau and cognac or rum. Pour batter into prepared cake pans. Bake in a 300-degree oven for 30 minutes; reduce heat
to 250 degrees, and continue baking for 1 ¼ to 1 ½ hours.

Note: This recipe doubles perfectly to make lovely presents. The
cakes are moist and keep very well.

SOUTHERN EGGNOG

12 eggs, separated

1 cup sugar

1 pint bourbon

1 cup brandy

1 pint heavy cream

1 quart half-and-half

1 pint vanilla ice cream, softened

Freshly grated nutmeg

Beat egg yolks and sugar with electric mixer or whisk until pale and
thickened. Add bourbon and brandy, stirring carefully. The liquor
"cooks" the eggs. Add cream and half-and-half, beating at medium speed.
Break up ice cream in spoonfuls and add. Beat egg whites until stiff
and fold in. Refrigerate for at least 30 minutes. Before serving, sprinkle
with nutmeg. Serves 15.

A Gala Christmas

Dinner for Eight

Smoked Salmon
Smoked Trout with *Horseradish Cream
Brown Bread, Sweet Butter, Lemon Wedges
*Caviar Tarte (see Index)
*Roast Turkey or Capon with *Gravy and *Oyster Dressing
*Spinach with Walnuts
*Julienne of Celery Root
  Salad of Endive, Watercress, and Beets with *Parsley
    Vinaigrette (see Basic Recipes)
*Suffolk Syllabub

Here is a gala dinner that could ring in the Christmas season—a feast for all the seasons—rich and traditional. Take the seasonal approach to decorating your home. Use fragrant boughs, colorful garlands, and of course a tree trimmed with all your traditional and treasured ornaments. And because the Christmas spirit is best expressed in its music, be sure to have some playing in the background. Plan this as a festive, gracious evening with good friends gathered—perhaps you could ask your guests to come in evening clothes.

Forgo regular cocktails this very special night: celebrate Christmas with champagne. With it, after guests arrive, serve the first course in the living room. Be sure to pass lemon wedges and a pepper grinder. The customary bar can be set with the wine cooler and glittering fragile glasses, the coffee or side table set for the first course with forks, plates, and snowy napkins.

The evening will then progress to the dining room where the table should be set in its grandest manner to honor this most festive roast turkey or capon. What sets this roast bird apart from any other bird is its simple yet sensational stuffing. It consists of plump, succulent oysters—three dozen of them!—lightly herbed. The spinach with walnuts and julienne of celery root are simply prepared—good foils for the fragrant turkey and its stuffing. All this is followed with a salad bright with Christmas colors.

Why not serve dessert in any other room that, with a bit of rearrangement, lends itself well to this purpose? This variation of the old English syllabub, light yet rich with wine, could be beautifully enjoyed before a blazing hearth. Then, following the English custom, guests could sip their port or madeira with blanched almonds and stemmed raisins over an easygoing conversation followed by demitasses of perfect coffee. Joy to the World!

HORSERADISH CREAM

1 cup heavy cream

2 to 4 tablespoons prepared
horseradish

Salt, freshly ground pepper

Lemon juice

Whip cream until medium stiff. Fold in horseradish to taste (sauce should be delicate but have a bit of a bite), and season with salt, pepper, and a few drops of lemon juice. Serve with smoked trout. Serves 8.

Note: Sauce is also good served with hot or cold roast beef.

ROAST TURKEY OR CAPON

10- to 12-pound fresh-killed
turkey (a fresh turkey is
available from your
butcher on special order)
or an 8- to 9-pound capon

Gravy (see recipe below)

Oyster Dressing (see recipe
below)

¼ pound butter, softened

1 tablespoon coarse salt

Preheat the oven to 325 degrees.

Wash the turkey and pat dry, reserving the giblets for the gravy. Stuff the turkey with oyster dressing and truss or secure with poultry pins. Rub the bird well with softened butter, and sprinkle with salt. Put cheesecloth over the roasting rack in the roaster, and cook the turkey, breast side down, for 45 minutes to 1 hour. This moistens the breast meat. Meanwhile, begin preparing giblet stock (see below). Turn the turkey, breast side up, butter again if necessary, and continue roasting for 3 hours for a 10- to 12-pound bird or until it reaches 175 to 180 degrees on meat thermometer. Prick the thigh; juices should run clear. Remove to a warming tray, and finish making the gravy. Serves 8.

Gravy

Giblets from the turkey or
capon

Salt, freshly ground pepper

4 tablespoons flour (for 2
cups broth)

While the turkey is roasting, simmer the giblets in a saucepan with water to cover, about 2½ cups, and salt and pepper to taste. When the bird is done, pour ½ cup water into the roaster, and scrape up any brown bits. Pour this into a bowl. Skim off the fat, and put 2 tablespoons of the fat from the roaster into a heavy saucepan. Stir in flour and cook until it is brown. Strain the giblet broth and add to the broth from the roaster. Skim any remaining fat, and stir the broth into the flour, whisking until smooth and thickened. Season with salt and pepper to taste.

Note: If roasting a capon, prepare as directed for turkey. Roast for 2½ to 3 hours' total cooking time, then test for doneness.

Oyster Dressing

6 cups fresh-cut bread cubes	4 tablespoons butter
3 dozen oysters	1 teaspoon thyme
1 small onion, finely chopped	Salt, freshly ground pepper
3 ribs celery, finely chopped	Butter

Preheat oven to 250 degrees.

Dry the bread cubes in the oven for 30 minutes. If the oysters are large, cut into pieces with kitchen scissors. Cook the oysters in their liquor in a large skillet just until their edges curl. Remove with a slotted spoon, reserving the oyster liquor. Sauté the onion and celery in the butter in a heavy sauté pan. Toss the oysters with the bread cubes, mixing carefully, and add the onion, celery, and butter mixture. The dressing should be just moist, not wet. If the dressing seems too dry, moisten carefully by adding the oyster liquor, a spoonful at a time. Season with thyme and salt and pepper to taste. Stuff the turkey or capon gently; *do not pack* dressing into the bird. Butter a 4-cup baking dish and fill with excess dressing. Cover and bake with the bird for about 20 minutes.

SPINACH WITH WALNUTS

4 pounds fresh spinach or 4
  10-ounce boxes frozen
  spinach
6 tablespoons butter

½ cup coarsely chopped
  walnuts
Salt, freshly ground pepper
Freshly grated nutmeg

Wash fresh spinach thoroughly and cook in a large pot in the water clinging to its leaves for 4 to 6 minutes, just until wilted. Cook frozen spinach according to directions on box. Drain well, squeeze to extract as much excess moisture as possible, and spread on paper towels to dry thoroughly. Chop coarsely.

Melt butter in a heavy 10-inch skillet and sauté the walnuts for 2 minutes, shaking the pan occasionally. Remove the walnuts from the pan and reserve. Put the spinach into the skillet and heat through. Add the walnuts and toss, and season to taste with salt, pepper, and grated nutmeg. Serves 8.

CELERY ROOT JULIENNE

3 pounds celery root
12 tablespoons unsalted
  butter
Salt, freshly ground pepper

1 to 2 lemons
5 to 6 tablespoons chopped
  parsley

Peel the celery root and cut into very thin julienne strips, or shred coarsely. Melt butter in a large heavy skillet, add celery root, and sauté, tossing and stirring constantly, for 2 to 3 minutes. Cover and cook over moderate heat about 5 to 8 minutes, until tender but still retaining texture. Season with salt, pepper, the juice of the lemons to taste, and parsley. Serve immediately. Serves 8.

SUFFOLK SYLLABUB

1 envelope unflavored gelatin
Juice of 1 lemon
½ cup medium-dry sherry
⅓ cup cognac
½ cup superfine sugar
Freshly grated nutmeg

Grated zest of 1 lemon
3 cups heavy cream
2 egg whites
Salt
Glacéed cherries or candied
   violets, blanched
   almonds, and angelica

Soften the gelatin in the lemon juice in a small bowl. Put bowl in a
larger bowl of hot water and stir until dissolved. Combine sherry, cognac,
sugar, nutmeg to taste, and lemon zest. Whip cream until very stiff, mix
in sherry mixture, and thoroughly fold in gelatin. Refrigerate. Beat egg
whites with a pinch of salt until stiff. When cream mixture starts to
thicken and set, put bowl over a bowl of ice and fold in egg whites.
Fill 8 sherbet or coupe champagne glasses with mixture, or put in a
crystal bowl (do not use a silver bowl; it would discolor). Refrigerate
until set. Garnish with cherries or flowers made of violets, almonds, and
angelica. Serves 8.

A Chili Supper for a

Chilly Sunday for Six

*Avocado Soup
*Chili
*Red Beans with Onions
  Rice (see Index)
  Chopped Onions
  Hot Peppers
  Romaine Salad with *Vinaigrette (see Basic Recipes)
*Margarita Pie

If you like a chili that bites back when you bite into it—this menu is for you. It is a "pure" chili, unadulterated by beans or tomato sauce. The beans and onions are served separately. The recipe for the chili was the gift to this book of an old chili aficionado who has spent time researching authentic chili recipes, hours cooking, and happy evenings eating and comparing. In his opinion, this is the best. It is forceful and fiery, but you can adjust the heat to your taste by reducing the amount of cayenne and chili pequins. Chili pequins are tiny dried chili pods bottled by well-known spice merchants.

A subtle, mousselike avocado soup is a creamy prelude to the chili itself. Dessert is an unusual tart Margarita pie, inspired by the famous Mexican cocktail. And, of course, you'll want to serve plenty of iced beer or sangria in pitchers throughout the meal.

Try covering the table with a brightly colored serape, a blanket available in Mexican import shops. Use wooden plates, or for really unusual dishes, buy terra cotta or clay plant saucers from your local garden supply shop and sterilize them in the dishwasher. Carry the theme through with a pottery centerpiece: put a Styrofoam or florist's clay base in a clay pot, and anchor a pretty curved branch in it. Disguise the Styrofoam base with pebbles and stones or crushed pottery—old clay pots. Decorate the branch with lots of brightly colored felt and feather birds, available from party supply stores. They'll come in handy later for decorating packages or a gift plant.

One word of caution: consider checking with your guests as to whether they like spicy, hot food. This menu is definitely not for timid taste buds.

CHILLED AVOCADO SOUP

2 ripe avocados
1 cup chicken broth
4 to 6 tablespoons sour cream
4 to 6 tablespoons heavy
  cream
2 tablespoons lemon juice

½ teaspoon salt
1 shallot or small onion,
  finely chopped
Chopped cilantro
  (coriander)

Scoop out the avocado flesh, and put in a blender with chicken broth, sour cream, heavy cream, lemon juice, salt, and chopped shallot or onion. Whirl until puréed. Check seasoning and add more salt, if necessary. Chill. Serve in chilled bowls, garnished with chopped cilantro. Serves 4 to 6.

Note: The mixture will be very thick. Add more chicken broth if a thinner soup is desired. It is best not to make it more than 1 to 1½ hours in advance.

CHILI

3 pounds lean beef, such as
  boneless sirloin or chuck
  in 1 piece
¼ cup olive oil
5 cups water
8 chili pequins (dried red
  peppers), or more to taste
1 tablespoon salt
12 cloves garlic, finely
  chopped

1 teaspoon ground cumin, or
  more to taste
1 teaspoon orégano
1 teaspoon cayenne pepper
1 tablespoon sugar
3 tablespoons paprika
2 tablespoons flour
5 tablespoons cornmeal
1½ to 2 cups chopped on-
  ions

Partially freeze beef, then cut into thin strips about 1½ to 2 inches long. Heat olive oil in a 6-quart pot. Add all the meat and sear over high heat, stirring constantly until meat is gray, not browned. Add 4 cups water. Cover and cook at a bubbling simmer for 1½ to 2 hours, until meat is quite tender. Add the chili pequins, salt, garlic, cumin, orégano, cayenne, sugar, and paprika, and cook 30 minutes at a bubbling simmer, uncovered. Mix the flour and cornmeal with remaining water, and add to the chili. Stir to prevent lumping and cook until thickened. Serve chili, beans, rice, and chopped onions in separate bowls. Serves 6 to 8.

RED BEANS WITH ONIONS

2 1-pound 4-ounce cans
  pinto or kidney beans

¼ cup minced onion
Salt

Cook beans, onions, and salt to taste until heated through and flavors have blended. Drain well before serving. Serves 6.

MARGARITA PIE

¾ cup pretzel crumbs
⅓ cup butter
3 tablespoons sugar
Vegetable oil for preparing
  pie pan
1 envelope unflavored gelatin
½ cup lime or lemon juice,
  or a little more to taste

4 eggs, separated
1 cup sugar
¼ teaspoon salt
1 teaspoon grated lime or
  lemon zest
⅓ cup tequila
3 tablespoons Triple Sec

Combine the pretzel crumbs thoroughly with the butter and sugar. Oil a 9-inch pie pan, and press the crumb mixture against the bottom and sides. Chill well before filling.

Soften the gelatin in the lime juice. Beat egg yolks in the top of a double boiler. Blend in ½ cup sugar, salt, and grated lime zest. Add the softened gelatin and cook over boiling water, stirring constantly until slightly thickened and the gelatin is completely dissolved. Remove to a mixing bowl and stir in the tequila and Triple Sec. Cool thoroughly but do not let the mixture thicken. Beat egg whites until foamy. Gradually add the remaining ½ cup sugar, and continue beating until the whites hold soft peaks. Gently fold egg whites into cooked mixture. Let the mixture set slightly. Swirl into the pie shell and chill until set. Serves 6 to 8.

January 1, Bowl Brunch

for Eight

*Red Lion Cocktail
  Champagne
*Cheese Biscuits
*Omelets with Smoked Capon, Pheasant, or Turkey and Oysters
  Warm Brioches and Croissants
  Sweet Butter
  Pots of Honeys and Jams
*Compote of Strawberries and Papaya

The day after New York's Eve can be a letdown if you let it be. In spite of all good resolutions, the first day of the year finds many people simply sitting around and watching the televised football bowl games. So don't fight it—let the bowl games serve as an inspiration. Gather six friendly football fans for this elegant but easy brunch and make New Year's Day cause for celebration.

The Sugar, Orange, and Rose Bowls can be reflected in the theme of the table centerpiece: a bowl of bright oranges interspersed with yellow rose buds and cubes of sugar. Plan to eat around the tree, the hearth, or the television if you must—but begin with a toast of champagne or a special Red Lion cocktail and a taste of cheese biscuits.

A three-egg, made-to-order omelet is the main idea here—and a very sumptuous omelet at that! Each is filled with diced smoked capon (use a welcome and savory Christmas gift), two plump, succulent oysters, and sliced mushrooms. If you can prepare a pretty omelet with no fuss —you might want to exhibit your expertise over a flame at the table. Serve the omelets with warm croissants and brioches and an array of jams and honeys in little pots.

Offer a refreshing cold dessert: a tropical compote of strawberries and papaya, subtly flavored with lime, rum, and Cointreau. And, of course, pour lots more champagne to ring in the new year with the proper spirit.

RED LION COCKTAIL

Mix 1 ounce gin, 1 ounce Grand Marnier, 1 tablespoon fresh orange juice, and 1 tablespoon fresh lemon juice. Shake over ice in cocktail shaker until chilled and serve. Makes 1 to 2 cocktails.

CHEESE BISCUITS

2 cups all-purpose flour
2 teaspoons salt
Freshly ground pepper
Cayenne pepper
½ to 1 teaspoon dry mustard
½ pound unsalted butter, softened

2 firmly packed cups grated sharp Cheddar cheese, or a mixture of Cheddar, Parmesan, Gouda, Edam, etc. —any hard cheese

Mix flour, salt, pepper to taste, a good pinch of cayenne, and mustard. Add butter and cheese and blend until it is a smooth dough. Taste and correct seasoning if necessary. Form dough into rolls about 1 inch in diameter. Refrigerate or freeze.

Preheat oven to 375 degrees.

Slice dough rolls (frozen or thawed but not soft) a little less than ¼-inch thick. Put on baking sheets and bake in a 375-degree oven for 12 to 15 minutes, until very lightly browned and just barely firm to the touch in the center. Let cool a few seconds before removing from baking sheets. Makes about 100.

Variations: Use 1 cup whole-wheat flour and 1 cup white flour. Vary the seasonings by adding 1 to 2 tablespoons sesame seeds *or* poppy seeds *or* slightly crushed cumin seeds.

OMELETS WITH SMOKED CAPON, PHEASANT, OR TURKEY AND OYSTERS

8 to 16 fresh mushrooms, ends trimmed, sliced lengthwise, 1 to 2 per omelet

6 tablespoon minced shallots, 1 heaping teaspoon per omelet

½ to ¾ pound unsalted butter, at room temperature

2 cups diced white and dark meat from smoked capon, pheasant, or turkey—¼ cup per omelet

1 ½ cups heavy cream, 3 tablespoons per omelet

16 oysters, 2 per omelet

24 extra large eggs, 3 per omelet

Salt, freshly ground pepper

Sprigs of parsley or minced fresh chives

Sauté the mushrooms and shallots lightly in 6 to 8 tablespoons butter, then add the diced meat from the capon, pheasant, or turkey and the cream. Cook the oysters in their liquor just until the edges curl. Keep warm, but do not cook further while preparing omelets according to any standard recipe. Fill each omelet with about ⅓ cup of the smoked bird mixture and 2 oysters. Serve each omelet as it is cooked; do not hold the others while waiting to cook the last. (Make it a house rule to eat hot food as soon as it is served.) Hot croissants and brioches, with a variety of jams are on the table, so no one is totally without food while waiting for his omelet. Each omelet takes about 1 ½ minutes to cook and roll. Garnish with a sprig of parsley, a soupçon of minced chives, or any leftover mushrooms.

COMPOTE OF STRAWBERRIES AND PAPAYA

2 ripe papayas, peeled

3 pints strawberries, washed and hulled

Juice of 1 to 2 limes

¼ cup Cointreau

¼ cup Barbados rum

Peel papayas, cut in half and remove the seeds. Cut into 1-inch dice. Combine with strawberries in a pretty crystal bowl, and add the lime juice, Cointreau, and rum. Mix gently. Refrigerate several hours before serving to allow flavors to blend. Remove from refrigerator ½ hour before serving. Serves 8.

Truffled Luxury

*Truffled Scrambled Eggs
*Truffes en Mousseline
*Poulet Vapeur with *Sauce Suprême Truffé

What is a truffle? What does one do with a truffle? To many, a truffle spells terror. A lot of people perhaps are put off by the expense—truffles have been called "black diamonds." However, when you consider that a single truffle can flavor many a dish, they may seem less prohibitive.

No one knows why truffles grow where they do; no one knows for sure whether they're fungus or tuberculum. French truffles—ebony black and about the size of walnuts—come from the Périgord. Knob-shaped, their surfaces are roughly pitted, ridged, and planed. They grow or evolve underground near the roots of random gnarled oak trees—no one knows how.

Man cannot plant or seed or reproduce truffles, and he must rely on certain pigs whose sensitive noses can detect that pungent truffle scent to root them out. Once harvested—and the harvest lasts a short time in December and January—truffles spoil quickly. They must be brushed of the soil that clings tenaciously, and then—to peel or not to peel? This has been the subject of considerable discussion, but if you peel the truffle carefully and save the peel in a small jar of madeira, you will make your truffle stretch that much further. For the price of a single truffle, you have the truffle itself to use luxuriously, and the infused madeira to use for a truffled sauce. Two for the price of one. And now three for the price of one: bury that fresh truffle with fresh, unshelled eggs in a tightly sealed Mason jar or plastic bag for two days. The heady fragrance is powerful enough to permeate the shells, allowing you truffle-flavored scrambled eggs, and the truffle itself—reserved for yet another use.

Fresh truffles are, of course, superior to canned or preserved ones, but they are so fragile and perishable that, except for their short season, you must rely on preserved ones. If you have a fresh truffle, keep it in a paper towel in a jar or bag. It must be kept dry. The minute it seems the slightest bit spongy, poach it in a thin broth of madeira and water, and keep it in its broth in a well-sealed Mason jar. It will keep indefinitely, and you'll have the infused broth for sauce.

This is not a menu as such, to be eaten in sequence. This is a selection of truffled dishes—three dishes and a sauce that can be prepared for four people with six truffles. The scrambled eggs are flavored with the truffle perfume, but the truffle itself is saved for two lavish dishes where one really tastes the truffle. One, a first course, is a delicate mousseline de volaille, a carefully seasoned forcemeat of breast of chicken in which a whole peeled truffle is buried. The dish is poached gently in a bain-marie and bathed with a delicate suprême sauce. The experience of cutting into the mold and finding a whole truffle is unforgettable.

The other lavish dish asks for truffle slices to be placed between the skin and flesh of a plump, fresh chicken. The chicken is wrapped for twenty-four hours to allow the truffle to infuse the chicken with its flavor and aroma, and then suspended over an extra-rich stock, reduced from twelve quarts to two, so that the chicken cooks in the vapor of the stock. A labor of love, this dish.

The 6 truffles will feed four people four times, not such a frightening luxury when you think you are really tasting the truffle, not just hoping for a bit of flavor from the tiny pieces used for garnishes on many dishes. Just once, brave the truffle and its incomparable frank sensuality. You will never forget the experience.

TRUFFLED SCRAMBLED EGGS

11 eggs
1 truffle

4 tablespoons unsalted butter

Put the eggs in their shells in a Mason jar or plastic bag with the truffle for 2 days. Remove the eggs and reserve the truffle for another use. You may, if you wish, peel the truffle and garnish the scrambled eggs with 1 teaspoon of the chopped peel. Melt 3 tablespoons butter in an 8-inch frying pan over gentle heat. Break 10 eggs into a large mixing bowl and blend quickly and thoroughly. Break the remaining egg into a small mixing bowl and reserve. Cook the scrambled eggs over very low heat, very gently scrambling them with a fork. The eggs should be creamy and liquid, not dry. When almost done, stir in the remaining egg and 1 tablespoon butter, and blend quickly. Serve at once. Serves 4.

TRUFFES EN MOUSSELINE

1 pound chicken breasts, boned and skinned
2 egg whites
½ cup heavy cream
½ teaspoon salt, or more to taste
Freshly ground white pepper

Butter for ramekins or custard cups
4 truffles, peeled
Sauce Suprême Truffé (see recipe below)

Preheat oven to 350 degrees.

Grind the chicken breasts finely. The meat should be almost a purée. Gradually add the egg whites to the chicken forcemeat, beating well. Put the bowl over crushed ice in another bowl, and continue beating until the forcemeat is cold. Stir in the heavy cream, a little at a time. You may not need the entire ½ cup; a firm yet soft consistency is ideal. Season with salt and pepper. Chill thoroughly.

Butter four ¾-cup ramekins or custard cups. Spoon chicken forcemeat into the custard cup. Put the truffle into the forcemeat, and cover with forcemeat to fill the ramekin and completely bury the truffle. Butter aluminum foil and cover the molds, buttered side down. Put the molds in a pan of boiling water—water should be about halfway up the molds—and bake in a 350-degree oven 30 to 35 minutes, until done. They draw slightly away from edge and an inserted knife comes out clean. Run a knife around the inside of the molds and unmold to serve. Serve with sauce suprême truffé. Serves 4.

Note: If you don't have truffles, a nice "surprise" idea would be a quickly sautéed seasoned chicken liver buried in the forcemeat.

POULET VAPEUR

5- to 6-pound finest-quality roasting chicken
2 large truffles, peeled and thinly sliced
12 quarts rich homemade Chicken Stock (see Basic Recipes)

6 tablespoons butter
Salt, freshly ground white pepper

The day before serving the poulet, rinse the chicken under cool water and pat dry. Slide the tips of the fingers carefully between the skin and flesh of the chicken, and separate the skin from the flesh, taking care not to puncture the skin. Work under the skin from the breast meat and down over the thigh and leg. Slide truffle slices between the flesh and skin of the chicken, working them down over the thigh and leg. Most of them should be under the breast skin. Wrap the fowl loosely in plastic wrap and put it in the refrigerator overnight to enable the chicken to absorb as much aroma from the truffles as possible.

Reduce 12 quarts of rich homemade chicken stock to about 2 quarts. You may have to use 2 large pots to do so.

The day of the dinner, rub the chicken all over with butter and lightly salt it. Wrap the chicken in cheesecloth, allowing extra cheese-cloth at both ends of the chicken. Bring the reduced stock to a gentle simmer in a large, deep casserole or stockpot, wide enough to accommo-date the chicken and deep enough to suspend the chicken over the stock. The chicken must not be in the stock. Suspend the chicken over the stock, tying or pinning the ends of the cheesecloth to the handles of the pot. Cover the pot and make sure it is tightly sealed, either with more cheesecloth or with a flour and water paste. Let the chicken steam in the vapor for 1 ½ hours, until done. Remove to a warm platter and carefully remove the cheesecloth. Serve with sauce suprême and champagne. Serves 4.

SAUCE SUPRÊME TRUFFÉ

3 tablespoons butter
3 tablespoons flour
1 cup extra-rich chicken
   stock over which the
   chicken was steamed
1 cup heavy cream

3 egg yolks
½ cup champagne (brut)
1 tablespoon lemon juice
1 tablespoon truffle peel,
   chopped

Melt butter in the top of a double boiler or a heavy-bottomed saucepan. Stir in the flour. Blend well and add the chicken stock, stirring constantly. Add the heavy cream and continue stirring until smooth and thickened. Add a bit of the sauce to the egg yolks, and stir to blend well. Return the egg-yolk mixture to the sauce, stirring constantly. Just before serving, stir in the champagne, lemon juice, and truffle peel. Makes 2 ½ cups.

Basic Recipes

BÉCHAMEL SAUCE

4 tablespoons butter
4 tablespoons flour
2 cups milk, boiling
¼ teaspoon freshly grated
  nutmeg (optional)

Salt, freshly ground white
  pepper

Melt the butter in a heavy-bottomed saucepan. Stir in the flour and
blend well over medium heat for about 2 minutes, stirring carefully to
avoid burning. Add the milk, and continue cooking over medium heat
until thickened, stirring constantly. Remove from heat and season to
taste with nutmeg, salt, and pepper. Makes 2 cups.

Note: White pepper is traditionally used by French chefs so that
the appearance of the finished sauce is an unblemished creamy white.

SAUCE VELOUTÉ

⅓ cup butter
⅓ cup flour
3 cups white stock, chicken
  or veal (if using canned
  chicken broth, chill and
  degrease before using),
  boiling

Salt, freshly ground white
  pepper

Melt the butter in a heavy-bottomed saucepan over medium heat. Add
flour and blend thoroughly, stirring constantly for several minutes. Add
the stock all at once, stirring constantly with a large wire whisk until
the sauce is smooth and well thickened. Continue cooking over low heat
until the sauce is reduced to about 2½ cups, stirring carefully. Taste
and season with salt and pepper.

EASY AND HONEST
HOLLANDAISE SAUCE

4 egg yolks
2 to 4 tablespoons lemon
    juice, depending on tart-
    ness desired

8 tablespoons butter, *thor-
    oughly* chilled
Salt, freshly ground pepper
Tabasco sauce (optional)

Combine egg yolks, lemon juice, butter, and salt, pepper, and Tabasco sauce to taste in a heavy enameled saucepan 1 or 2 hours before serving. Cover and refrigerate. Just before serving, put the pan over very low heat and stir constantly until butter melts, all ingredients are blended, and the sauce is thickened and warm. Makes about 1 cup. May be doubled or tripled.

MAYONNAISE

3 large egg yolks
¾ teaspoon dry mustard
¾ teaspoon salt
2 tablespoons vinegar or
    lemon juice

1 cup corn or peanut oil
¾ cup best-quality olive oil
Additional vinegar, salt, mus-
    tard, or pepper
2 tablespoons boiling water

Bring ingredients to room temperature. Rinse out bowl in hot water and dry well. Add egg yolks, mustard, salt, and vinegar and beat well for 1 to 2 minutes. Combine oils and begin adding by tablespoonfuls, beating until last trace of oil has disappeared before adding another spoonful. Continue in this manner until an emulsion has formed, then you may add oil in larger amounts, beating it in until no trace is left after each addition. When all the oil has been added, taste critically for seasonings, adding more as necessary. Beat in 2 tablespoons boiling water to stabilize the mayonnaise and store in a cool place. Makes about 2 cups.

RÉMOULADE SAUCE

½ cup celery, finely chopped
½ cup green onion, finely
  chopped
3 cloves garlic, finely chopped
⅓ cup tarragon vinegar
1 cup olive oil
2 tablespoons paprika

¼ to ½ teaspoon cayenne
  pepper
½ teaspoon salt
3 tablespoons Creole or
  Dijon prepared mustard
2 heaping tablespoons prepared horseradish

Combine all ingredients in a blender and whip thoroughly. Chill several hours before serving. Good with shellfish. Makes about 3 cups.

VINAIGRETTE SAUCE

Vinaigrette sauce may be prepared in quantity and stored in the refrigerator. Allow to come to room temperature before serving, then shake or stir well. Do not use too much; the sauce should just lightly coat the greens of a salad, with no excess remaining in the bottom of bowl. A good rule of thumb is to allow about 1 tablespoon of oil, plus the proper proportion of other ingredients, per person; thus, for an ample salad for eight, about ¾ cup of vinaigrette is needed. It is easiest to prepare it in a screw-top jar so it may be well shaken to blend ingredients.

Basic vinaigrette sauce

¾ cup best-quality olive oil
¼ cup wine vinegar

½ teaspoon Dijon mustard
Salt, freshly ground pepper

Combine oil, vinegar, and mustard in a jar. Season with about 1 teaspoon salt and pepper to taste. Shake well and correct seasoning if necessary. Makes 1 cup.

Lemon vinaigrette

Substitute lemon juice for the vinegar in the basic recipe, and omit the mustard.

Mustard vinaigrette

Increase Dijon mustard to 1 teaspoon, or more if desired. For an even more pungent sauce, beat in ¼ teaspoon dry mustard.

Thyme or other herb vinaigrette

Use only ¼ teaspoon Dijon mustard in basic recipe, and add ½ teaspoon dried, or 2 teaspoons chopped fresh, thyme or other herb. Just before serving, 1 tablespoon minced fresh parsley may be mixed in.

Watercress or parsley vinaigrette

Prepare 1 cup basic vinaigrette sauce. Wash, dry, and remove thick stems from 1 bunch watercress or parsley. Just before serving, put sauce and watercress or parsley in blender and whirl until green is well chopped. This must be done just before serving or the bright green flecks lose their color.

White wine vinaigrette

½ cup dry white wine	Salt, freshly ground pepper
Juice of ½ lemon	4 to 5 scallions, minced, green
½ cup basic vinaigrette	parts as well if desired

Combine wine, lemon juice, vinaigrette, and salt and pepper to taste. Add scallions just before serving. This is good with any green salad, especially one made of delicate greens, and even more so with a salad bowl lined with endive leaves and heaped in the center with watercress sprigs and sliced mushrooms.

BREAD CRUMBS

Fresh bread crumbs are infinitely superior to the commercially prepared crumbs. They are easy to prepare and have on hand if you save stale bits and ends of bread, crusts, etc., in the freezer. To prepare, break bread into smaller pieces and whirl, a handful at a time, in blender until they are of the desired consistency.

If a recipe specifies *fresh bread crumbs*, use a good-quality fresh white bread, remove the crusts, cut into cubes, and whirl in blender. These may be frozen.

To prepare *buttered bread crumbs*, heat 2 tablespoons clarified butter (see directions below) in a small, heavy skillet. Stir in 1 cup bread crumbs and cook over low heat, stirring, until butter and crumbs are well mixed and mixture has reached desired color.

To prepare *dry bread crumbs*, dry bread slices in a 300-degree oven until lightly browned.

CLARIFIED BUTTER

Unsalted butter is preferable in most cooking procedures, especially for sautéing, because it has less of a tendency to burn than salted butter. But clarified butter is most important for all delicate sautéing, since all milky particles, which are the part of the butter that burns first, are removed.

To prepare it, melt butter in a small heavy saucepan over low heat. Skim off foam, then pour carefully through a cheesecloth-lined sieve, leaving the milky residue. Do not press down on the cheesecloth to extract all the butter; the milky particles will go right through.

BASIC PASTRY

1 ¾ cups sifted flour	1 egg yolk
¼ pound unsalted butter, chilled	¼ cup cold water
Salt	1 tablespoon peanut or corn oil

Put flour in a bowl. Cut the butter into tiny bits and put in bowl with a pinch of salt. Quickly blend the flour and butter with a pastry fork, pastry blender, or 2 knives (unless you are very adept at doing this rapidly, the fingers are too warm and melt the butter) until mixture has the texture of oatmeal. Combine egg yolk, water, and oil, pour into the center, and quickly blend until dough can be gathered into a ball. If it seems too dry, sprinkle with a few drops of cold water. It is all right if small particles of butter remain; this will produce an even flakier dough. Wrap in plastic wrap and refrigerate until firm before rolling. Makes enough for a 9-inch round shell and about eight 1½ to 2-inch tartlet molds. Use for quiches and other savory dishes.

To make a *sweet pastry* for desserts, mix 2 tablespoons sugar with flour, then proceed with recipe.

Note: Cream Cheese Pastry (see Index) may also be used for any recipe calling for a pastry shell. Use unsweetened for savory dishes; for desserts, combine 2 tablespoons sugar with flour, then proceed.

To partially cook a pastry shell, preheat oven to 400 degrees. Roll out pastry thinly, line mold, and trim edge decoratively. Line with foil and raw rice or dried beans, or prick bottom and spread lightly with either Dijon mustard (for savory tarts) or melted sieved apricot jam (for dessert tarts). Refrigerate until pastry is firm again. Bake 10 to 12 minutes, until pastry is lightly colored and the edge is just beginning to draw away from mold.

CRISP MELBA TOAST

1 loaf unsliced bread: white,   Butter (optional)
   whole-wheat, or rye

Preheat oven to 250 degrees.

Slice bread *very* thinly, remove crust. Brush with melted butter if desired, and put slices on baking sheets. Put on middle rack of oven and bake for 30 to 40 minutes, until golden brown and crisp.

Note: Bread may be cut into desired shapes before baking: smaller squares, strips, triangles, rounds.

VARIATIONS

Brush Melba toast with melted butter, sprinkle with freshly grated Parmesan cheese, about 1 tablespoon per slice, and return to oven just before serving, to melt the cheese.

Brush Melba toast lightly with olive oil, then spread with Pesto (see Index) and heat through for an unusual accompaniment to fresh summer hors d'oeuvres.

DUXELLES

2 pounds mushrooms	Salt, freshly ground pepper
12 tablespoons unsalted butter	2 to 3 tablespoons dry madeira
6 to 8 shallots, finely chopped	

Wipe the mushrooms with a damp cloth and mince as finely as possible. Put into the corner of a dish towel a handful at a time and wring to extract liquid (reserve liquid to use in soups). Melt butter, and cook shallots over low heat until soft. Add mushrooms, and cook over low heat, stirring occasionally, until all liquid is evaporated and mixture is very dark. Season to taste with salt and pepper, stir in madeira, raise heat slightly, and cook 2 to 3 minutes more. Duxelles may be frozen. Makes about 4 cups.

A NOTE ON STOCK

There is nothing more delicious than a homemade stock made of meat or poultry, yet people seem to be afraid of it. There is really nothing to it: it is inexpensive (much more economical to use than canned stocks), easy to make, and extremely nutritious. The best way to go about it is this: "save" bones—always remember to ask your butcher if he has any available, then store them in the freezer; if you notice a special on shank or stew meat, buy and freeze; reserve and freeze bones whenever you bone chicken, and also save the chicken innards. Then when you have a sufficient supply, defrost, prepare the other ingredients, and you are ready to go.

Several rules apply to stock making: always use the lowest heat possible and if necessary set pot over an asbestos pad; if stock boils, it will not be clear. Never cover stock completely while cooking or until completely cooled or it will sour. Cook it for as long as possible, until the last bit of flavor has been imparted from the ingredients to the stock—overnight if possible.

BROWN MEAT STOCK

6 to 8 pounds beef or veal bones and meat (if possible, use half bones, sawed into 2- to 3-inch pieces, and half beef shank meat or inexpensive stew meat)
2 carrots, scrubbed and cut into chunks
2 onions, peeled and quartered

2 stalks celery
2 leeks, cleaned (optional)
Salt
Bouquet garni made of ½ teaspoon thyme, several parsley sprigs, 1 bay leaf, and 6 to 8 black peppercorns, tied in cheesecloth

Preheat oven to 450 degrees.

Put meat and bones, carrots, and onions in roasting pan. Put in oven and roast, turning pieces occasionally, until browned all over. This will take 30 to 40 minutes.

Put bones, vegetables, celery, leeks if desired, and bouquet garni in a 8- to 10-quart stock pot. Add water just to cover and 1 tablespoon salt. Put over very low heat, bring to a simmer, and cook at a very low simmer (with bubbles barely perceptible) for at least 6 hours. The best thing to do is to leave stock cooking overnight. Ingredients should always be covered with water; add boiling water if necessary. Skim off scum and fat as necessary. When ready, strain into a large bowl and refrigerate. When fat has risen to the top and solidified, skim off. Taste carefully: if flavor is weak, put into a clean pot and boil down until flavor is full and strong. Taste again carefully, this time adding salt if necessary. Draw strips of paper towel carefully across the top to remove any remaining fat. Strain through a damp linen towel. When completely cool, put into containers and refrigerate or freeze. If storing in refrigerator, boil every 3 to 4 days or stock will sour. Makes 2 to 3 quarts.

CHICKEN STOCK

6 to 8 pounds chicken
    bones, wings, innards
    (do not use livers),
    gizzards, and pieces of
    chicken if desired
2 carrots, scraped and quar-
    tered
2 onions, peeled and quar-
    tered
2 stalks celery, with leafy
    green tops if possible

2 leeks, cleaned (optional)
Bouquet garni made of 6
    parsley stems (the leaves
    make stock darker), ¼ to
    ½ teaspoon thyme, 1 bay
    leaf, and 6 to 8 pepper-
    corns, tied in cheesecloth
Salt

Put chicken bones, etc., carrots, onions, celery, leeks if desired, and
bouquet garni in 8- to 10-quart stock pot. Cover with water by 2
inches and add 1 tablespoon salt. Put over low heat and bring to a simmer.
Cook at a very low simmer (with bubbles barely perceptible) for at
least 6 hours. The best thing to do is to leave stock cooking overnight.
Ingredients should always be covered with water; add boiling water
if necessary. Skim off fat and scum as necessary. When ready, strain
into a large bowl and refrigerate. When fat has risen to the top and
solidified, skim off. Taste carefully: if flavor is weak, put into a clean
pot and boil down until flavor is full and strong. Taste again carefully,
this time adding salt if necessary. Draw strips of paper towel carefully
across the top to remove any remaining fat. Strain through a damp linen
towel. When completely cool, put into containers and refrigerate or
freeze. If storing in refrigerator, boil every 3 to 4 days or stock will
sour. Makes 2 to 3 quarts.

Lagniappe

To extract juice from grated zucchini, cooked spinach, etc., squeeze in a potato ricer.

Freeze juiced citrus shells; the zest can then be easily grated when needed.

Store washed fresh greens in a pillowcase in refrigerator to dry and chill, or roll them in a terrycloth towel.

To heat food in broiler while oven is in use (if broiler is separate section from oven but heated by the same flame), cover dish to be heated with foil, then put in broiler. Food will just warm.

To slice hard-cooked eggs easily, use a hot, wet knife.

Use coarse or kosher salt rather than the fine iodized salt; it has a much better flavor.

To retain flavor, color, aroma, and freshness of dried herbs, store in refrigerator or freezer if possible; in any event, keep away from light and heat—they dissipate flavor. For the same reason, store spices away from light and heat.

To store fresh herbs, wash the leaves, put in small plastic bags with the water clinging to the leaves, and freeze. To use, thaw on paper towel and blot well to remove excess moisture.

Superfine sugar is preferable in most desserts to regular granulated sugar; it dissolves faster and more thoroughly.

To peel garlic easily, shave off ends of cloves, then smash garlic with flat of knife. Peel falls away.

To peel tomatoes, tiny white onions, shallots, peaches, and nectarines, drop into boiling water for 15 to 30 seconds, then remove. Run under cold water to stop cooking. Skin is then easily peeled off. Another method for peeling tomatoes is to rub all over with dull side of knife blade, then peel easily and quickly.

To prepare whipped cream that may be made several hours in advance and stored in refrigerator without separating or "watering," either put bowl of cream into a larger bowl filled with ice and whip, or chill bowl and beater(s) for at least 30 minutes before whipping cream. For best results, use cream that is one or two days old and make sure that it is well chilled.

Copper mixing/beating bowls should be wiped out with vinegar, then salt, before each use; this removes any remaining tarnish and stains and cleans the bowl without leaving any trace of flavor. This is also an old, and excellent, method for cleaning if one does not have a commercial powder or cleanser on hand; it is not tough enough for really soiled or stained pots, however. Clean a cheeseboard with vinegar.

To determine if egg whites are sufficiently beaten, turn bowl upside down. If they do not slide out, they are ready to use. If they start to slide as bowl is turned, beat some more before testing again.

The best sweet and bittersweet chocolate is Swiss; its flavor is far superior to any other available. The "extra bittersweet" is perfect for recipes calling for semi-sweet chocolate. "Triple-vanilla" is superb for chocolate mousse, cakes, etc., and there is no need to adjust such things as sugar and vanilla proportions.

To make a superb vanilla, to be used with discretion in desserts such as any chocolate or nut dessert, but not a delicate lemon one, take 4 to 5 whole vanilla beans, put in a large bottle, cover with a good dark rum or a good cognac, and let stand, tightly covered, for at least one week before using. Fill with rum or cognac when necessary, and occasionally add a new vanilla bean. Use as specified in any recipe calling for vanilla, except, of course, in a delicate fruit-flavored dessert.

When straining stock, it is preferable to use a damp linen dishtowel instead of cheesecloth; the closer weave really strains out all particles.

Get in the habit of checking 10 to 20 minutes before specified cooking time is up—burner and oven heat differences can really affect "doneness." It is a good idea to keep an oven thermometer always in the oven and check it each time.

A famed French cook suggests using a cut raw potato on burns; we can enthusiastically attest to its effectiveness!

Use a meat thermometer to determine temperature of water when working with yeast.

Index